The Weekly Mitzva

Yeshivat Har Etzion ישיבת הר עציון

מגיד
MAGGID

Binyamin Tabory

THE WEEKLY MITZVA

Yeshivat Har Etzion
Maggid Books

The Weekly Mitzva

First Edition, 2015

Maggid Books
An imprint of Koren Publishers Jerusalem Ltd.

POB 8531, New Milford, CT 06776-8531, USA
& POB 4044, Jerusalem 9104001, Israel
www.korenpub.com

Cover design: Tani Bayer

The publication of this book was made possible
through the generous support of *Torah Education in Israel.*

ISBN 978-1-59264-425-4, *hardcover*

A CIP catalogue record for this title is
available from the British Library

Printed and bound in the United States

מוקדש באהבה רבה לנוות ביתי, אשת נעוריי, נעמי

When the idea of Torah MiTzion *kollels* was first proposed, Rabbi Binyamin Tabory immediately jumped at the opportunity to pioneer a transformational concept for Religious Zionist communities outside of the State of Israel. He helped actualize the prophecy that Torah would emanate from Zion with his unique appreciation that fulfillment of the prophecy required exporting the Torah of the Land of Israel (*Torah MiTzion*) from Israel's *yeshivot hesder* to Jewish communities around the world. So Rabbi Tabory became the founding *rosh kollel* of the international Torah MiTzion Kollel movement. His example, his leadership, and his Torah brilliance have inspired hundreds of Torah MiTzion Kollel members, over many years, to disseminate *Torat Tzion* to the rest of the world as community leaders, teachers, and role models. The impact of their efforts has dramatically changed the Modern Orthodox world and significantly increased the number of people making *aliya* every year.

Bob Stark
CEO, Stark Enterprises

ספר זה מוקדש על ידי תלמידי הרב בנימין תבורי,
תלמיד חכם המאמין בשילוב של עם ישראל, מדינת ישראל ותורת ישראל.
אשרינו שזכינו ללמוד מאישיותו, אשרינו שזכינו להתחנך מתורתו,
אשרינו שזכינו להיות מתלמידיו.
אנו תקווה שהרב תבורי ימשיך ללמדנו בשנים הבאות.
משפחת קושיצקי

Dedicated to our dear friend Rabbi Binyamin Tabory, in honour of and in perpetuation of his many years of Torah teaching in North America and in Israel.

Faygie and Phil Schwartz

Kehillat Alei Tzion in London pays tribute to Rabbi Binyamin Tabory for his inspirational *shiurim* and Torah leadership when he served as rabbi of the community in 5768.

Contents

SEFER SHEMOT

SEFER DEVARIM

בפתח הספר

"פִּקּוּדֵי ה׳ יְשָׁרִים מְשַׂמְּחֵי לֵב". פסוק זה עולה בתודעתי מיד בחשבי על תורתו של ידיד נפשי ותלמידי משכבר הימים, הרב בנימין תבורי שליט"א. החן, השמחה והלבביות הם מסימני ההיכר הבולטים של תורת ר׳ בנימין. כל מי ששוחח עמו בדברי תורה - ורבים מאוד עשו כן לאורך השנים - חש מיד באושר הקורן מאישיותו ובשמחה הגלומה בתורתו. בין שהמפגש עמו היה בבחינת "בשבתך בביתך" בבתי המדרש הרבים שבהם קבע הרב תבורי את מקום מושבו, בין שהיה בבחינת "בלכתך בדרך", תמיד ידעתי, כרבים אחרים, שבכל מפגש כזה תהיה שיחה בדברי תורה ושהתורה המובעת בה תהיה נעימה וערבה לשומע, הן בתוכן הן בהגשה. אמרותיו של נעים זמירות ישראל "מה אהבתי תורתך, כל היום היא שיחתי" ו"זְמִרוֹת היו לי חֻקֶּיךָ" מצאו להם אוזן קשבת בנפשו של ר׳ בנימין והן מיטיבות לבטא את תורתו. העין הטובה והלב השמח שליוו את תורתו כל השנים הרבות שבהן למד ולימד, מוכרים היטב לכל תלמידיו ומכריו ואיני צריך להעיד על המפורסמות.

היכרותי עם הרב תבורי הינה רבת שנים ושורשה עוד בבית אמא ז"ל בליטא. הרב צבי תבורי ז"ל, אביו של ר׳ בנימין, ואמא ע"ה פעלו שם יחדיו בשדה החינוך היהודי, וזכינו שקשר של קיימא זה המשיך וליווה את משפחותינו לאורך הדרך ובמשך עשורים רבים. כד הוינא טליא והחילותי את לימודי הגמרא בצעירותי, ר׳ צבי היה ממוריי הראשונים. הקשר המשיך ביתר שאת וביתר עוז בישיבת ר׳ יצחק אלחנן בניו יורק כאשר ר׳ בנימין למד בכולל שעמדתי בראשו, והקשר הלך והתפתח בארץ הקודש בתקופה של למעלה משלושים שנה שבהן לימדנו יחדיו בישיבת הר עציון.

לאורך תקופה זו האירה תורתו את הסביבה, כשחוט של חן אנושי משוך עליה בזכות הנופך האישי המיוחד שהרב תבורי יצק בה. סיפוריו המרתקים על רבותיו וגדולי ישראל שבא עמם במגע היו לשם דבר. דברי הגמרא בחגיגה (ה:) על החיוניות המיוחדת שיש למי שרואה חכמים ומתבונן באישיותם היו תדיר לנגד עיניו ובדרך זו השכיל להפוך את התורה שבעל־פה ליצירה חיה ותוססת שבני אדם מעורבים ומחדשים בה. התורה שלימד בשיעוריו הייתה מורכבת לא רק ממושגים מופשטים ותובנות שכליות, אלא חכמי המסורה ובני אדם בשר ודם הופיעו תדיר בבית מדרשו לנגד עיני תלמידיו. הסיפור והמעשה שהיה הפכו בידו לכלי חינוכי מהמדרגה הראשונה.

בהקשר זה אי־אפשר שלא להזכיר את זיקתו העמוקה של ר' בנימין למו"ח הרב יוסף דוב הלוי סולוביצ'יק זצ"ל. כל העובר בין דפי הספר הזה יחוש זאת וכל מי ששוחח עם הרב תבורי, ולו לכמה דקות, הבחין מיד בהערצתו לרבו ובחיבה שהרב רחש לתלמידו.

"נעניתי עד מאד, ה' חיֵני כדברך". השמחה ורחבות הנפש המוכרת הוחלפו בשנים האחרונות בייסורים ובמאבק קשה ועיקש במחלה איומה. לאורך תקופה זו זיקתו של ר' בנימין לתורה ככוח חיוני וקיומי נשארה איתנה ויציבה, ואנו, שכניו ומכריו, זכינו להיחשף לפן אחר באישיותו של ר' בנימין, של אשתו נעמי העומדת לצדו כסלע איתן של תמיכה וטיפול, ושל בני משפחתו - והיא הגבורה הנפשית. דברי המדרש על גבורתם הרוחנית של בני אדם הנתונים בשלשלאות ומושג גבורת הנפש שהוא כה משמעותי בהגות רבו הגרי"ד, באים לידי ביטוי מרשים בתלמידו המסור ומעידים על עוז רוח.

ספר זה משקף את שני הצדדים הללו של תורת הרב תבורי. הורתו בעתות של שמחה והארת פנים ולידתו בעת צרה ומשבר. תקוותי היא שפרקי הספר שכתיבתם הייתה מתוך שמחה, תסיסה וחיוניות, וחתימתם בגבורה ובכאב המלווים את התקופה האחרונה, יבטאו וישקפו בתכניהם את השמחה, החום ואהבת התורה שאפיינה את תורת הרב תבורי בכל השנים, יעשירו את הלומדים בהם בתורה ערבה לחיך ונעימה לאוזן, בעוד הנחישות להביאם לעולם למרות כל הקשיים תיתן ביטוי לעוז הרוח והגבורה של השנים האחרונות.

יהי רצון שהספר יפיץ את מעיינותיו של הרב בנימין החוצה, ולמעגל השומעים שכה נהנה מתורתו עד עתה, יתווסף חוג של קוראים וישמחו גם הם בתורה זו.

בברכת התורה והמצווה,
אהרן ליכטנשטיין

Foreword

"The statutes of the Lord are righteous, rejoicing the heart" (Tehillim 19:9). This verse immediately arises in my mind when I think of the teachings of my dear friend and former student Rabbi Binyamin Tabory, *shlita*. Joy, charm, and warmth are notable hallmarks of Rav Binyamin's teachings. Anyone who has ever discussed Torah matters with him – and very many have done so over the years – immediately senses the happiness radiating from his personality and the joy contained in his Torah.

Whether meeting Rabbi Tabory in one of the many Torah institutions in which he has taught, or just happening upon him "when you travel on the way," I, like many others, have always known that conversation with him will center on Torah matters, and that the Torah would be pleasant to hear, both in its content and in its presentation.

The maxims of King David, that sweet singer of Israel, "O how I love Your Torah! It is my meditation all the day" (Tehillim 119:97) and "Your statutes have been my songs" (v. 54) resonate in Rav Binyamin's soul, and they express his teachings in excellent manner. The generous and joyful heart that have accompanied his teachings during the many years that he has studied and taught are well known to all of his students and acquaintances; I do not need to testify to that which is common knowledge.

My long-standing acquaintance with Rabbi Tabory is rooted in my late mother's home in Lithuania. Rav Binyamin's late father, Rabbi Zevi Tabory, worked together with my mother in the field of Jewish education, and it has been our privilege that this lasting bond has continued to accompany our families for many decades. When I was a young boy just beginning to study Talmud, Rav Zevi was among my first teachers. My connection with Rav Binyamin was strengthened at the Rabbi Isaac Elchanan Theological Seminary in New York when he studied in the *kollel* that I headed, and further developed in Eretz Yisrael during more than thirty years that we taught together at Yeshivat Har Etzion.

Throughout this entire period, his teachings illuminated his surroundings, graced by the charm of Rabbi Tabory's unique personal touch. His fascinating stories about his teachers and the other Torah luminaries with whom he came into contact are well known. The words of the Gemara (Ḥagiga 5b) about the special vitality bestowed upon someone who sees Torah sages and contemplates their personalities were constantly in his awareness. Consequently, he could bring the Oral Law to life for his students, engaging them and allowing them to innovate within it. The Torah he taught in his classes was not composed of mere abstract concepts and intellectual insights: the Sages of the *mesora* and real flesh-and-blood people appeared regularly in his *beit midrash* and before his students. Stories and anecdotes became first-rate educational tools in his employ.

In this context, mention must be made of Rav Binyamin's deep relationship with my father-in-law, Rabbi Joseph B. Soloveitchik, *zt"l*. Anyone who reads this book or speaks with Rabbi Tabory, if only for a few minutes, will immediately detect the adoration he had for his teacher and the affection that his teacher showed to his student.

"I am afflicted very much; revive me, O Lord, according to Your word" (Tehillim 119:107). Rabbi Tabory's well-known joy and effusiveness have been challenged in recent years by afflictions and a hard and unyielding struggle with a terrible disease. Throughout this period, Rav Binyamin's bond with Torah as an essential and existential force has remained strong and stable. We, his neighbors and acquaintances, have merited witnessing another aspect of the personality of Rav Binyamin; of his wife, Naomi, who has stood by him as a rock of support and care; and of the other members of his family – namely, spiritual heroism. The words of the Midrash about the spiritual heroism of men shackled in chains, and the concept of spiritual heroism that is so significant in the thought of his teacher Rabbi Soloveitchik, find impressive expression in his devoted student and attest to his courage of spirit.

This book reflects these two sides of Rabbi Tabory's teachings. It was conceived in periods of joy and illumination and emerged to the world at a time of distress and crisis. It is my hope that the chapters of this book, which were written in joy, vibrancy, and vitality, and sealed with the courage and pain that have accompanied the recent period, will express and reflect in their content the joy, warmth, and love of Torah that have characterized Rabbi Tabory's teachings over all the years, that they will enrich his readers with Torah that is pleasant to the palate and delightful to the ear, while his determination to bring them to fruition despite all the difficulties will give expression to the bravery and heroism of the past few years.

May this book cause Rav Binyamin's teachings to spring forth, so that the circle of those who have heretofore so greatly enjoyed his teaching will be joined by a new circle of readers who also will delight in this Torah.

With blessings of Torah and mitzvot,
Aharon Lichtenstein

Preface

The history of this book began years ago, when my father, Rabbi Binyamin Tabory, began a series of *shiurim* in Yeshivat Har Etzion entitled "The Mitzva of the Week." Each *shiur* focused on a topic in halakha connected to that week's *parasha*.

A few years later, Rabbi Uri Dasberg *z"l*, editor of the weekly Torah pamphlet *Shabbat BeShabbatto*, asked my father to contribute a weekly column. These columns, written in Hebrew, later formed the basis for an English-language course posted on Yeshivat Har Etzion's Israel Koschitzky Virtual Beit Midrash (VBM).

This book presents these articles in a new format. One of my father's unique qualities is that every *shiur* he gives speaks to both scholars and laymen alike. It is our hope that these weekly discussions will succeed in conveying classic concepts of *lomdus* (traditional halakhic analysis) in a manner that is both comprehensible and engaging to a broad audience.

Unfortunately, due to illness, my father is unable to write the introduction to this book. Nevertheless, I have tried to imagine the people he would like to thank.

Debra Berkowitz, the VBM's office manager, devotedly typed up the *shiurim*. In addition to the articles reproduced here, Rabbi Ezra Bick encouraged my father to write additional articles and lectures for the VBM, as well as to record several series of shiurim on the VBM's audio branch. (These can be found, respectively, on etzion.org.il and kmtt.libsyn.com.) Of course, our thanks also go to Matthew Miller, Rabbi Reuven Ziegler, and the staff at Maggid Books for bringing this book to print. Special thanks as well to Rabbi Alan Haber for editing the text and David B. Greenberg for proofreading it.

We also thank the patrons of this book, who are among my parents' friends from all over the world. Although my father has spent most of his time teaching Torah in Yeshivat Har Etzion, he and my mother have also traveled far and wide to spread Torah and mitzvot. Friends, *talmidim*, and congregants from Los Angeles, Toronto, Cleveland, and London have generously contributed to the making of this book.

Special thanks also go to Ezra Rozenfeld, a close friend of my parents, for all his help.

My father asked me to dedicate this book to my mother. Her commitment, love, and strength have been an inspiration not only to our family but also to our friends and to my father's many students who visit on a regular basis.

In the name of my entire family, I pray that my *abba* continues to see *naḥat* from his children, grandchildren, and *talmidim*. May Hashem bless him with better health and strength as he continues his courageous battle.

Aviad Tabory
Pesaḥ 5775

Sefer Bereshit

Parashat Bereshit

Peru URevu

S*efer HaḤinnukh* states that procreation is the first mitzva in the Torah. Bereshit 1:28 reads, "God blessed them and God said to them, 'Be fruitful and multiply (*peru urevu*).'" The *Sefer Yere'im* (413) says that the Torah commanded us in four different places regarding this mitzva. He cites only two of these, the present verse and the commandment given to Noaḥ when he left the ark (Bereshit 9:7). The commentary *To'afot Re'em* also cites God's words to Yaakov (Bereshit 35:11), which are written in singular (*pereh ureveh*) as opposed to the plural (*peru urevu*).

There is a dispute among *Tanna'im* (Yevamot 65b) as to whether women are commanded to perform this mitzva. The *tanna kamma* maintains that women are exempt, either because the verse relates procreation to *kibbush,* i.e., conquering or dominion, or because the command was given to Yaakov in singular form, indicating that it applies to a man and not to a woman. The *Tosafot* (ad loc.) point out that the statement to Adam, which is phrased in the plural, should be construed as a blessing given to both man and woman, rather than a mitzva. R. Yoḥanan b. Beroka, however, maintains that the original statement to Adam and Ḥava is the source of the mitzva; therefore women are equally obligated.

Rambam (*Hilkhot Ishut* 15:2) and the *Shulḥan Arukh* (*Even HaEzer* 13) codify the halakha according to the *tanna kamma*. In *Meshekh Ḥokhma,* Rabbi Meir Simḥa HaKohen suggests that the mitzva given to Adam and Ḥava was indeed incumbent upon both of them. However, the mitzva given to Noaḥ applied only to him and his sons, and similarly Yaakov's mitzva was addressed only to him. The reason for this change may be that God did not command mitzvot that were painful, dangerous, and even life-threatening. Before the sin of eating from the Tree of Knowledge, childbirth was a relatively simply process, and therefore man and woman were commanded equally. However, after the sin, when God mandated that childbirth be accompanied by pain and difficulty, women could no longer be commanded to bear children. Women would desire to have children because of an inherent maternal instinct rather than a divine commandment.

Rabbi Meir Simḥa also gives an additional rationale. Since under biblical law a man is entitled to be polygamous, if his wife is incapable of having children, he does not have to divorce her in order to fulfill the mitzva: he can simply marry a second wife. However, since a woman must be monogamous, if her husband were incapable of siring children, she would need to obtain a divorce from him in order to fulfill the mitzva. This would create an acrimonious situation, and thereby contradict the principle that the ways of the Torah are pleasant (Mishlei 3:17). One may also add that this reasoning did not apply to Adam and Ḥava, as they received God's blessing to procreate, and furthermore could not have married anyone else even if the blessing were not realized.

It is obvious that even if women are not obligated to have children, they certainly fulfill the mitzva if they do. Similarly, women can fulfill the mitzva of *kiddushin* (betrothal) even though they are not commanded to marry. The Gemara (Kiddushin 41a) says that although a woman could become halakhically engaged by proxy, it is a greater mitzva for her to do so in person. Rishonim raise the obvious question: if women are not commanded to marry and to have children, why does the Gemara state that it is a greater mitzva for them to be personally involved in the betrothal process? The Ran (ad loc.) says that a woman fulfills the mitzva since she enables her husband to fulfill his obligation. The Ḥida (*Birkei Yosef, Even HaEzer* 1:16) cites an anonymous Rishon according to whom women fulfill the mitzva even though they are not obligated by it, just as they can fulfill the mitzvot of sukka, shofar, and lulav even though they are not obligated. This Rishon also suggests that although women are exempt from the biblical mitzva, they may be obligated by rabbinic law. This concept, namely, that the Rabbis required women to fulfill a mitzva from which the Torah exempts them, seems to be a novel one.

The mitzva of procreation appears to be independent of any other mitzva, and therefore the Rosh (Ketubbot 1:12) says that if one fathered children with a concubine, he would not have to marry. However, Rabbi Aḥai Gaon (*She'iltot* 165) writes that "the Children of Israel are required to marry, have children, and engage in procreation." He cites as a proof text Yirmiyahu 29:6: "Marry and have sons and daughters." Since this source is not from the Torah but from Nevi'im, it does not seem to be a Torah requirement. Yirmiyahu's admonition begins with advice to people going into exile to invest in real estate and work the land, as life will go on. He further adds that they should ensure that their children marry and have children. This is definitely not a Torah requirement (see Kiddushin 29a; Rambam, *Hilkhot Ishut* 20:1). It therefore seems that the verse in Yirmiyahu may indicate a rabbinic commandment. Alternatively, it may merely represent sage advice to marry prior to having children.

Sefer HaḤinnukh concludes its discussion of this mitzva by saying that one who negates this mitzva will be sorely punished, as he thus demonstrates that he does not wish to realize God's desire to populate the world.

Parashat Noaḥ

Noahides' Obligation to Honor Their Parents

The mitzva of *kibbud av va'em* (honoring parents) that was given to the Jewish nation is not one of the seven Noahide laws that obligate all non-Jews. Nevertheless, there are a number of sources that seem to indicate that this mitzva applies to Noahides, as well.

For example, the Torah relates that some time after the Flood, Noaḥ became intoxicated and left himself exposed in his bed. His son Ḥam informed his other sons, Shem and Yefet, who took a blanket and covered their father's nakedness (Bereshit 9:21–24). Rashi (ad loc.), citing the Midrash, says that it was Shem who took the initiative to perform this mitzva involving a textile, and therefore his descendants were rewarded with the mitzva of affixing fringes to their garments (*tzizit*). Similarly, *Tanna DeBei Eliyahu* (16) explains that the Torah calls Noaḥ righteous due to his diligence in sustaining his father. These sources seem to imply that a Noahide who honors his parents fulfills a mitzva.

Another example of a Noahide who engages in *kibbud av va'em* is Esav. The Midrash (Devarim Rabba 1:14) relates that Rabban Shimon

b. Gamliel initially declared that no one was as meticulous in *kibbud av va'em* as he himself was, but later recanted when he discovered that Esav had been even more respectful towards his parents. The Midrash explains that Rabban Shimon served his father while wearing ordinary clothes and would put on more elegant clothing when he went out to the market. Esav, however, would put on his best finery whenever he served his father, Yitzḥak. This information is related incidentally in the Torah: Rivka advises Yaakov to don Esav's best clothes in order to impersonate him (Bereshit 27:15), out of concern that Yitzḥak might feel Yaakov's clothes and thus realize that he was an imposter. (Yitzḥak was virtually blind and could not discern visually what clothing Esav was wearing.) The Midrash then goes on to say that Esav was amply rewarded for this act, again implying that he thus fulfilled a mitzva.

A possible explanation of these sources is that the mitzva of *kibbud av va'em* does not actually obligate Noahides, but it nevertheless is certainly considered meritorious for them to honor their parents. Therefore, Noaḥ, Shem, and Esav were each rewarded for treating his father properly, even though they were not obliged to do so.

The Gemara (Kiddushin 31a) spells out this approach clearly with the well-known story of Dama b. Netina, a non-Jew from Ashkelon, who did not awaken his father even when he had a chance to conclude a very profitable business deal. The key needed to access the merchandise was under his father's head; since he refused to disturb his father to get the key, the merchandise was inaccessible and he forfeited the sale. As a reward for this great sacrifice, a red heifer, which was extremely valuable, was born into Dama's flock. The Gemara's account concludes with a comment by R. Ḥanina that if this is the case for one who is not commanded regarding *kibbud av va'em*, how much more must it be for one who is commanded.

The Gemara (Nazir 61a) states that a non-Jew cannot vow to become a Nazirite, as a vow that prohibits becoming defiled for one's deceased parents can pertain only to a person who is generally obligated by *kibbud av va'em*. This gemara is cited by Rabbi Meir Simḥa HaKohen in his *Or Same'aḥ* as a final, convincing proof that *kibbud av va'em* is not obligatory for Noahides.

In contrast, though, other sources seem to imply that Noahides are commanded regarding *kibbud av va'em*. For example, Rabbi Shmuel ben Ḥofni Gaon enumerates *kibbud av va'em* as one of the mitzvot incumbent upon all mankind. In his commentary on Bereshit 9:22, he points out that Ḥam was cursed for not fulfilling this mitzva, which implies that it is in fact an obligation, not merely a meritorious act.

The Malbim (Devarim 27:16) also comments that, although we do not find an explicit commandment that requires Noahides to fulfill *kibbud av va'em*, they are enjoined from cursing their parents. Since blasphemy is prohibited for Noahides, and since respect for one's parents is akin to respect for God (Kiddushin 32a), it follows that every person is required to honor his parents. Of course, this proves only that it is prohibited to curse or otherwise act disrespectfully towards one's parents. It does not prove that one is obligated to actively respect or serve his parents.

The *Shulḥan Arukh* (*Yoreh De'ah* 241:9) rules that a convert may not shame or curse his parents, lest it be said that conversion leads to a lowering of moral standards, which would imply that the convert has become less holy. Many commentators (such as Rabbi Akiva Eiger, *Beit Hillel*, and *Yad Shaul* ad loc.) raise the question, since Noahides are not required to fulfill *kibbud av va'em*, what reduction in behavior would be discerned? Rabbi Akiva Eiger suggests that although there is no commandment incumbent on Noahides, most people respect their parents. If a convert ceased acting in the customary manner, this would be viewed with disapproval. Alternatively, *Yad Avraham* suggests that while Noahides are not commanded to actively respect their parents, the halakha here refers to the prohibition of cursing and shaming one's parents. That prohibition does apply to Noahides, as indicated by the story of Noaḥ's sons.

None of these commentators cites Rambam's *Hilkhot Mamrim* 5:11, which seems to be the source of the *Shulḥan Arukh*'s ruling. This text contains an additional phrase that is not cited in the *Shulḥan Arukh*: "He should show him partial honor." (See the Frankel edition of the Rambam for variant readings.)

Rabbi Moshe Feinstein (*Iggerot Moshe, Yoreh De'ah,* II:130) suggests that the concept of partial honor is a function of the fact that *kibbud av va'em* is predicated upon the requirement of showing gratitude, a value that is certainly incumbent upon all mankind. Despite the lack of an explicit commandment to act morally or ethically, there are obvious moral obligations that apply to all people. While the laws of *kibbud av va'em* given to Jews are very detailed, a Noahide must show only partial honor to demonstrate his gratitude to his parents. It might be added that the Yerushalmi (Pe'ah 1:1) says that the obligation of *kibbud av va'em* is actually a form of repaying a debt, and this would certainly apply to Noahides.

In summary, Noahides are not bound by a specific requirement to honor their parents, but are forbidden to disgrace or curse them. It is meritorious for them to honor their parents, and they may be required to show partial honor as an expression of gratitude or payment of a debt, which are universal values.

Parashat Lekh Lekha

Circumcision Performed by a Non-Jew

The mitzva of *brit mila* (circumcision) was given to Avraham and his descendants as part of the covenant with God. The Torah emphasizes the centrality of this commandment with the compound phrase "*himmol yimmol,*" "shall surely be circumcised" (Bereshit 17:13). The supreme importance of this mitzva also is demonstrated by the fact that it is one of only two positive mitzvot that carry a penalty of *karet,* being cut off from the Jewish people.

Despite the centrality of circumcision to God's covenant with the Jewish people, the Gemara (Avoda Zara 26b) raises the question of whether circumcision may be performed by a non-Jew. R. Meir maintains that this is not allowed, as a non-Jew may maliciously harm the child. The Sages maintain that it is permissible, provided there are observers present to ensure that no harm is done. According to both opinions, circumcision performed by a non-Jew is intrinsically effectual.

However, the Gemara then cites a dissenting opinion according to which circumcision performed by a non-Jew is inherently invalid.

According to this approach, the phrase "you shall observe my covenant" (Bereshit 17:9) indicates that only Avraham and his progeny may perform the *brit,* to the exclusion of non-Jews. R. Ḥisda then cites another source invalidating circumcision performed by a non-Jew: the compound phrase "*himmol yimmol*" implies that only one who is a member of the covenant can perform the *brit.* The Gemara explains that even a circumcised non-Jew is not included in the covenant, and therefore may not perform circumcision. Conversely, even an uncircumcised Jew may perform a *brit,* because he is included in the covenant. (An example of a Jewish male who is not required to be circumcised is one whose brothers died as a result of circumcision. He cannot undergo a *brit* because of concern that there may be some hereditary factor, such as hemophilia, that would endanger him.)

The *Minḥat Ḥinnukh* (2) cites the opinion of Rabbi Yonatan Eybeschutz that the mitzva of *brit mila* requires the father to either circumcise the child himself or appoint an agent (*shaliaḥ*) to do so. Indeed, common practice is for the father to explicitly designate the *mohel* as his agent to fulfill the mitzva. The *Minḥat Ḥinnukh* thus questions the need for a specific source to invalidate a *brit* performed by a non-Jew, inasmuch as the law of agency does not apply to non-Jews (Kiddushin 41b).

Responding to this question, the *Rid* (*Tosefot Rid,* Avoda Zara 26b) argues that *mila* does not require agency. His proof is from the very fact that there is an opinion allowing a non-Jew to serve as the *mohel.* The *Rid* posits that agency is not necessary since the mitzva is not to actually circumcise the child, but merely to see to it that a proper circumcision is performed. According to this approach, the father need not appoint the *mohel* as an agent, and if a non-Jew performs a circumcision as required by halakha, this fulfills the mitzva. (The *Rid* also uses this principle to explain why *brit mila* is not considered a mitzva that is incumbent at a specific time: while it is true that the circumcision itself must be performed on the eighth day, the father's mitzva, namely, arranging the *brit,* can be fulfilled at any time.)

Notwithstanding, according to the opinion that the father is required to appoint the *mohel* as his agent, we might suggest the following answer to the question posed by the *Minḥat Ḥinnukh*: Assuming that *mila* should be done by the father or his agent, what would happen if another Jew performed the *brit* without the father's permission? Undoubtedly the *brit* would be valid, although the father would not have fulfilled his mitzva. In fact, the *mohel* might be considered to have stolen the mitzva and be required to indemnify the father (*Shulḥan Arukh, Ḥoshen Mishpat* 382). Similarly, a non-Jew who performs a *brit* may fulfill the technical requirements of *mila* although the father does not thus fulfill his mitzva. Conversely, if a non-Jew is disqualified from performing the mitzva, the circumcision itself must be ruled invalid and the child requires a minor additional surgical procedure.

Rambam (*Hilkhot Mila* 2:1, cited in *Shulḥan Arukh, Yoreh De'ah* 264:1) rules that a non-Jew should not perform the *brit*. However, if he does, there is no need to do so again. (*Beit Yosef* ad loc. cites a disagreement about whether this means that nothing more need be done, or that there should be only minor additional surgery.) The *Kesef Mishneh* (ad loc.) opines that Rambam was unsure of whether the halakha allowed a non-Jew to perform a *brit* and therefore said that he should not do so; since the halakha may permit it, it is valid ex post facto.

The *Shaagat Arye* (54) questions this approach. If the halakha is unclear, then the general rule requires us to be stringent regarding a biblical law, such as circumcision, and resort to another surgical procedure. Thus according to the *Shaagat Arye*, a *brit* performed by a non-Jew is definitely invalid and cannot be repaired at all.

To summarize, there is a dispute as to whether a non-Jew may circumcise a Jew. While the halakha clearly states that he should not do so, there is a major dispute among the *posekim* regarding the ex post facto validity of such a circumcision.

Parashat Vayera

Visiting the Sick

Our *parasha* opens with God's appearing to Avraham while the latter is sitting at the entrance of his tent in the plains of Mamre (Bereshit 18:1). Rashi (ad loc.) comments that He came to visit Avraham because Avraham was recuperating from his circumcision. Apparently Rashi deduced this from the fact that the verse gives no reason for God's appearance, and no divine statement is made to Avraham at the beginning of the *parasha*.

R. Ḥama b. R. Ḥanina explained that the verse "You shall walk after Hashem, your God" (Devarim 13:5) commands us to emulate God's behavior. Just as He clothed Adam and Ḥava (Bereshit 3:21), so must we clothe the needy. Just as God visited Avraham in Mamre, so must we visit the sick. Just as God comforted Yitzḥak when he was mourning the loss of his father, Avraham (Bereshit 25:11), so must we comfort mourners. Just as God buried the dead (Devarim 34:6), so must we (Sota 14a).

R. Yosef interpreted the verse "you shall show them the path that they should take" (Shemot 18:20) to mean that we are required to perform general acts of lovingkindness, including visiting the sick and burying the dead (Bava Metzia 30b).

Rabbi Yitzḥak of Korbeil counted *bikkur ḥolim* (visiting the sick) as one of the 613 mitzvot (*Sefer Mitzvot Katan* 47), citing the verse "you shall walk in His ways" (Devarim 28:9) as the source of this mitzva. Likewise, the *Behag* counted *bikkur ḥolim* as an independent mitzva, for which he was criticized by Rambam (*Sefer HaMitzvot,* principle 1). Rambam argues that rabbinic laws and enactments are not to be counted in the list of mitzvot. Therefore, unlike the *Behag,* Rambam does not count such precepts as *bikkur ḥolim,* comforting mourners, reading the Megilla, and Hallel among the 613 commandments.

Rambam further elucidates his position regarding this mitzva in principle 2 of *Sefer HaMitzvot* as well as in the *Mishneh Torah* (*Hilkhot Evel* 14:1). He maintains that all specific acts of lovingkindness, such as comforting mourners, visiting the sick, hosting guests, and arranging funerals, are not biblical mitzvot, but rather mandated by rabbinic law. However, he then adds that these obligations fall under the general rubric of the biblical mitzva "love your neighbor as yourself" (Vayikra 19:18).

At first glance, this position is somewhat puzzling. Since the Torah commands us to love our neighbors and since Rambam says that *bikkur ḥolim* is included in that requirement, it should follow that this is indeed a biblical obligation! Moreover, the commandment "you shall walk in His ways" is certainly a biblical obligation. In fact, Rabbi Soloveitchik writes in his "Reflections on the *Amidah*" (translated in his book *Worship of the Heart,* ed. Shalom Carmy, Jersey City: Ktav, 2003) that the central mitzva of the 613 mitzvot is that of following the ways of God (*imitatio Dei*).

In his book *Od Yosef Yisrael Beni Ḥai* (Chicago: Yeshivat Brisk, 1993, p. 4), Rabbi Ahron Soloveichik solves this issue by demarcating the exact parameters of "love your neighbor" and "walk in His ways." He explains that these mitzvot are in the realm of *ḥovot halevavot* (duties of the heart): the obligation is to internalize love of one's neighbor and develop character traits modeled for us by God's actions, such as mercy and compassion.

However, the biblical mitzva does not require making these feelings manifest by performing any specific action. It was our Rabbis who dictated specific directions and guidelines as to how to express these internal feelings. Therefore, when an individual carries out the specific deeds commanded by the Rabbis, he externally demonstrates internal feelings that are the fulfillment of the biblical mitzva.

Rabbi Aḥai Gaon, in his *She'iltot* (93), stipulates that Jews are obligated to perform the mitzva of *bikkur ḥolim*. Apparently, Rabbi Aḥai Gaon assumes that non-Jews are not similarly obligated. However, if the mitzva is predicated upon love of one's neighbor or following the ways of God, one may consider the possibility that these obligations actually are incumbent upon non-Jews.

The Gemara (Nedarim 40a) relates that a student of R. Akiva took ill. No one visited this student until R. Akiva himself visited and personally attended to his needs. When R. Akiva left, his student called out, "You have saved my life." R. Akiva then declared, "Anyone who does not visit the sick is tantamount to a murderer!" This comment is codified by Rambam (*Hilkhot Evel* 14:4):

> *Bikkur ḥolim* is a mitzva that is obligatory upon all. Even people of higher stature are required to visit people of lower stature. Numerous visits daily should be made as long as this does not inconvenience the patient. Whoever visits is considered to have taken away part of the illness, and whoever does not visit is akin to a murderer.

Inasmuch as the prohibition of murder is one of the seven Noahide laws, one might argue that any requirement based on an extension of murder, such as that formulated by R. Akiva, also is obligatory upon non-Jews.

Other actions have likewise been compared to murder, and how literally we should relate to these comparisons is unclear. For example, the Gemara (Sota 10b) advises that it is better to jump into a burning furnace than to shame someone. The *Tosafot* (ad loc.) raise the issue that shaming someone is not included in the three cardinal sins for which one must give up his life. While some Rishonim respond that the Gemara is not to be interpreted literally and one need not actually give up his life to avoid shaming someone, the *Tosafot* accept the literal meaning of the Gemara. They maintain that shaming is not listed in Pesaḥim (25a) among the sins for which one must give up his life because the three cardinal sins listed there are those explicitly mentioned in the Torah, while the prohibition against shaming a person is deduced only by inference. According to the reasoning of the *Tosafot*, it may similarly be argued that a non-Jew is required to perform *bikkur ḥolim*, as an extension of the prohibition against murder.

No *berakha* (blessing) is recited on the performance of this mitzva. In fact, there is no *berakha* on any mitzva *bein adam laḥavero* (a mitzva directed toward one's fellow man). Rabbenu Baḥya (Bemidbar 35:8) explains that *berakhot* are made only on mitzvot not done by non-Jews, as we thereby demonstrate that God "sanctified us through His mitzvot." However, this implies not that non-Jews are obligated to perform these mitzvot, but merely that non-Jews can fulfill them.

Parashat Ḥayei Sara

Birkat Eirusin: The Blessing on Betrothal

The Gemara (Ketubbot 7b) distinguishes between the *Sheva Berakhot* recited at a marriage and the *berakha* recited on betrothal. (Halakhic betrothal, known as *kiddushin* or *eirusin,* is generally performed today under the *ḥuppa*. The groom gives the bride a ring and makes a declaration that causes her to become *mekudeshet,* betrothed, to him. The arrangement popularly known in modern Hebrew as *eirusin* and in English as engagement, i.e., when a couple decides to get married, has no halakhic significance.)

Following *kiddushin,* the actual marriage (*nissu'in*) is effected when the couple enter the *yiḥud* room (according to Rambam, *Hilkhot Ishut* 10:1). The *Sheva Berakhot* are recited in the wedding hall at the time of the marriage. They should be said in the presence of a *minyan,* as Boaz assembled a *minyan* before his marriage (Ruth 4:2). However, the blessing over betrothal (*Birkat Eirusin*) is recited at the time of betrothal. The Gemara does not mention a requirement for a *minyan,* nor a source for this *berakha*.

The *Tosafot* (Ketubbot 7b) point out that Tractate Kalla cites a source for this *berakha*. When Eliezer left the house of Lavan with Rivka, her family blessed her (Bereshit 24:60). The *Tosafot* explain that the *berakha* recited by Boaz is the source for the *berakhot* at the wedding, while Eliezer was an agent (*shaliaḥ*) for *eirusin*, and thus his *berakha* is the source for the *berakha* of betrothal. The *Tosafot* suggest that perhaps the derivation from Rivka is merely an *asmakhta* (an allusion used as support for an oral law), as the blessing given to her is stated in the Torah ("Our sister, may you be the mother of thousands of myriads") and does not really refer to *Birkat Eirusin*. The *Tosafot* further add that *Birkat Eirusin* apparently may be recited by a *shaliaḥ*, based on the precedent of Eliezer.

Rambam (*Hilkhot Ishut* 3:23) writes that the procedure of *kiddushin* requires a *berakha* immediately prior to its performance, "as is done with all mitzvot." This *berakha* should be recited by the groom or by his agent. If one performed the *kiddushin* without a *berakha*, he may not recite the *berakha* afterwards, as this would constitute a *berakha levattala* (a *berakha* for no purpose), since the mitzva has already been performed. This conforms to the opinion of Rambam (*Hilkhot Berakhot* 11:5–7) that a *berakha* on a mitzva must precede the mitzva and may not be recited once the mitzva has been completed. The *Or Zarua* (*Hilkhot Keriat Shema* 25) disagrees, maintaining that all *berakhot* meant to be recited prior to a mitzva may still be said even if the mitzva has been completed.

Inasmuch as this is a *berakha* recited on a mitzva, the common custom that the rabbi performing the ceremony recites the *berakha* is surprising. While there is a general rule that one may recite a *berakha* for someone else, this is true only when the person reciting the *berakha* also is involved in the mitzva (e.g., on Rosh HaShana, one who has already heard the shofar may recite the *berakha* for someone who has not). Since the rabbi is not personally involved in a betrothal, he should be unable to recite the *berakha* on the groom's behalf.

In fact, the custom in Yemen and some other communities was for the groom himself to recite the *berakha*. The *Noda BiYehuda* (*Even HaEzer Tinyana* 1) cites a responsum of Rambam stating that if anyone but the groom recited the *berakha*, this would constitute a *berakha levattala*. Rabbi Yosef Kapaḥ, the great Yemenite scholar and expert in the writings of the Rambam, told me that although this position seems logically accurate, the alleged responsum does not exist.

Apparently, common custom is based on the opinions of Rishonim who disagree with Rambam. The Rosh (Ketubbot 1:12) says that the *berakha* is not recited over the mitzva of *kiddushin*. In his opinion, there actually is no mitzva of *kiddushin* at all. Rather, there is a mitzva of procreation, which could theoretically be fulfilled without *kiddushin*. Moreover, the *berakha* must be recited even in a case where it is clear that the couple will not have children. Additionally, the unusual text of the *berakha* ("who sanctified us through His mitzvot and commanded us regarding forbidden relations") also implies that this is not an ordinary *berakha* over a mitzva. Rather, this blessing seems to fall in the category of *birkhot shevaḥ* (blessings marking special events or circumstances, such as thunder, a rainbow, and seeing a king).

In fact, the Ritva (Ketubbot 7b), who agrees with the Rosh, argues that this cannot be a *berakha* on the mitzva because the custom is that the groom does not recite it. Rather, he maintains that the *berakha* is similar to Kiddush: we praise God for sanctifying the Jewish people by forbidding illicit relations and formulating laws to govern procreation. The Ritva therefore maintains that although the general practice is to recite the *berakha* prior to *kiddushin*, logically it should be said afterwards, just as we recite Kiddush when the holy Shabbat day has already begun.

According to the view that this *berakha* is a *birkat shevaḥ* and not a *birkat mitzva*, who is obligated to recite it? One might argue that the *berakha* should be made by the person or persons who experience the mitzva of *kiddushin*, namely, the groom and the bride. There is a similar situation in the case of a *brit mila*: the *mohel* recites the *berakha* over the mitzva itself, and then, after the actual circumcision, the father recites a *berakha*: "who commanded us to bring him into the covenant of our father Avraham." There is a discussion as to whether anyone other than the father may recite this *berakha* (*Shulḥan Arukh, Yoreh De'ah* 265:1).

In fact, the *Tevuot Shor* (1:59) maintains that recitation of this *berakha* is clearly not incumbent upon the groom, and the rabbi does not even have to intend for him to fulfill an obligation to recite it. This approach solves the dilemma that the rabbi is faced with if the groom does not want to hear or relate to the *berakha*. In such a case, although according to Rambam it would seem to be a *berakha levattala,* according to the *Tevuot Shor* (and presumably the Rosh and Ritva) the *berakha* fulfills the obligation of others, including the rabbi himself, and is therefore not in vain.

This may be the reasoning of the *Tosafot,* who prove from the case of Eliezer that an agent may make the *berakha.* If the *berakha* is recited over the mitzva, then obviously the agent who performs the mitzva may make the *berakha* (Shabbat 137a). However, if the *berakha* is over the event, perhaps it should not be recited by proxy. First, the *berakha* still may be incumbent on any other parties involved. More important, perhaps it is not the type of event that requires a *berakha.* Therefore, *Tosafot* cite the proof involving Eliezer to show that the *berakha* is still to be made.

There are other ramifications to the dispute between Rambam and the Rosh. According to Rambam, the mitzva is incumbent upon the groom and perhaps the bride, as well (*Noda BiYehuda, Even HaEzer Tinyana* 1). If so, the party or parties required to recite the *berakha* should choose the rabbi who helps them fulfill this requirement. However, according to the *Tevuot Shor* (as well as the Rosh and Ritva), the obligation is incumbent upon everyone attending the wedding. Rabbi Herschel Schachter (*BeIkvei HaTzon,* Jerusalem, 1997, p. 271) comments that the attendees should choose the rabbi according to the above criteria.

While it is proper decorum for people to remain silent and listen at the betrothal ceremony, according to Rambam this does not seem to be a halakhic obligation, as they are not involved in the *berakha.* However, according to *Tevuot Shor* (and others), they must listen and have the intention of fulfilling their obligation.

Our custom that the rabbi recites the *berakha* seems to follow the opinion that this *berakha* is not a *birkat mitzva.* However, we recite the *berakha* before the *kiddushin,* even though, according to the Ritva, it preferably should be said after the event (as is the case with Kiddush). The Ritva justified the prevalent custom by saying that, since the *berakha* is said at the time of the mitzva, it was instituted similarly to a *birkat mitzva,* and therefore the custom should not be abolished.

Parashat Toledot

A Blind Person's Duty to Fulfill Mitzvot

In our *parasha,* we read that Yitzḥak asks Esav to sharpen his equipment, hunt an animal, and prepare a meal (Bereshit 27:1–4). Rashi comments that the seemingly superfluous request to sharpen his equipment indicates that Yitzḥak instructed Esav to prepare his knife properly so that the animal would be slaughtered correctly and thus kosher. From Yitzḥak's instructing Esav to *hunt* for the animal, Rashi understands that Yitzḥak specified that he did not want Esav to steal one. Esav's reply, however, implies that if he were unsuccessful in hunting for an animal, he would steal one for his father's meal.

The *Keli Ḥemda* (Rabbi Meir Dan Plotzki) and other Aḥaronim raise the question of why Yitzḥak deemed it necessary to exhort Esav regarding these halakhic requirements. Would Esav, who was so meticulous in honoring his father, have brought him non-kosher food? Even if Esav was personally inclined to steal, would he have given stolen food to his revered father?

One answer is that since Yitzḥak was legally blind, Esav felt that his father was exempt from all halakhic obligations. Therefore Yitzḥak technically could have eaten non-kosher or even stolen food without violating any prohibition. Nevertheless, despite the letter of the law, Yitzḥak asked Esav to bring him kosher food.

In order to see whether this answer is tenable, let us try to determine the halakhic status of a blind person with regard to mitzva observance. The Gemara (Kiddushin 31a) cites the opinion of R. Yehuda that a blind person is exempt from all mitzvot. Apparently this issue was subject to dispute, as can be deduced from an incident related there: R. Yosef, who was blind, offered to host a festive meal in celebration if informed that the halakha follows R. Yehuda's opinion, as he felt that fulfilling the mitzvot despite not being obligated to do so would reflect a great commitment to God. However, once told that a person who is obligated by the mitzvot and fulfills them is greater than one who fulfills them although not obligated, he reversed his position and said he would host such a meal if told that the halakha is not in accordance with R. Yehuda, and a blind person is obligated to perform mitzvot.

The *Peri Megadim* (*Shulḥan Arukh, Oraḥ Ḥayim,* introduction, part 3) maintains that, even according to R. Yehuda, a blind person is exempt only from positive mitzvot, but is restricted by all prohibitions. According to this opinion, no authority would permit a blind person to eat non-kosher or stolen food.

However, the *Noda BiYehuda* (Responsa, *Oraḥ Ḥayim* 112) questions this assertion. He cites the statement of the *Tosafot* (Bava Kamma 87a) that according to R. Yehuda, rabbinic law requires a blind person to observe all biblical laws even though he is fundamentally exempt. (The Rashba [Bava Kamma 87a] clearly argues with this view, describing R. Yehuda as understanding that the Rabbis did not obligate a blind person to perform mitzvot.) The *Tosafot* assume that this rabbinic obligation is intended to prevent blind people from appearing to be non-Jews. The *Noda BiYehuda* asks, if the *Peri Megadim* is right in arguing that a blind person is forbidden to violate prohibitions, then there should be no need for a rabbinic measure to prevent him from appearing non-Jewish: is it not very clear that he is Jewish since he is not allowed to work on Shabbat, consume non-kosher food, or eat *ḥametz* on Pesaḥ? Further, it is possible that according to the *Peri Megadim* a blind person would be obligated to make Kiddush on Shabbat and eat matza on Pesaḥ, inasmuch as these positive mitzvot are associated with prohibitions and the Gemara states that anyone who is enjoined from eating *ḥametz* must eat matza (Pesaḥim 43b) and that anyone who is forbidden to work on Shabbat must make Kiddush (Berakhot 20b). The *Noda BiYehuda* thus understands the statement of the *Tosafot* that, in the absence of the rabbinic enactment, a blind person would appear non-Jewish, as implying that he is exempt from all biblical laws and would, in fact, be allowed to eat non-kosher food.

Would he also be permitted to steal? The *Minḥat Ḥinnukh* (2) maintains that even if a blind person is exempt from biblical mitzvot, his status is not lower than that of a Noahide, and he therefore must observe the seven Noahide laws. The *Minḥat Ḥinnukh* (26) further states that the status of a blind person is unique and different from that of a non-Jew in several respects. First, if he violates a law, he is not punished as is a Noahide. Second, whereas a Noahide is not allowed to observe Shabbat, a blind Jew is certainly permitted to do so. Presumably, the restriction of teaching Torah to a non-Jew (Ḥagiga 10a) also would not apply to him.

To summarize, there is an opinion that a blind person is obligated to observe all biblical and rabbinic laws, while R. Yehuda maintains that he is exempt from biblical mitzvot. There are two ways to understand R. Yehuda's position: (a) he is exempt from positive mitzvot but restricted by prohibitions (*Peri Megadim*); (b) he is exempt from prohibitions, as well (*Noda BiYehuda*). However, it seems inconceivable that he is not obligated to observe at least the Noahide laws (*Minḥat Ḥinnukh*).

Inasmuch as R. Yosef was undecided as to which opinion was accepted as halakha, there is a dispute among the *posekim*. The Ran (Kiddushin 31a) says that since R. Yehuda argued with the Sages, the halakha is in accordance with the view of the Sages, based on the general rule of following the majority. The Ran maintains that R. Yosef, as well, knew this and his discussion was merely theoretical. Rabbenu Yeruḥam (*Sefer Adam* 5:4) is one of the few scholars who ruled in accordance with the opinion of R. Yehuda. Latter day *posekim*, such as the *Arukh HaShulḥan* (58a) and the *Mishna Berura* (53:41), all follow the majority opinion that a blind person is obligated to observe all mitzvot. Even according to Rabbenu Yeruḥam, a blind person is required by rabbinic law to observe all mitzvot.

It therefore follows that no authority would allow a blind person to steal, and it therefore remains puzzling that Yitzḥak felt it necessary to tell Esav not to steal. On the other hand, according to the *Peri Megadim*'s understanding of R. Yehuda, it is permitted by biblical law for a blind person to eat non-kosher food. Nevertheless, Yitzḥak did not wish to eat non-kosher food and therefore told Esav to slaughter the animal properly.

Parashat Vayetzeh

Arvit: Obligatory or Not?

On the way from Be'er Sheva to Haran, Yaakov arrived at what the Torah describes simply as "the place" (Rashi identifies it as Mount Moriya.) The Torah uses the verb "*vayifga*," which may be interpreted as "reached" or "prayed." Therefore, *Ḥazal* interpret the verse to mean that Yaakov prayed the Arvit (evening) prayer.

Rambam (*Sefer HaMitzvot* 4; *Hilkhot Tefilla* 1:1) maintains that there is a biblical obligation to pray once daily. Ramban (*Sefer HaMitzvot* 4) disagrees, arguing that daily prayer is a rabbinic requirement. According to him, the only biblical obligation of prayer is at a time of crisis. Both Rambam and Ramban agree that the requirement of praying three times daily is a rabbinic law.

The Gemara (Berakhot 26b) cites the opinion of R. Yosei b. R. Ḥanina that the three daily prayers were instituted by the Rabbis in accordance with the prayers of our forefathers: Avraham instituted Shaḥarit, Yitzḥak instituted Minḥa, and Yaakov instituted Arvit. On the other hand, R. Yehoshua b. Levi says that our daily prayers were instituted as substitutes for the Temple service: Shaḥarit was instituted in place of the daily morning sacrifice, Minḥa in place of the afternoon sacrifice, and Arvit in place of the remains of the sacrificial animals that were left to burn on the Altar all night.

Rambam (*Hilkhot Tefilla* 1:5–6) codifies the opinion that our prayers correspond to the daily sacrifices. He adds that the obligation of Arvit is not as stringent as that of Shaḥarit and Minḥa. Nevertheless, it is the custom of all Jews worldwide to pray Arvit, and it has therefore become accepted as an obligation.

If Arvit is derived from the burning of the sacrificial remains on the Altar, it is understandable that this prayer is not obligatory, since there is no requirement to leave any remainder of the sacrifices. Inasmuch as this was not an obligation, it follows that Arvit should not be as stringent as the other prayers.

On the other hand, if the prayers were instituted by the forefathers, then why should Yaakov's prayer be different from those of Avraham and Yitzḥak? This question is so compelling that the *Tosafot* (Yoma 87b) say that Arvit is not really optional. Rather, they say, it is obligatory, but not as obligatory as Shaḥarit and Minḥa, and it may therefore be waived under unusual circumstances (such as if there is a pressing mitzva to be fulfilled). The reason for this is that Arvit was the prayer of Yaakov and therefore cannot be taken lightly.

While the *Tosafot* believe that Arvit is a basic obligation, they agree that it is still less of an obligation than Shaḥarit and Minḥa. Therefore, the question remains: why is this prayer different? Moreover, Rambam, who says that Arvit is not as stringent as the other prayers, also codifies (*Hilkhot Melakhim* 9:1) that Yaakov prayed Arvit. The *Or Same'aḥ* (*Hilkhot Tefilla* 3:9) explains that Rambam mentioned this because he believes our prayers were instituted for both reasons. The time constraints of prayer parallel the times of the sacrifices, but the basic obligation is also due to the prayer of our forefathers. Why, then, is the obligation of Arvit not the same as that of the other prayers?

The *Torah Temima* (Bereshit 28:11) suggests that Yaakov was not really obligated to pray Arvit. In fact, the Gemara (Eiruvin 65a) states that one need not pray while traveling, as it is difficult to have proper concentration (*kavvana*) while praying. (Many authorities hold that since today our *kavvana* is not very intense at any time, we must pray under all conditions.) Since Yaakov himself was not obligated to pray, his prayer was voluntary. It therefore follows, argues the *Torah Temima*, that Arvit would never be obligatory. Nevertheless, as mentioned, the halakha today is that one must pray Arvit, either because of the virtually universal acceptance of the obligation (Rambam) or because of the qualification that it may be waived only under extreme circumstances (*Tosafot*).

Our custom is that the *ḥazan* repeats the *Amida* at Shaḥarit and Minḥa but not at Arvit. Rambam (*Hilkhot Tefilla* 9:9) explains that since Arvit is not really obligatory, there is no individual who must pray. Therefore, not only is there no need to say the *Amida* for one who is unable to recite it himself (the usual rationale for the *ḥazan*'s repetition of the *Amida*), but doing so would constitute a *berakha levattala* – an unnecessary, wasteful *berakha*.

In order to determine the proper time to pray Arvit, we should take into account that *Shema* must be said at night (Berakhot 2a, mishna; *Tosafot* and Rishonim ad loc.). The *Amida* itself may be said throughout the time that the remains of the sacrifices would be on the Altar.

The *Torah Temima* (Vayikra 6:2) maintains that inasmuch as the remains stayed on the Altar all night, we may pray Arvit all night. Even though the Sages generally instituted that all nightly obligations be performed by *ḥatzot* (halakhic midnight), this may not apply to burning what remains of sacrifices (as is evident from the first mishna of Berakhot). Therefore, he says, it should not apply to Arvit, either.

If we follow the opinion that our prayer corresponds to Yaakov's, we should determine when he actually prayed. The *Tosafot* (Berakhot 26b) prove from the Gemara that Yaakov actually prayed before dark, and thus ask why the Gemara assumes that one may pray only at nighttime. They respond that we follow the opinion of R. Yehuda that one may pray earlier (at *plag haminḥa*), and that indeed this is preferable.

The Mishna (Berakhot 20a) says that women are obligated to pray. Sephardic women, who follow the opinion of Rambam, may be obligated only by the biblical mitzva of prayer (once daily). This, in fact, is the opinion of Rabbi Ovadia Yosef as recorded by his son Rabbi Yitzhak in *Sefer Otzar Dinim* (Jerusalem, 1989).

Those who follow Ramban and the other Rishonim would not distinguish between Shaḥarit and Minḥa (*Mishna Berura* 106:4). However, there is a controversy among the codifiers as to whether a woman must pray Arvit. The *Mishna Berura* (ibid.) says that women did not accept the obligation of Arvit and observes that most women indeed do not pray Arvit. The *Arukh HaShulḥan* (106:5) disagrees, arguing that according to the Ashkenazic tradition, women should pray three times daily.

This discussion relates only to the weekday obligation of Arvit. The question of Arvit on Shabbat, Yom Tov, or Motza'ei Shabbat may be different, as special prayers are said on those occasions.

Parashat Vayishlaḥ

Pride and Humility

As Yaakov prepared to meet Esav, he prayed, "I have been diminished by all the kindnesses and by all the truth that You have done for Your servant" (Bereshit 32:11). Rashi explains that Yaakov was afraid that any merit he had accumulated had been dissipated by the reward that he had already received. Therefore, he was worried that he did not deserve to be saved from Esav.

The Gemara (Sota 5a) says in the name of R. Ḥiyya b. Ashi that a *talmid ḥakham* should have "one-eighth of one-eighth of pride." R. Naḥman b. Yitzḥak disagrees, saying that he should have no trace of pride at all.

Many commentators have attempted to explain the meaning of the expression "one-eighth of one-eighth." Rabbi Tzvi Hirsch Chajes commented that this measure is less than one-sixtieth, and therefore is considered null and void. (If non-kosher liquid is mixed with sixty times as much kosher liquid, the non-kosher segment is null and void and the mixture may be eaten.)

It has been written in the name of the Vilna Gaon (*Kol Eliyahu*, p. 81) that "one-eighth of one-eighth" alludes to the statement

"I have been diminished." The eighth *parasha* of the Torah is *Toledot*, and the eighth verse begins, "I have been diminished." The Gaon explains that when someone prays, he should not ask God to help him for his own sake. Rather, he should ask for help in the name of our ancestors and forefathers. However, after his prayers are answered, a *talmid ḥakham* should feel that God has rewarded him for his own merits, thus reducing his accumulated merit.

While it is obvious that humility is a positive virtue and it certainly is inappropriate to display hubris, this may not be an independent mitzva. An interesting incident is recorded in the introduction to the *Sefer Mitzvot Gadol* (*Semag*) and reiterated in greater detail in Mitzva 64. After the author finished his compilation of the 613 mitzvot, he received a message in a dream informing him that he had forgotten to include the principle "Be careful lest you forget Hashem, your God" (Devarim 6:12; 8:11). He then realized that this is an important foundation of the fear of God. Although Rambam did not count this mitzva in his list, the *Semag*, who generally follows the list of Rambam, realized that he should enumerate it as an independent mitzva. After a while, the *Semag* saw that the Gemara (Sota 5a) said that R. Naḥman b. Yitzḥak had utilized this verse (among others) to derive that it is forbidden to be haughty.

The *Sefer Yere'im* (332:22) cites Rabbi Yehudai Gaon as saying that there is a positive mitzva to be modest and humble. Although the author (Rabbi Eliezer of Metz) finds no positive or negative commandment about humility stated explicitly in the Torah, he notes that the Torah praises Moshe for being exceedingly humble (Bemidbar 12:3). He infers from this that there is a mitzva to be humble.

Besides the obvious problem with this approach – that it derives a general obligation from a statement about a particular individual – commentaries on the *Yere'im* raise another objection. It seems obvious that Moshe was praised for having a unique attribute. How, then, could this statement be employed to require the average person to reach such a level? Perhaps the Torah implies an *a fortiori* argument: if Moshe Rabbenu could be modest, every person can and should be humble.

Rabbenu Yona (*Shaarei Teshuva* 3:34) finds another source in the Torah that forbids pride. The Torah imposes certain laws and restrictions upon a king so that "his heart not become haughty" (Devarim 17:19).

Rabbenu Yona adds that pride is one of the most severe transgressions and ultimately leads to perdition of the soul.

Although Rambam did not count pride or modesty as either a positive or a negative mitzva, he certainly felt that modesty is an extremely important trait to possess. In fact, Rabbi Ahron Soloveichik wrote that the reason Rambam declined to count the mitzva of humility is precisely its importance. The prohibition of pride is associated with the prohibition of forgetting God (as the *Semag* explains) and therefore is a mitzva that encompasses the entire Torah. According to Rambam, mitzvot that are all-embracing are not to be counted among the 613 mitzvot (*Paraḥ Matteh Aharon, Sefer HaMadda*, p. 66).

Rambam (*Hilkhot De'ot* 3:3) states that one should be exceedingly humble, as the Torah uses the adjective "very" when it describes Moshe's humility. Rambam cites *Pirkei Avot* 4:4, which says that one should be "very, very" modest. Many commentators (e.g., *Leḥem Mishneh, Hilkhot De'ot* 1:4) point out that Rambam (ibid.) says that one should always take the middle road, which he terms "the golden path," in regard to all character traits, including modesty. How, then, can he say that one must be "exceedingly humble?"

Rabbi Menaḥem Krakowsky (*Avodat HaMelekh, Hilkhot De'ot* 3:3) raises an objection to the position of the *Semag* and the *Yere'im*. Inasmuch as there is a general obligation to emulate the attributes of God ("you shall walk in His ways," "*vehalakhta biderakhav*"), why is there a specific commandment to be modest? He then says that, according to Rambam, the general halakha of *vehalakhta biderakhav* would require us to follow the golden mean. The additional point – to be exceedingly modest – is merely a rabbinic law.

To summarize, Rambam feels that there is no specific biblical mitzva regarding pride and humility. The *Yere'im* argues that there is a positive mitzva to be humble, whereas the *Semag* and Rabbenu Yona derive from various sources that there is a prohibition to be haughty.

Rabbi Yona Mertzbach (*Aleh Yona*, p. 195) points out that the different sources cited by the *Semag* and Rabbenu Yona reflect a difference in their understanding of this law. Rabbenu Yona derives the prohibition from the injunction that a king not be proud of his lofty status and thereby denigrate ordinary people. This implies that the basic prohibition of haughtiness is between man and his fellow man (*bein adam laḥavero*).

The *Semag*, on the other hand, feels that the prohibition of pride is connected to man's relationship to God, as was pointed out in his dream. Pride may lead to forgetting God Himself. A person may feel that he earned and deserves the abundance of good that he has received. Therefore, the prohibition is to be defined as one between man and God (*bein adam laMakom*).

Obviously, the comment of the Vilna Gaon that one should always feel that "I have been diminished" goes hand in hand with the position of the *Semag*.

Parashat Vayeshev

Yibbum in Ancient Israel

After Yehuda's eldest son, Er, died without children, Yehuda instructed his younger brother, Onan, to perform *yibbum* (levirate marriage) in order to establish offspring for his brother (Bereshit 38:8). Rashi (ad loc.) says that the product of such a union would be named for the late uncle.

However, Ramban (ad loc.) disagrees, maintaining that although the purpose of *yibbum* is to remember the deceased brother, there is no requirement to name the child accordingly. He points out that when Boaz married Ruth, he said (Ruth 4:10) that the purpose of the marriage was for the deceased to be remembered, yet the child was named Obed and not Mahlon (the name of Ruth's late husband). Ramban goes on to explain that the ancient sages knew that there is a great benefit in levirate marriage. In his notes on Ramban's commentary, Rabbi C. D. Chavel cites mystical works such as the *Zohar* that attempt to explain these benefits.

Prior to the giving of the Torah, levirate marriage was performed by a father, a brother, or any other relative of the deceased man. When the Torah was given, a prohibition of marrying a daughter-in-law or sister-in-law was introduced. However, due to the importance and value of *yibbum*, the Torah allowed a man to marry his sister-in-law if her husband had died and left no progeny.

According to Ramban, there was no mitzva of *yibbum* before the Torah was given. Nevertheless, it was practiced voluntarily by those who understood its value. It is possible that this custom predated the incident of Er and Onan but was not previously recorded in the Torah. However, Bereshit Rabba (85:6) says that Yehuda originated the mitzva of *yibbum*. This statement might be understood to mean that Yehuda was the first to institute the practice of levirate marriage, or that it was already an established custom but Yehuda was the first to institute it as a mitzva and not merely a voluntary act.

The Mishna (Kiddushin 82a) says that Avraham fulfilled all the mitzvot of the Torah before they were given. Presumably, his descendants also were taught to observe mitzvot even though they were not commanded to do so. On the other hand, another midrash says that Yehuda first received the commandment of *yibbum*. This midrash (Shir HaShirim Rabba 1:16) traces the evolution of the 613 mitzvot, explaining that Adam and Noaḥ were commanded to observe the Noahide laws, Avraham received the mitzva of *mila*, Yitzḥak was the first to be obligated to perform *mila* on the eighth day, Yaakov was prohibited to eat the thigh tendon, and Yehuda received the mitzva of *yibbum*.

The *Tosefot Yeshanim* (Yevamot 2a) ask why Yevamot was chosen as the first tractate in the order Nashim. After all, the topics discussed in Kiddushin and Ketubbot ("betrothal" and "marriage contracts") chronologically precede any application of *yibbum*. One of the answers given is that *yibbum* is the first mitzva that was fulfilled by a woman. This seems difficult, as the mitzva of *peru urevu* (procreation) had obviously already been fulfilled since the beginning of history.

Perhaps the *Tosefot Yeshanim* meant that not only is *yibbum* a mitzva that preceded the giving of the Torah, but women were commanded by this mitzva as well, and it was therefore the first time that a woman performed a mitzva in fulfillment of an obligation. Even though women certainly fulfill the mitzva of *peru urevu* when they have children (Ran, Kiddushin 41a), the halakha follows the opinion that women are exempt from this mitzva (Yevamot 65b; cf. *Parashat Bereshit* above).

Apparently, the question of whether Yehuda was commanded regarding *yibbum* or merely observed it as a custom is debated by Rishonim. As we have seen, in his commentary to the Torah, Ramban says that it was a custom. However, in his novellae (Yevamot 98a), Ramban asserts that Noahides are forbidden to engage in sexual relations with blood relatives (such as mother or daughter), but are permitted to marry relatives through marriage. He attempts to prove this point by the fact that Yaakov was permitted to marry two sisters (however, see his commentary to Vayikra 24:10 for another, seemingly contradictory, explanation), and that Yehuda was allowed to marry his daughter-in-law. He does not refer to *yibbum* as a mitzva.

However, the Rashba (ad loc.) refutes the proof brought from the incident of Tamar and Yehuda. He argues that even if relatives through marriage are forbidden to Noahides, Tamar was permitted to Yehuda, since the mitzva of *yibbum* would overcome any prohibition. According to the Rashba, the mitzva was incumbent upon all family members prior to the giving of the Torah, and was limited by the Torah to brothers of the deceased. Why, then, did Yehuda first instruct Er to perform *yibbum*, instead of doing it himself? He answers that Yehuda wished to have the mitzva fulfilled according to Torah parameters. This idea is similar to the tradition that our ancestors fulfilled the entire Torah before it was given.

It therefore appears that Ramban feels that *yibbum* was a voluntary custom, and the Rashba considers it a mitzva.

When Tamar was found to be pregnant, Yehuda initially sentenced her to death. For what sin was this punishment to be imposed? The Ḥizkuni (Bereshit 38) points out that if a widow who is awaiting levirate marriage has relations with someone, this is punishable by stripes (*malkot*) but not by death. He explains that the reason for the more stringent punishment is the severity of the Noahide laws. Rabbi M. Kasher, in his *Torah Shelema,* cites a manuscript of the *Baalei HaTosafot* as stating that Tamar was thought to be guilty of a form of adultery, since she was awaiting *yibbum*. This obviously implies that the mitzva of *yibbum* applied to her.

We have learned that according to Ramban, there was no mitzva of *yibbum*. Why, then, would Tamar be punished? Ramban explains that Tamar was deemed rebellious for violating Yehuda's instruction to wait until she would be given to his youngest son in marriage. He assumes that the household of Yehuda was considered to be royalty, and anyone who rebels against the king or his kingship is punished by death (see Rambam, *Hilkhot Melakhim* 9:14).

There is a dispute in the Gemara (Yevamot 39b) regarding whether it is preferable to perform *yibbum* or *ḥalitza* (a ceremony that frees the widow from the requirement of levirate marriage). *Responsa Beit Yosef* (*Even HaEzer* 1) comments that *yibbum* is preferable because historically it preceded *ḥalitza*. He feels that while Noahides practiced *yibbum*, whether as a mitzva or as a custom, *ḥalitza* was an alternative given only at *mattan Torah*.

We have discussed the issue of *yibbum* prior to *mattan Torah*. Today, the mitzva and obligation of *yibbum* and *ḥalitza* are certainly in force, yet the accepted custom is that only *ḥalitza* is done (Yevamot 39b; *Shulḥan Arukh, Even HaEzer* 165:1).

Parashat Miketz

Is It Permissible to Sell Oneself as an *Eved Ivri*?

After Yosef's agent accused Yosef's brothers of stealing his cup, they protested their innocence and explained that they were so honest that they had returned the money that had been found in their pouches. Assured of their innocence, they said that if the cup were to be found in their possession, the guilty one should be given the death penalty and the rest of the brothers should become slaves. Yosef's agent answered that indeed the guilty one would become a slave and the others would be absolved of guilt.

According to Rashi's explanation, the agent implied that although the sentence suggested by the brothers was just, he would indulge them with extra leniency. Ramban points out that the brothers' offer implied that there is a distinction between the actual thief and his brothers. Presumably, if one had stolen the cup, the others knew nothing about it. Why, then, did they all offer to be slaves if the cup were to be found in the possession of one of them? Ramban answers that they imposed an extra penalty upon themselves, which was subsequently waived by the agent. (See Bereshit 44:7–11; Rashi and Ramban ad loc.)

Is a Jew allowed to voluntarily become a slave, either to another Jew or to a non-Jew? The Torah (Vayikra 25:42) says, "The Children of Israel are slaves to Me... whom I took out of the land of Egypt; they are not to be sold as slaves." The *Torat Kohanim* (ad loc.) explains, "My deed of ownership preceded any sale; they were redeemed from Egypt with the stipulation that they cannot be sold as slaves." It then offers another interpretation: "They are not to be sold on an auction block." There seems to be a major difference between the two explanations. According to the first interpretation, there is a fundamental principle that Jews may not be sold at all, while the second explanation implies that they may be sold as slaves, provided the sale is conducted in a dignified manner.

If a Jew is convicted of theft and has no means to repay that which he stole, the court (*beit din*) may sell him as a slave (Shemot 22:3). Rambam (*Hilkhot Avadim* 1:3) says that the *beit din* may sell the thief only to a fellow Jew. However, if a Jew transgressed and sold himself to a non-Jew, the sale is valid, as it says in the Torah explicitly, "or to the offshoot of a stranger's family" (Vayikra 25:47). The *Minḥat Ḥinnukh* (42) points out that Rambam mentioned that the sale is valid only in the case of one selling himself to a non-Jew, implying that the *beit din* does not have the legal power to sell a thief to a non-Jew. This can be easily explained. After all, the *beit din* does not own the Jew; they are merely given the power to sell him in strict accordance with judicial procedure. Hence, any deviation from the letter of the law would nullify the sale.

However, if a person sells himself as a slave, this is a different situation. Rambam (*Hilkhot Avadim* 1:1) says, "The *eved ivri* (Hebrew slave) referred to in the Torah is a Jew who was sold against his will or one who sold himself voluntarily." He adds, "If a Jew became totally impoverished, the Torah gave him permission to sell himself." Why does he need the Torah's permission? Why would there be a prohibition against selling oneself?

According to the first explanation of the *Torat Kohanim*, since we are slaves to God Himself, we have no ownership of our bodies, and hence cannot sell them. We belong to God, and His deed preceded any sale. On the other hand, according to the second explanation, why would it be prohibited for a Jew to sell himself if he does so in a dignified manner? Perhaps we can suggest that the prohibition stems from the fact that by selling oneself, one becomes unable to perform certain mitzvot.

Rabbi Yosef Karo (*Kesef Mishneh, Hilkhot Issurei Mizbe'aḥ* 5:10) states clearly that an *eved ivri* is relieved of certain mitzvot. Although the *Mishneh LaMelekh* and others find this statement puzzling and wonder to which mitzvot he was referring, there may be a number of explanations. The Rishonim (Kiddushin 14b) debate whether an *eved ivri* is allowed to marry a non-Jewish slave. (One who is sold by the *beit din* is certainly permitted to do so.) Moreover, in the Yerushalmi (Berakhot 3:1) it says that an *eved* is not required to say *Shema*. Presumably, he cannot accept the total yoke of Heaven if he is enslaved to another human being.

What would happen if one transgressed and sold himself without the permission of the Torah? If we assume that a Jew is automatically enslaved to God, then even ex post facto, the sale would be invalid. This is indeed the position of the *Minḥat Ḥinnukh* (42). However, if the prohibition of selling oneself is due to the reduced obligation to perform mitzvot caused by the sale, it can be argued that although the individual violated a prohibition by selling himself, the sale should nonetheless be valid. In fact, the Tosefta (Arakhin 5:3) states explicitly that although one is permitted to sell himself only if he is indigent, anyone who sold himself under any condition is legally sold.

The *Sefer HaMikna* (Kiddushin 14b) disputes this ruling for a different reason. There is a general ruling of Rava (Temura 4b) that any action that is taken against the Torah's wishes is invalid. If so, then even if the prohibition is due to the reduction of mitzvot, the sale may be null and void. However, Professor E. Shochetman ("*Maaseh HaBa BaAvera*," Jerusalem: Mossad HaRav Kook, 1981, p. 55) has questioned whether this principle applies to sales.

We therefore see that the *beit din* may not sell a Jew to a non-Jew, and one may sell himself only to a Jew and only if he is impoverished. If someone sold himself under any other conditions, the Tosefta says the sale is valid, although the *Minḥat Ḥinnukh* and the *Sefer HaMikna* disagree.

Interestingly, after the death of Yaakov, the brothers were nervous that Yosef would punish them for their treatment of him, and again offered to become his slaves (Bereshit 50:18). Yosef rejected their offer, asking, "Am I in place of God?" Yosef's reply can be interpreted homiletically to mean that we are all slaves of God. Therefore, Yosef explained that he could not own them, as he was not in the place of God.

Parashat Vayigash

Learning Torah While Driving

Yosef sent his brothers back to Canaan in order to bring Yaakov to Egypt. He cautioned them, "Do not become agitated on the way" (Bereshit 45:24). Rashi explains that Yosef was afraid that the brothers would be so ashamed of their actions that they would argue and blame each other, which would only exacerbate the situation.

However, Rashi also cites a gemara (Taanit 10b) that offers two other interpretations of Yosef's exhortation. An anonymous source says that Yosef warned them not to travel too quickly and not to travel at night. Apparently, according to this opinion, Yosef worried that the brothers were so excited with the news that he was alive that they would not take proper caution in their haste to inform Yaakov.

The other opinion, that is cited first in the Gemara and by Rashi in his commentary on the Torah, is that of R. Elazar: Yosef cautioned them not to learn Torah on the road, out of concern that involvement in Torah might cause them to lose their way. The Gemara then contrasts this opinion with a statement of R. Ilai that two scholars who travel without learning deserve to be burned. Although the Gemara does not provide any source for R. Ilai's position, it seems to be based on the command "You shall teach [Torah] to your children, and you shall talk about [it] while you are at home and when you travel" (Devarim 6:6), implying an obligation to study Torah while traveling. The Gemara answers that there is no contradiction: studying by rote is permitted, but analytical discussion of Torah topics (*iyyun*) is forbidden.

However, the Midrash (Bereshit Rabba 94) disagrees with this gemara and interprets Yosef's words to mean that the brothers actually should learn Torah while traveling. Apparently, the Midrash felt that it is dangerous to travel without learning, as R. Ilai said in Taanit. Therefore, Yosef instructed his brothers to learn in order that there would be no problems on the road. According to this source, it would seem that even intense analytical learning is permitted.

Rabbi Kasher, in his *Torah Shelema* (Jerusalem, 1992), cites a manuscript of the *Moshav Zekenim* with a completely different understanding of Yosef's statement. According to this source, Yosef meant that the brothers should not involve themselves with halakhic stringencies (*ḥumrot*) while traveling. Rather, they should avail themselves of the leniencies extended to travelers, such as eating *demai* (produce not known to have been tithed properly).

Another interpretation was given by *Midrash Devek Tov*. Yosef told his brothers that they should study Torah diligently, and should not treat it casually. They should not interrupt their learning for sightseeing or to view the scenery. We are reminded of the mishna (Avot 3:9) that says that one who interrupts his learning to admire the scenery bears guilt ("*mitḥayyev benafsho*").

According to most of the opinions cited above, there would be no halakhic problem with learning while driving. However, according to R. Elazar, it seems that intense learning would be forbidden while driving, as it could cause one to lose concentration and to lose his way, or worse.

Rabbenu Gershom explained that according to R. Elazar, the reason that one should not learn intensely while traveling is that passersby who would observe the brothers delving intensely into a halakhic topic might think that they are quarreling and battling each other. This would cause animosity between the brothers and the passersby.

The Divrei Shalom (IV:2) points out that according to Rashi, it would seem that only the driver is forbidden to learn intensely, whereas there would be no restriction on the passengers. However, according to Rabbenu Gershom, no one should learn. Conversely, according to Rabbenu Gershom, if one is driving alone, without any passengers, even he would be allowed to learn intensely. However, according to Rashi, this situation may even be worse, as no one is there to caution the driver to be observant of the road.

One might argue that this entire discussion is not halakhic in nature. Perhaps Yosef's advice was limited to this specific case; perhaps he simply told his brothers that they should hasten and not tarry, as he was very anxious to reunite with his father.

It goes without saying that one should use common sense and be careful while driving. If learning interferes with a driver's concentration, it would certainly be wrong for him to learn under those conditions. I was once a passenger in a car driven by Rabbi Eliezer Simcha Wasserman, and on the way I asked him a halakhic question. He replied that he has a tradition that it is forbidden to discuss halakha while driving.

Although no such halakha is codified in the *Shulḥan Arukh*, the *Magen Avraham* (*Oraḥ Ḥayim* 110:10) says that although one should learn while traveling, one should not do so intensely, in order to avoid becoming distracted. He adds that if one is only a passenger, perhaps this may not apply and he may learn intensely. The *Shulḥan Arukh HaRav* (of the *Baal HaTanya*) cites this ruling unequivocally, and maintains that a passenger may learn intensely.

The Divrei Shalom (IV:2) pointed out that the *Magen Avraham* was unsure of whether the passengers could learn, and suggested that perhaps he accepted the reasoning of Rabbenu Gershom that such learning could create animosity. However, *Shulḥan Arukh HaRav* may have accepted the opinion of Rashi that the fear of losing concentration would apply only to the driver, and passengers are certainly allowed to learn.

Today many drivers listen to recordings of Torah lectures while driving. If this is considered to be intense learning, it would be forbidden by the *Magen Avraham* and the *Shulḥan Arukh HaRav*. It may, however, be permitted for passengers to listen to such a recording if the driver cannot hear it.

In any event, care must obviously be taken while driving. We must remember the talmudic principle (Ḥullin 10a), "Danger is to be taken more stringently than a prohibition."

Parashat Vayeḥi

Aveilut

The Torah tells us that after Yaakov passed away and was embalmed, the Egyptians bewailed him for seventy days. Yosef then asked Pharaoh for permission to bury Yaakov in the grave that had been prepared in Canaan. Pharaoh acceded to this request and a great entourage accompanied them until they reached Goren HaAtad, where eulogies were delivered and seven days of mourning were observed (Bereshit 50:1–12).

The Gemara (Moed Katan 20a) seeks a biblical source for the seven days of *aveilut* (mourning). The *Tosafot* (ad loc.) point out that they cannot be derived from this incident, as the seven days of mourning for Yaakov were observed prior to interment. However, the Yerushalmi (Moed Katan 3:5) appears to say that this actually is the source for *aveilut*. The Yerushalmi then comments, "We learn this [from an incident that occurred] before the Torah was given." The *Tosafot* (ibid.) interpret this as a rhetorical question meant to discount that source: is it possible to learn a halakha from an event that took place prior to *mattan Torah*?

There is a major controversy among Rishonim as to whether *aveilut* is biblically mandated. Rambam (*Hilkhot Evel* 1:1) maintains that the Torah commanded us to observe *aveilut* only on the day of death and burial, and that Moshe innovated seven days of mourning (as well as seven days of rejoicing for newlyweds). He also points out that one cannot deduce a full week of *aveilut* from our *parasha,* because this halakha was established when the Torah was given. Apparently, Rambam understood the Yerushalmi as the *Tosafot* did.

Although there are opinions that all *aveilut* is of rabbinic origin (Rosh and Rabbenu Tam cited in Rabbenu Yona, Berakhot 9b in Rif), the Rif (ibid.) cites an opinion that there is a biblical obligation to mourn for seven days, and the source is the event at Goren HaAtad. He apparently understands the Yerushalmi according to the simpler reading: that the Gemara declared that such a law could be deduced from an event that preceded *mattan Torah,* and did not question it. However, this opinion still seems to be quite difficult, as the *Tosafot* pointed out. Didn't the mourning for Yaakov take place before burial? How, then, could this be the source of seven days of *aveilut* after interment?

In order to understand this point and the chain of events, let us analyze the entire story. In the beginning of the *parasha,* Yosef was called to Yaakov, who asked his son to perform an act of kindness and truth: "Do not bury me in Egypt." Instead, Yaakov asked to be buried with his ancestors. Although Yosef immediately said that he would fulfill the request, Yaakov insisted that Yosef take an oath assuring that he would comply. It is interesting to note that Yaakov did not specify the exact place of burial (*Me'arat HaMakhpela*).

Later on, after the blessings were given, Yaakov commanded his children to bury him in *Me'arat HaMakhpela* and he explained that his ancestors and wife Leah were all buried there (Bereshit 49:29–32). Why did Yaakov command Yosef first, and separately, later also command the brothers? Why did Yaakov specify where he wished to be buried only to the brothers and not to Yosef? Why was Yosef required to swear that he would fulfill his father's request but the brothers were not so required?

Moreover, Yosef related the account of these events to Pharaoh a little differently from the way they are related in the Torah. He told Pharaoh that his father had administered an oath to bury him in the burial ground that had already been prepared for him in Canaan. He did not mention that his father's main point seemed to have been not to be buried in Egypt. (The interested reader can find a different analysis of the events in Rabbi Mordechai Breuer's book *Pirkei Bereshit,* Alon Shevut: Tevunot Press, 1998, pp. 716–720.)

It may be suggested that Yaakov split his wish into two parts. He did not feel comfortable asking Yosef to bury him in *Me'arat HaMakhpela,* as Yaakov had not buried Raḥel, Yosef's mother, there. Furthermore, there was no assurance that Yosef would be allowed to leave Egypt. After all, he was a ruler of the country and people may have suspected that he would not return. Perhaps the residents of Canaan would not allow him to enter, as they would fear his power and would assume that he wished to conquer Canaan. On the other hand, Yaakov could not ask the brothers to take him out of Egypt, as they did not have any authority or power to do so. The Egyptians, who respected and revered Yaakov, would insist that his burial take place in Egypt, where his tomb would become a shrine. Yaakov commanded Yosef, who had the authority, to take him out of Egypt. He insisted that Yosef take an oath in order to "force" Pharaoh to acquiesce to this request. Indeed, Pharaoh said, "Go and bury your father *as he adjured you*" (Bereshit 50:5). After Yosef took the body out of Egypt, the other brothers were to bring Yaakov to *Me'arat HaMakhpela,* where Leah was buried.

Following this analysis, it is possible that the entire entourage went until Goren HaAtad, which is in Trans-Jordan, and Yosef thereby fulfilled his obligation. He then gave over responsibility to the brothers to perform the actual task of bearing Yaakov to *Me'arat HaMakhpela.* Inasmuch as Yosef had finished his part of the agreement and therefore turned back to return to Egypt, he (and only he) was required to fulfill *aveilut.* This is in accordance with the principle that once the mourners transfer the body to the pallbearers, *aveilut* begins (Moed Katan 22a).

Thus, we could derive from this event that *aveilut* of seven days is biblically mandated. In fact, Rabbi Kasher (*Torah Shelema,* Jerusalem, 1992, VIII:1902) cites a manuscript of the *Moshav Zekenim* that claims that the kings of Canaan did not allow Yosef to enter Canaan, so he had to return to Egypt and therefore had to sit shiva.

Additional proof could be added from the details of the story. "They came to Goren HaAtad, which is in Trans-Jordan, and they eulogized him greatly and he observed a seven-day mourning period"

(Bereshit 50:10). Although *they* (all the entourage) came there and eulogized, only *he* observed shiva. Immediately afterwards, it says that the brothers did as they had been commanded. Originally, it said that Yosef went to bury his father, along with everyone else, and now the Torah mentions the brothers. It seems that Yosef had the responsibility of taking Yaakov out of Egypt and coming to Goren HaAtad. At this point, the brothers assumed their responsibility and Yosef sat shiva.

A somewhat similar approach was taken by Rabbi Meir Simḥa in his *Meshekh Ḥokhma*. He said that *aveilut* was observed by the Egyptian part of the entourage, who were not allowed to enter Canaan. Although the idea is similar, it would seem a bit strange that the Yerushalmi derived *aveilut* from the Egyptians. It therefore seems to be more logical to assume that it was Yosef who mourned; furthermore, the singular "he observed" implies that one person mourned.

Midrash Lekaḥ Tov observes that the seven days of mourning parallel the seven days of Creation. Man was created alone in order to teach us that one person is comparable to the entire universe (Sanhedrin 33a). Therefore, when someone dies, we should mourn for seven days.

Sefer Shemot

Parashat Shemot

Jewish Language and Clothing

According to a well-known midrash, Benei Yisrael merited redemption from slavery in Egypt for their having retained particular mitzvot and symbols of Jewish identity. R. Huna said in the name of Bar Kappara (Vayikra Rabba 32:5) that they did not change their names or their language, did not speak *lashon hara* (slanderous speech), and observed the laws of *arayot* (forbidden relationships).

Arayot and *lashon hara* are, needless to say, forbidden by the Torah. But is there any law requiring us to speak or familiarize ourselves with *leshon hakodesh* (the holy language)? The Tosefta (Ḥagiga 1) says that once a child develops the ability to speak, his father should teach him Torah and *leshon hakodesh*. If he does not do so, the Tosefta adds, then "it would have been more appropriate for him not to have been born." The *Sifrei* (Devarim 11:20) comments that if a father did not do this, he is considered as having buried his son. The *Sifrei* derives this from the Torah's juxtaposition of the mitzva of teaching children and the reward of long life, implying that if one teaches his children Torah and *leshon hakodesh*, they will enjoy longevity. Apparently, the converse is also true: if a father does not do so, their days will be shortened.

Although Rambam does not codify the obligation to speak *leshon hakodesh* in *Mishneh Torah*, elsewhere he states explicitly that such a mitzva indeed exists. The Mishna (Avot 2:1) instructs us to be as meticulous concerning minor mitzvot as we are with major ones. Rambam, in his commentary on the Mishna, portrays the study of *leshon hakodesh* as an example of a minor mitzva.

If, indeed, studying *leshon hakodesh* constitutes a mitzva, why does Rambam make no mention of it in his *Mishneh Torah*? Let us first inquire as to whether this mitzva of studying and speaking *leshon hakodesh* is an independent mitzva, or is merely a prerequisite to the mitzva of learning Torah. The *Sifrei* and the Midrash cited the mitzva of learning Torah together with the requirement of teaching *leshon hakodesh*. The Yerushalmi (Sukka, end of chapter 3) formulates the halakha as follows: "Once a child can speak, his father should teach him *leshon haTorah* (the language of Torah)." These sources might imply a strong relationship between the study of *leshon hakodesh* and Torah learning. This may mean that the study of *leshon hakodesh* is significant because it helps to facilitate study of Torah, but it does not stand on its own as an independent mitzva.

Rabbi Yaakov Emden was asked whether it is permissible to study Hebrew grammar in the bathroom. He replied that it was forbidden, since the only proper way to study Hebrew grammar is through the study of biblical grammar. Consequently, one who studies grammar will inevitably be reminded of sections of Tanakh. Since the study of Tanakh is forbidden in the bathroom, he held it was also forbidden to study Hebrew grammar there. Rabbi Y. Gershuni pointed out that if the study of *leshon hakodesh* were an independent mitzva, then it would be intrinsically forbidden in the bathroom. Since Rabbi Yaakov Emden forbade it only due to the inevitability that it would lead to studying Tanakh, he apparently felt that learning *leshon hakodesh* is only a prerequisite to Torah study.

We may, therefore, suggest that Rambam felt that although there is a mitzva to study and to speak *leshon hakodesh*, it need not be mentioned in *Mishneh Torah*, as it is merely a *hekhsher mitzva* (a prerequisite to the performance of a mitzva).

The *Torah Temima* (Devarim 11:19) mentions that he wrote an extensive treatise entitled *Safa LeNe'emanim* about this mitzva. In this essay, he raised the question as to why no codes of halakha mention the requirement to speak *leshon hakodesh*. He suggested that perhaps the mitzva applies only in the Land of Israel, whereas in the Diaspora, it would be impossible to fulfill for many reasons. Despite this rationale, he was not satisfied and tried to suggest another reason for its omission.

In our world today, when so much of Torah literature is available in translation, one might wonder how important it is to study *leshon hakodesh*. In truth, however, besides the fact that much of Torah has not been translated, it is obviously better to study Torah in the original. The nuances and style of language are lost in translation. *Lehavdil* (to separate the holy from the secular), if one reads great literature such as the works of Shakespeare in translation, does he get the full meaning and depth of that literature?

Let us now turn our attention to the issue of clothing. Although it is common to attribute the idea that Benei Yisrael did not change their names, language, or style of clothing to a midrash, S. Buber (note to *Pesikta DeRav Kahana* 10:3) observes that there is no extant midrashic source regarding clothing. However, the Ritva apparently knew of such a midrash, as he mentions it in his commentary to the Haggada and explains it to mean that Benei Yisrael wore tzitzit and were thus immediately recognized as Jews by their special garments.

The *Kol Bo* (commenting on the Haggada's remark that Benei Yisrael were "*metzuyanim*" – "exceptional") writes that Benei Yisrael's unique clothing prevented assimilation. Interestingly, though, Moshe Rabbenu himself seems not to have observed this custom. As we read in this *parasha*, when Moshe arrived in Midian, he did not identify himself, and when Yitro asked his daughters who had assisted them, they answered that it was an Egyptian. Apparently, Moshe did not wear any special garb that would identify him as a Jew.

Is this issue only a question of Jewish custom and identity, or does halakha mandate wearing clothing that is different from that of the gentiles?

Rambam (*Hilkhot Avoda Zara* 11:1) codifies a prohibition against following the laws of gentiles, among other things forbidding us from imitating their dress or hairstyle. He says that a Jew should be recognizable by his clothes and distinguishable from gentiles through his mode of dress. However, the *Yere'im* (313) writes that it is forbidden merely to resemble the seven nations that inhabited Israel or to conduct ourselves like the Egyptians. Moreover, the Me'iri (Avoda Zara 52b) limits the prohibition to dressing or coifing oneself in a style resembling idolatrous practices. The Rema (*Shulḥan Arukh, Yoreh De'ah* 178) rules that clothing similar to non-Jewish style is forbidden only if it would lead to immoral behavior. He also forbade wearing clothes that were worn as part of special customs that had no objective value. However, any special clothing used for specific purposes, such as a uniform identifying doctors, is permitted.

Whether there is a halakhic imperative for Jews to distinguish themselves in their dress or not, the popular midrash implies that it is certainly a positive value. In fact, the prophet Tzefanya said, "It shall happen on the day of the sacrifice that I will remember [i.e., punish] the officers and princes and all those who dress themselves in gentile garb" (Tzefanya 1:8).

Parashat Va'era

Arba Kosot

The Yerushalmi (Pesaḥim 10:1) inquires about the source for the obligation of the *arba kosot* (four cups of wine at the Pesaḥ Seder), and cites a number of possible sources. The prevalent opinion is that the four cups correspond to the four expressions of redemption stated towards the beginning of *Parashat Va'era*: "I shall take you out… I shall rescue you… I shall redeem you… I shall take you to Me" (Shemot 6:5–7). Interestingly enough, the *Keli Ḥemda* maintains that drinking the *arba kosot* constitutes a biblical requirement, as it is derived from biblical sources. We may draw further support for this thesis from a variant text of the Yerushalmi, as it appears in the *She'iltot* of Rabbi Aḥai Gaon: "What is the source of the *arba kosot* from the Torah?" Nevertheless, it is generally assumed that this mitzva was instituted by the Rabbis, who based it upon the language of the Torah. The Gemara (Pesaḥim 117b) clearly states, "Our Rabbis instituted *arba kosot* to be drunk in a manner expressing freedom."

Despite the presumed rabbinic origin of *arba kosot*, we nevertheless find a number of stringent halakhot associated with this mitzva. First, even if wine affects a person's physical condition, he must force himself to drink *arba kosot* (*Shulḥan Arukh, Oraḥ Ḥayim* 372:1). Rabbi Ovadia Yosef (cited in *Yalkut Yosef*, v:387) qualified this ruling, claiming that it refers only to a person who may develop a minor ailment such as a headache or some stomach discomfort. If, however, drinking will cause one to be bedridden or trigger an internal illness, he is exempt from this obligation.

Another stringency is stated in the Mishna (Pesaḥim 10:1). A poor person who depends on the public dole for his livelihood must be provided with wine for the *arba kosot*. The *Shulḥan Arukh* (*Oraḥ Ḥayim* 372:13) ruled that an indigent person should sell his clothes, borrow, or hire himself out as a laborer in order to obtain money for wine. Rambam (*Hilkhot Ḥanukka* 4:12) extended this halakha, requiring a poor person to resort to such measures to obtain Ḥanukka candles, as well. The *Maggid Mishneh* explained that both Ḥanukka and Pesaḥ have an element of *pirsumei nissa* (the requirement to publicize a miracle) and thus share this stringency.

The Gemara (Pesaḥim 112a), commenting on the aforementioned mishna, notes that the mishna does not mean to inform us that the supervisors of the charity funds should supply wine as part of the Pesaḥ provisions. This point is obvious and does not require an explicit clause to this effect. Rather, the mishna refers to a case where the person has enough money to buy all his needs except wine. In such a situation, the mishna establishes that one should resort to charity, and suffer the resulting shame and debasement, rather than avoid purchasing wine and thus forfeit the mitzva of *arba kosot*. R. Akiva maintains that if a person receives charity, he should be given three meals for Shabbat. If, however, he can independently afford two meals, he should treat Shabbat as a weekday (and eat only two meals) rather than begin taking charity to pay for the third meal. Yet, the Gemara notes, even R. Akiva agrees that when it comes to *arba kosot*, an otherwise self-sufficient person should accept charity to purchase wine, because this obligation involves *pirsumei nissa*.

The *Avnei Nezer* (*Oraḥ Ḥayim* 501) explains that a poor person who sincerely desires to fulfill a mitzva but whose financial difficulties do not allow him to do so is ordinarily considered as if he had fulfilled the mitzva. However, this rule applies only to ritual obligations, such as putting on tzitzit. *Pirsumei nissa*, by contrast, cannot be achieved through good intentions. After all, when all is said and done, in such a case the desired publicity has not occurred. Therefore, he reasons, being poor does not excuse one from fulfilling this mitzva, and one must therefore beg for, borrow, or somehow obtain the money needed for the performance of this mitzva.

The Gemara (Megilla 18a) ascribes the quality of *pirsumei nissa* to the obligation of Megilla reading, as well. It would seem that these three mitzvot represent three different forms of *pirsumei nissa*. On Ḥanukka, the basic idea is to light the candles outdoors and proclaim the miracle to the entire world. Megilla reading, on the other hand, is required only within the framework of the Jewish community. And the *pirsumei nissa* of *arba kosot* pertains only to one's family or the *ḥavura* (group) that attends that particular Seder.

Rambam (*Hilkhot Ḥanukka* 4:13) rules that if a person does not have enough money to buy both wine for Kiddush and Ḥanukka candles, he should buy candles instead of wine. The *Kesef Mishneh* bases this ruling on the fact that there is an element of *pirsumei nissa* with regard to candle lighting, but not to Kiddush.

The *Avnei Nezer* (*Oraḥ Ḥayim* 501) questioned the assumption that Friday night Kiddush is not considered *pirsumei nissa*. After all, Shabbat commemorates both the creation of the world and the redemption from Egypt. These events, both of which we refer to in the text of Kiddush, certainly qualify as miracles, and reciting Kiddush indeed publicizes these miraculous events. Why, then, is Kiddush not an expression of *pirsumei nissa*? He answered that *pirsumei nissa* means that the miracle should be publicized to others, whether it be the entire world, the Jewish community, or the immediate family. However, Kiddush is inherently a purely personal obligation; no one else need be present for a person to fulfill the mitzva of Kiddush. Therefore, Kiddush cannot be considered a mitzva of *pirsumei nissa*.

Although, as we have seen, the Gemara explicitly connects the *arba kosot* with the concept of *pirsumei nissa*, this should strike us as somewhat surprising. The miracles of Ḥanukka and Purim – which are not recorded in the Torah – understandably require publicity to ensure their place within the collective memory of Am Yisrael. Furthermore, needless to say, we have no biblical requirements to fulfill on Ḥanukka and Purim that would facilitate the continuous memory of these miracles. However, Pesaḥ, its history, and its laws comprise such an integral part of the Torah that it hardly needs any additional publicity. The Ten Commandments begin with a reference to the Exodus from Egypt. We also have the biblical requirements of the Pesaḥ sacrifice; eating matza; and, above all, the biblical obligation of relating the story to our children and grandchildren. Do we really require more *pirsumei nissa*?

Rabbi Moshe Sternbuch (*Mo'adim UZemanim,* VII:97) raises another point relevant to this issue. The Gemara (Pesaḥim 108b) says that the *arba kosot* contain elements of *ḥerut* (freedom) and *simḥa* (joy). If the Gemara there establishes the primary reason(s) for the *arba kosot,* then why did the Gemara cited earlier feel that *pirsumei nissa* is also a factor? Despite the lack of a response to this question, Rabbi Sternbuch suggests that all the obligations of the Seder constitute *pirsumei nissa.* This radical approach implies that a person should beg for or borrow money even to buy *maror* (bitter herbs) for the Seder, despite the fact that today, in the absence of the Pesaḥ sacrifice, eating *maror* constitutes a rabbinic obligation.

Several Rishonim raise the question of why we do not recite a *berakha* before we drink the *arba kosot.* Among the answers given is that this mitzva is not performed all at once. Indeed, a *hefsek* (interruption) between the *kosot* necessarily occurs, given that each of the cups has a specific text to be recited before it is drunk (Kiddush, the main section of the Haggada, *Birkat HaMazon,* and Hallel). The *Or Zarua* (I:140) compared this to the three meals of Shabbat: since they, too, are to be eaten at intervals, one does not recite a *berakha* over the mitzva of eating Shabbat meals. Rabbenu David (Pesaḥim 109b) assumes that the *arba kosot* are four components of one mitzva, and goes so far as to say that if one should drink only one or two cups, he fulfills nothing at all until he drinks all four. (The editor of Rabbenu David's novellae, Rabbi A. Shoshana, cites other opinions in note 9.) Since this one mitzva is divided into four parts and must be done at intervals, it follows that there is no *berakha* recited.

In light of this discussion, another question arises. Two of the mitzvot involving *pirsumei nissa,* Ḥanukka candles and Megilla reading, feature the special *berakha* of *SheAsa Nissim* ("who performed miracles"). Given that the entire Pesaḥ Seder also involves *pirsumei nissa,* and the mitzva of the *arba kosot* certainly constitutes *pirsumei nissa,* why is no such *berakha* recited at the Seder? Some Rishonim (*Sefer HaOra* 90; cf. *Orḥot Ḥayim,* Avudraham, and other commentators on the Haggada) explain that in truth, such a *berakha* indeed exists. Just before we drink the second cup, we recite the *berakha* of *Asher Ge'alanu VeGaal et Avotenu* ("who redeemed us and our fathers"), which is akin to the *berakha* of *SheAsa Nissim.* The question, however, could still be raised: even if this is true, why is it recited before the second cup and not the first?

Perhaps the answer lies in a unique requirement that exists on the night of Pesaḥ: one must experience the redemption as if he himself has left Egypt. Therefore, before reciting the *berakha,* we begin the Seder and attempt to feel the slavery to Pharaoh in Egypt. As we recite the Haggada, we relive the *geula* process. As we realize the full meaning of the redemption and say Hallel, we fully appreciate the miracle and therefore, only then is it appropriate to say the *berakha* of *SheAsa Nissim,* transformed into a different form as *Asher Ge'alanu.*

Parashat Bo

Matza

The Torah in *Parashat Bo* (Shemot 12:8) commands us to eat the *korban Pesaḥ* (the Paschal lamb) together with matza and *maror*. Inasmuch as today we cannot offer sacrifices, including the *korban Pesaḥ*, there is currently no biblical obligation to eat *maror*, which is to be eaten in conjunction with the *korban Pesaḥ*. Nevertheless, our sages instituted a rabbinic requirement to eat *maror* independently of the *korban*.

However, the Gemara (Pesaḥim 120a) tells us that according to Rava, the obligation to eat matza has an independent status as a biblical requirement even in the absence of a *korban Pesaḥ*, since the Torah explicitly states, "On [that] evening you shall eat matzot" (Shemot 12:18). The Gemara then cites a *baraita* that supports this opinion, observing that in one place, the Torah requires eating matza on all seven days of the festival (Shemot 12:15), whereas elsewhere it obligates eating matza for only six days (Devarim 16:8). The *baraita* employs an exegetical principle to conclude that once the second verse excludes the seventh day from the obligation, the entire obligation dissolves. Seemingly, then, the consumption of matza on Pesaḥ should be entirely optional. However, the Torah specifically mentions the obligation to eat matza together with the *korban* on the first night of Pesaḥ. And even if there is no *korban*, the Torah still reiterated "on [that] night you shall eat matzot" in order to establish an independent mitzva to eat matza. Based on this, Rambam (*Sefer HaMitzvot, Aseh* 158), as well as other codifiers, writes that there is a biblical requirement to eat matza on the first night of Pesaḥ, even without a *Beit HaMikdash*.

The Ḥizkuni (Shemot 12:18) understands the Torah's seemingly convoluted presentation of this mitzva to imply that although one is obligated to eat matza only on the first night of Pesaḥ, one who does so during the rest of the week nevertheless fulfills a mitzva. He explains that when it comes to most mitzvot, one not only merits reward for observing them, but also deserves punishment if he is negligent and fails to fulfill them. There is, however, another category of mitzvot, such as eating matza during the remainder of Pesaḥ, that are not obligations and therefore do not entail any punishments but do nevertheless bring reward to those who fulfill them optionally.

Another possible source for a mitzva to eat matza throughout the entirety of Pesaḥ is the juxtaposition of the prohibition against eating *ḥametz* and the requirement to eat matza (Devarim 16:3). The Gemara (Pesaḥim 43b) derives from this textual association that women (who are forbidden to eat *ḥametz*) must eat matza (despite its being a *mitzvat aseh* caused by time, from which women are ordinarily exempt). Furthermore, according to R. Shimon (Pesaḥim 28b), these two mitzvot are also mutually dependent in terms of the times of their application. R. Shimon maintains that there is no biblical prohibition to eat *ḥametz* before or after Pesaḥ. His argument is that *ḥametz* is only biblically forbidden at the time that matza is to be eaten. The *Penei Yehoshua* (ad loc.) writes that Rashi's interpretation of R. Shimon shows that there is a biblical requirement to eat matza all Pesaḥ.

We find another indication that the mitzva of eating matza is required (or at least fulfilled) throughout Pesaḥ in the discussion regarding tefillin on Ḥol HaMoed. The Gemara (Menaḥot 36b) explains that since tefillin are called "*ot*" (a sign), and Shabbat and Yom Tov are themselves *ot*, there is no need to put on tefillin on those days. The *Tosafot* (ad loc.) raise the issue of whether one must wear tefillin on Ḥol HaMoed, and they claim that Pesaḥ is an *ot* since *ḥametz* is forbidden, and Sukkot is an *ot* because of the obligation to sit in the sukka. The Rosh (Responsa 23:3), however, cites the Geonim as saying that Pesaḥ is an *ot* due to the *obligation* of eating matza. Indeed, it seems far more logical that an *ot* should involve a demonstrative act such as eating matza, rather than passively refraining from eating *ḥametz*. Although the Rosh maintains that one should put on tefillin on Ḥol HaMoed, he does not take issue with the opinion that the obligation of matza creates an *ot*.

It is well known that the Vilna Gaon maintained that eating matza is an optional mitzva during all of Pesaḥ. It is related (*Maaseh Rav* 175) that he attributed immense value to this mitzva. In fact, he would make a point of eating *Seuda Shelishit* on the last day of Pesaḥ (although he did not usually eat *Seuda Shelishit* on Yom Tov), in order to fulfill the mitzva of eating matza in its waning moments, before Yom Tov was over.

If we indeed assume that there is a mitzva to eat matza all Pesaḥ, we must ask why there is no *berakha* attached to it. Even if it is an optional mitzva, it should not be exempt from a *berakha*. On Sukkot, for example, there is no obligation to eat in the sukka throughout the festival: the obligation to eat in the sukka applies only on the first night. Thereafter, it is prohibited to eat anything substantial outside the sukka, but technically, one could avoid eating in the sukka throughout the remainder of Sukkot by living the entire week on snacks. If, however, one does eat in the sukka, he fulfills a mitzva and also recites a *berakha*. Why should we not similarly require a *berakha* over the consumption of matza after the first day of Pesaḥ?

This question, originally posed by the *Baal HaMaor* (end of Pesaḥim), has become the subject of much discussion, and various answers have been suggested. The *Baal HaMaor* himself answered by saying that one need not eat matza the rest of Pesaḥ, as it is possible to subsist on rice (for those whose custom permits it) or other foods. However, since a person cannot refrain from sleeping for an entire week, one must be in the sukka at some point during the week, and therefore that mitzva requires a *berakha*. The *Mikhtam* (Sukka 27a) and the Me'iri (Pesaḥim 91b) reject the entire thesis and maintain that there is no mitzva at all to eat matza after the first night of Pesaḥ. By contrast, the *Sedei Ḥemed* (*Ḥametz UMatza* 14:10) cites a prevailing custom to recite a *berakha*, and the Netziv (*Meshiv Davar* 77) expresses uncertainty as to whether such a *berakha* would be considered a *berakha levattala* (an unnecessary *berakha*). In any event, this custom of making a *berakha* has been resoundingly rejected (see *Responsa Yeḥavveh Daat* 1:22).

It is told that certain people who were known as extremely meticulous in mitzva observance did not eat matza at all after the first night of Pesaḥ. Apparently, they were concerned about the intricacies of baking matza and feared that it could become *ḥametz* quite easily. Rabbi Eliezer Waldenberg (*Tzitz Eliezer* 13:65) disputed this position very strongly for a number of reasons. He thought that there was an inherent contradiction in this practice. If the adherents of this custom were truly afraid that the matza was not baked according to halakha, how could they eat it on the first night of Pesaḥ? Furthermore, Rabbi Waldenberg argued that there is a mitzva to eat bread (which obviously must be matza) on every day of Pesaḥ, especially Shabbat and Yom Tov, and questioned how they could ignore this obligation. Additionally, if we accept the opinion of the Ḥizkuni and Vilna Gaon, then the followers of this practice also negate the fulfillment of eating matza all Pesaḥ.

Rabbi Waldenberg also cites an opinion that, given the Karaitic doctrine requiring eating matza all Pesaḥ, as the Torah says, "You should eat matza seven days" (Shemot 12:15), there were those who refrained from eating matza after the first night to demonstrate their opposition to the Karaitic position. Nevertheless, Rabbi Waldenberg strongly advised eating matza all week.

We have shown that there is some dispute as to whether there is a mitzva to eat matza throughout Pesaḥ. On the first night of Pesaḥ, however, everyone agrees that there is an obligation. In general, any mitzva that requires eating has a minimum requirement of a *kazayit* (the volume of an olive). The Mishna (Pesaḥim 10:1) says that a waiter who takes a moment at the Seder to recline and eat this amount of matza fulfills his obligation. The Maharal of Prague (*Gevurot Hashem* 48) inferred from the formulation of this halakha that the waiter fulfills his requirement only ex post facto, since he satisfied the minimum requirement of eating while reclining. Ideally, though, the mitzva involves all the matza that one eats on the first night of Pesaḥ and therefore all of it should be eaten while reclining. He states that this is the position of Rambam, as well.

The Maharal did not specify to which halakha codified by Rambam he refers, and attempts have been made to deduce this from various halakhot. (See Rabbi Y. B. Zolty, *Mishnat Yaavetz* 16, for one possible source.) It seems fairly clear to me, however, that the Maharal referred to Rambam in *Hilkhot Ḥametz UMatza* 6:1. There Rambam writes, "There is a biblical requirement to eat matza on the night of the fifteenth.... Once one has eaten a *kazayit,* he has fulfilled the mitzva." Rambam could have said simply that there is a mitzva to eat a *kazayit* of matza. By writing instead that there is a mitzva to eat matza and one need not eat more than a *kazayit,* he implies that all of one's matza consumption constitutes a fulfillment of the mitzva, though the minimum requirement is a *kazayit.*

We have thus learned that according to one view (*Penei Yehoshua*'s understanding of R. Shimon) there is an obligation to eat matza all week, whereas another opinion (Ḥizkuni, Vilna Gaon) maintains that although there is no obligation, one fulfills a mitzva by eating matza all week. This latter opinion was disputed by Me'iri and others. Finally, we have seen that the Maharal felt that on the first night, although one fulfills the requirement by eating a *kazayit,* all matza eaten is a fulfillment of the mitzva.

Parashat Beshallaḥ

Leḥem Mishneh

Benei Yisrael received a daily portion of manna that sustained them throughout their sojourn in the desert. On the first Friday after the manna began to fall, they were surprised to find a double portion. Since Moshe had not yet informed them of the laws of Shabbat, they did not understand the reason for this double portion. Thereupon, Moshe explained that the extra portion was to be eaten on Shabbat, as the manna would not fall.

Since the custom was to eat two meals a day, the manna that arrived on Friday sufficed for four meals. Assuming that each portion consisted of one loaf, there must have been three loaves for the Shabbat meals. Apparently, on Friday night and Shabbat day the loaves were set on the Shabbat table, and one loaf would be eaten at each meal. Obviously, this would mean that at *Seuda Shelishit* (the third meal of Shabbat), only one loaf remained and was then eaten.

The Gemara (Shabbat 117b) says in the name of R. Abba that on Shabbat, "*ḥayyav adam livtzoa al shetei kikkarot*" – one must cut two loaves of bread, since it says in the Torah that "*leḥem mishneh*" – a double portion – fell on Friday for Shabbat, as well. Although we might have understood R. Abba to mean that one must in fact cut the two loaves, as the term "*livtzoa*" ("to cut") seemingly implies, Rashi comments that the obligation is merely to recite the *berakha* over two loaves, whereas only one must be eaten at the meal. Rabbi Ḥayim Soloveitchik is reported to have understood that if the host recited the *berakha* and the guests did not eat from the *leḥem mishneh*, they have nevertheless fulfilled their obligation. He likened this to the law of Kiddush: anyone who hears Kiddush fulfills his obligation even if he does not drink wine at all. (See *Mesorah* 4, p. 16.) The *Mishna Berura* (167:83), however, says clearly that all must hear the *berakha* and partake of the *leḥem mishneh*.

The Gemara continues by noting the custom of R. Kahana, as recorded by R. Ashi, to take two loaves and cut just one. The Gemara explains this practice as based on the *pasuk* "they *gathered leḥem mishneh*." The verse does not say that they actually cut both loaves – which they obviously did not, since this would not leave enough loaves for the three meals of Shabbat – but rather that they gathered two loaves. Thus, on Shabbat R. Kahana would take two loaves but slice only one of them.

The Gemara reports another custom, that of R. Zeira, who would cut all of *sheiruteh*. (The meaning of this word is unclear. Indeed, the text of the Gemara and the names of the sages cited vary in different versions of the Talmud. The interested reader is referred to a scholarly article on the topic by my brother, Prof. Yosef Tabory: "*Lesugyat Leḥem Mishneh BeShabbat*," *Kovetz Zikkaron LaRav Shimon Katz* (Bnei Brak, 5747), pp. 116–29. Rashi explains that R. Zeira sliced a large portion of bread that would suffice for the entire meal. The Gemara goes on to explain why this custom does not appear gluttonous.

In summation, according to Rashi's explanation of the Gemara, everyone agrees to the following points: the *berakha* should be recited over two loaves, only one loaf must be sliced, and there was a custom to cut an unusually large portion.

The Rashba (Shabbat 117b) cites Rashi's interpretation of R. Zeira but disagrees, arguing that the generous host should always cut a large portion, not only on Shabbat. Furthermore, why would the Gemara raise the issue of gluttony if the host cut a large slice in order to appear generous? The Rashba therefore explained that R. Zeira cut all the loaves placed before him, thus requiring the Gemara to explain why this did not appear gluttonous. The Rashba gives no explanation, however, as to why all the loaves must be sliced.

The custom of the Ari, based on Kabbala, was to slice twelve *ḥallot* at each meal on Shabbat. The Vilna Gaon (*Shulḥan Arukh, Oraḥ Ḥayim* 274:1) commended and approved of the opinion of R. Zeira as understood by the Rashba, and indeed it is reported (*Maaseh Rav* 123) that the Gaon generally sliced two *ḥallot* at each meal. Once, however, he happened to have many *ḥallot* before him, and he sliced them all. Apparently, the Gaon thought the Rashba recommended slicing *all* the *ḥallot* at each meal.

However, the Rashba himself paints an entirely different picture in his responsa (VII:530). He says that Rava (the Rashba apparently had an alternate text of the Gemara; the standard edition says "R. Zeira") sliced two *ḥallot* – not all of them – at each meal. He explained that many aspects of Shabbat (such as the two sheep of the *korban musaf*, the ideas of *zakhor veshamor*, etc.) are double. Therefore, one should slice twice as many loaves as one ordinarily does. As the Rashba notes, however, this could not possibly correspond to what was done at the time of the manna, when they had to leave the loaves for the other meals. He therefore recommended that we follow the custom of R. Kahana (R. Huna in variant texts) to recite the *berakha* over the *leḥem mishneh* but to slice only one of the loaves.

According to the Rashba, then, there is one opinion (R. Kahana or R. Huna) that says only one *ḥalla* should be cut, another opinion (R. Zeira) requiring slicing two *ḥallot*, and yet another opinion (the Vilna Gaon's understanding of the Rashba's explanation of R. Zeira) that all *ḥallot* should be cut.

At first glance, R. Zeira's opinion has nothing to do with the manna; therefore, all Shabbat meals, including *Seuda Shelishit*, should require *leḥem mishneh*, despite the fact that Benei Yisrael did not have enough loaves for *leḥem mishneh* for *Seuda Shelishit*. The *Shulḥan Arukh* (*Oraḥ Ḥayim* 29:1) rules accordingly. In addition, the Rema cites the position of the Avudraham that if one were to eat more than three meals on Shabbat, he must have *leḥem mishneh* at each meal.

On the other hand, R. Kahana (or R. Huna) maintains that we should cut only one *ḥalla* at each meal, as was done by Benei Yisrael. It would follow, therefore, that there is no need for *leḥem mishneh* at *Seuda Shelishit,* since only a single portion of manna remained for this meal. It has been argued, however, that remembering the manna does not necessarily mean reenacting the experience. The *leḥem mishneh* reminds us of the manna, and therefore we could be required to have *leḥem mishneh* even at *Seuda Shelishit.* Although in the wilderness Benei Yisrael did not have *leḥem mishneh* for their third meal, we are still reminded of the manna by having two loaves at this meal (Ritva, Shabbat 117b). The *Tur* and *Beit Yosef* (*Oraḥ Ḥayim* 291) quote a number of authorities who debate this point.

The question arises as to whether women are obligated to have *leḥem mishneh.* In general, women are exempt from positive mitzvot caused by time. However, Rabbenu Tam (Responsum 70; also cited in responsa of Rabbi Meir of Rothenburg, Prague edition, no. 473) claimed that since women were involved in the miracle of the manna, they are therefore obligated with respect to *leḥem mishneh.* The Ran (Shabbat 44a in Rif) agrees with Rabbenu Tam that women are obligated in *leḥem mishneh,* albeit for a different reason. Since, in general, men and women are equally obligated in all laws of Shabbat, we need not base women's obligation to have *leḥem mishneh* on their inclusion in the miracle of manna.

However, there is an opinion of the Ari (cited in *Avodat Yisrael* of the Maggid of Kozhnitz) that says women are exempt. Some Aḥaronim (e.g., Rabbi Shlomo Kluger) have contested both points of the Rav and Rabbenu Tam and maintained that women are exempt from *Seuda Shelishit* just like any other positive mitzva caused by time. It should be noted that in many communities men joined together to eat *Seuda Shelishit* and generally women did not participate. The *Mishna Berura* (291:1) comments that women are obligated because of their involvement in the manna, and the *Arukh HaShulḥan* (*Oraḥ Ḥayim* 274:4) writes that women are obligated to have *leḥem mishneh* because all Shabbat laws pertain equally to men and women.

Parashat Yitro

Kibbud Av VaEm

There are two positive mitzvot pertaining to children's relationship with their parents. The Torah commanded us to honor our father and mother (Shemot 20:12) as well as to treat them with reverence (Vayikra 19:3). The Gemara (Ketubbot 103a) deduces from the extra word "*et*" that appears in the command to honor parents before both "your father" and "your mother" ("*et avikha ve'et immekha*"), that one is also obligated to honor his father's wife and his mother's husband. The Gemara further comments that the extra letter *vav* ("*ve'et*") teaches that one must similarly respect his older (or perhaps only oldest) brother.

In his discussion of the principles governing the count of the mitzvot (*Sefer HaMitzvot*, principle 2), Rambam elucidated his opinion that mitzvot derived from seemingly extraneous letters or words should not be enumerated in the list of the 613 mitzvot. He argued that anyone who disagrees with this theory should list as three separate mitzvot the obligations of honoring one's father's wife, mother's husband, and older (or oldest) brother.

Ramban (in his comments ad loc.) explained that these three people are not really the focal point of the mitzva. The basic mitzva is to honor one's father and mother, but the obligation to honor one's father would include a requirement to honor his wife, honoring one's mother would include honoring her husband, and honoring parents would include honoring one's older (or oldest) brother. Since parents would wish to have their older children respected by the younger siblings, the obligation to honor an older brother is part of the mitzva of *kibbud av va'em* and does not constitute a separate mitzva. The halakhic ramification of this position is that the obligation of honoring a stepmother, stepfather, or older brother would not, according to Ramban, apply after the parent's death. Presumably, the parent could also waive these obligations, even without the consent of the spouse or older brother.

One might still ask why *kibbud av va'em* is counted as a single mitzva. After all, the requirement to honor one's mother is just as strict and mandatory as that of honoring one's father. I recall a comment in this regard made by Rabbi Soloveitchik shortly after the death of his mother. After the death of the Rav's father, the Rav delivered his annual *yahrzeit shiur* in his memory. When the Rav's mother died (more than two decades after her husband, but within a few weeks of his *yahrzeit*), he said that in principle, whatever he did in memory of his father should be done for his mother, as well, as *kibbud av* and *kibbud em* are identical. However, he felt that he did not have the strength to deliver two *yahrzeit shiurim* so close to one another.

Ramban suggested that since the verse presents the two obligations with a single verb ("*Honor* your father and your mother"), they should be considered a single mitzva. He then argued that even if the obligation to honor an older (or oldest) brother stands independently of the honor due to parents (and therefore would presumably continue even after the parents' death), it would still not qualify as a separate mitzva because it is also included in the general command.

One might argue, however, that although it is true that only one verb is employed, nevertheless, since one's father and mother are two separate people, and the Torah requires honoring each equally and independently, two mitzvot should be counted.

The *Semag* indeed appears to count the obligation to honor one's parents as two separate mitzvot. Although his elucidation of these mitzvot (111, 112) might imply that he referred to one mitzva of honor and another of reverence, some have interpreted his list to mean that indeed two individual mitzvot exist: a mitzva to honor one's father, and another to honor one's mother. Rabbi Tzvi Hirsch Chajes (Sanhedrin 56b) cites the *Mishneh LaMelekh* as saying that both Ramban and the *Semag* count two individual mitzvot. Rabbi Chajes notes, however, that this position becomes very difficult in light of the Gemara's explicit comment that ten mitzvot were given to us at Mara. Given that the Gemara there lists *kibbud av va'em* and nine other mitzvot, it follows that *kibbud av va'em* counts as a single mitzva.

This argument indeed seems conclusive, but it does not explain the conceptual basis for considering *kibbud av va'em* as one mitzva.

The *Minḥat Ḥinnukh* (33) mentions that if a child does not fulfill the mitzva of *kibbud av va'em* properly, he most certainly can and should do teshuva. He questioned, however, whether this mitzva should be classified under the category of *bein adam laMakom* (mitzvot between man and God) or *bein adam laḥavero* (between man and man). If we consider this a mitzva *bein adam laMakom*, then the violator need not ask his parents for forgiveness as part of his repentance. However, if it falls under the category of *bein adam laḥavero*, then he must appease his parents as a prerequisite for forgiveness. He reasoned that mitzvot *bein adam laḥavero* include all people and all relationships. Since honor of one's parents is obviously restricted to only two people, he suggests that perhaps it is "only" a mitzva *bein adam laMakom*.

In *Minḥat Asher* (Shemot, p. 251), Rabbi Asher Weiss questions the assumption that leads the *Minḥat Ḥinnukh* to classify *kibbud av va'em* under the category of *bein adam laMakom*. Why can't a mitzva *bein adam laḥavero* apply to one specific person? On the other hand, Rabbi Weiss cites Ramban and Rabbenu Baḥya, who explain that the obligation to honor parents derives from their partnership with God Himself in the birth of a child. Ramban finds an allusion to this special relationship in a phrase in Devarim (5:16). The Torah said that we must honor our parents "as Hashem, your God, commanded you." Although Rashi explains that this refers to God's having already commanded us with regard to *kibbud av va'em* in Mara, Ramban explains that we must honor our parents as we were commanded to honor God, since they are partners in birth. (The reader is advised to see the practical application of this concept in Ramban's commentary to Shemot 20:12.) Thus, according to Ramban and Rabbenu Baḥya, *kibbud av va'em* indeed falls under the category of *bein adam laMakom* (but not for the reason suggested by the *Minḥat Ḥinnukh*).

Rabbi Meir Simḥa HaKohen of Dvinsk (*Meshekh Ḥokhma*, Vayikra 19:3) suggested a slightly different approach. He cites the halakha that if a parent would ask a child to violate a law of the Torah, he need not and must not obey the parent. Rabbi Meir Simḥa asked why this halakha requires mentioning at all. Why should any mitzva *bein adam laḥavero* override a law between man and God? He therefore explained that the obligation to honor parents relates directly to one's relationship with God. One's parents, who are partners in his physical creation, also transmit to him the message of God. Therefore, one might have thought that one must always listen to his parents under all circumstances, and it was thus necessary to teach that God's commandments take precedence over parents' wishes.

If we assume the *bein adam laMakom* nature of the mitzva, then the mitzva is really to honor God's partners, and it can therefore be understood why the obligation to honor one's father and mother is really a single mitzva.

It should be pointed out, however, that Rambam (Pe'ah 1:1) writes quite clearly that *kibbud av va'em* is a *mitzva bein adam laḥavero*. One might suggest that perhaps there are actually two aspects of this mitzva, and it is both *bein adam laMakom* as well as *bein adam laḥavero*.

Parashat Mishpatim

Wife and Family Support

The first topic addressed in *Parashat Mishpatim* involves the treatment of Jewish slaves, both male and female. Ramban (ad loc.) explains that fair treatment of slaves serves as a reminder of the exodus from slavery in Egypt. He adds that this *parasha* is thus connected to the first of the Ten Commandments, the requirement to believe in God, who delivered us from slavery in Egypt.

The laws of the Jewish maidservant follow the laws of the male slave, who is generally a thief sold into slavery by the court because he could not repay his theft. The maidservant, by contrast, is a young girl "sold" by her father to a man who is expected to either marry her or arrange for his son to marry her. Thus the "sale" of a maidservant is actually a marriage arrangement for the future.

After the maidservant's marriage, she is subject to the same laws, customs, and regulations that apply to any other spouse. The Torah instructs, "He shall deal with her according to the manner of the young women... he shall not diminish her food, her clothing, or her conjugal rights" (Shemot 21:9–11). This translation of the biblical text reflects the opinion presented in the Gemara (Ketubbot 47b) by Rava and cited by

Rashi in his commentary on the Torah. Based on this understanding, Rambam (*Sefer HaMitzvot, Lo Taaseh* 262) lists as one of the 613 mitzvot the prohibition against withholding these rights from the maidservant-wife, and adds that the same applies to any other married woman. In principle 9 of his introduction to *Sefer HaMitzvot*, Rambam explains that although there really are three separate obligations, they are nevertheless to be counted as a single *mitzvat lo taaseh* (prohibition), since the Torah employed just one verb: "shall not diminish."

Rabbi Saadia Gaon likewise maintains that these obligations are of biblical origin, but claims that we must count them as three individual *mitzvot aseh* (positive commandments). He apparently understood that the basic obligation is, "He shall deal with her according to the manner of young women." When the Torah then enumerates three individual obligations, they are each to be counted as a separate mitzva.

However, other authorities maintain that supporting one's wife constitutes a rabbinic requirement. Ramban cites these opinions and explains that the obligations of the Torah refer only to marital relations and have nothing to do with financial arrangements.

The previous section establishes that if a male slave is married when he begins his term of slavery, his wife goes out of slavery together with him after six years of service (Shemot 21:3). Rashi (ad loc.) cites a gemara (Kiddushin 22a) that questions the meaning of the wife's exit, given that she was never enslaved in the first place, as a married woman cannot become a slave. The Gemara therefore explains that this verse refers to the master's obligation to support his servant's wife as long as the servant remains in his possession. When the servant goes free, so does his wife.

If we assume that the Torah requires a husband to support his wife, then it seems logical that when the husband becomes a servant and cannot fulfill his obligation, the Torah obligates the master to do so. However, if the husband is not required to support his wife, why did the Torah obligate the master to do so? Ramban (Shemot 21:3) explains that although there is no explicit obligation in the Torah to support one's wife, it is the normally accepted practice to do so. Although the Torah itself placed no specific obligation on the husband, it assumed that the wife would be well provided for. When the husband becomes a slave and thus cannot care for his wife, the Torah realized that the master would not automatically assume the responsibility to support his servant's wife, and it therefore imposed a biblical obligation to this effect upon the master.

Apparently, Ramban felt that there is no reason to obligate people to do something that should be self-evident and naturally done. Moreover, perhaps the Torah did not want a husband to support his family because of strict biblical requirement, but rather out of love and a sense of responsibility. The Sages, however, foresaw the possibility of recalcitrant husbands who would not fulfill this normal practice, and they therefore enacted a rabbinic obligation to support one's wife.

To summarize the basic positions, all acknowledge that an obligation exists for a husband to support his wife. Rashi and Rambam consider this a Torah requirement, whereas Ramban holds that while it is proper and normal to do so, it is legally mandated only as a rabbinic obligation.

The Gemara (Ketubbot 65b) states clearly that one is obligated to support his small children. Ramban understands this to be a rabbinic law: there is no biblical requirement of child support just as there is no Torah obligation of wife support. On the level of Torah law, the obligation to feed one's children should be self-evident and done as normal behavior and practice, but the Sages instituted a specific law in order to require the neglectful father to support his young children. Rambam (*Hilkhot Ishut* 12:14) codifies the obligation for a father to support his young children, and adds, "just as he must support his wife." This comparison drawn by Rambam between supporting children and supporting a wife suggests that in his view, feeding children likewise constitutes a biblical obligation.

The *Mishneh LaMelekh* (ad loc.) cites the position of the Ran that the obligation of child support is actually a derivative of the requirement of wife support. The obligation to support one's wife includes providing the means to support her children, as well. It therefore follows that the obligation of child support would cease with the wife's death. It would also follow logically from this position that a husband would have to support his wife's children even if he were not their father. By contrast, the Rosh and Rivash (cited in *Mishneh LaMelekh*) maintain that if a man sired a child out of wedlock, he is obligated to support the child. In that case, he certainly has no obligation to support the mother, as she is not his wife. These Rishonim thus disagree with the Ran and hold that there is an independent halakha of supporting children. This obligation would therefore continue after the wife's death and presumably would not require a husband to support his wife's children from another man.

In conclusion, halakha indeed obligates a father to support his children. The basic obligation seems to be a biblical obligation according to Rambam and a rabbinic obligation according to Ramban. It may be viewed as either an independent halakha (Rosh and Rivash) or a requirement subsumed under the obligation of wife support.

Furthermore, there might be different halakhot that apply to children of different ages. It is possible that the basic law applies only to children below the age of six, while various *takkanot* (ordinances) have been added throughout the ages to ensure that the rights of children are protected. For an example, see the history and analysis of the *takkanot* of the Chief Rabbinate in Israel in this regard written by Dr. Z. Warhaftig, which appeared in *Tehumin* 1 and has been included in his work *Meḥkarim BaMishpat HaIvri* (Ramat Gan, 1985).

Parashat Teruma

Leḥem HaPanim

The *Sefer HaḤinnukh* enumerates two positive mitzvot found in *Parashat Teruma*. The first is to build the *Beit HaMikdash* as a site for offering sacrifices and assembling all the Jewish people on the three major festivals. Following the opinion of Rambam (*Sefer HaMitzvot, Aseh* 20), the *Ḥinnukh* maintains that this mitzva also encompasses the requirement to build the various vessels of the *Mikdash*, such as the Altar, Candelabra, and Table.

Ramban (*Sefer HaMitzvot, Aseh* 37) disagrees with Rambam and argues that building the *Mikdash* should be counted as a single mitzva, and the fashioning of the various parts, such as the Ark and the *Kapporet* (cover), as separate mitzvot. He contends that since sacrifices can be offered even without these appurtenances, the *Mikdash* obviously constitutes an independent mitzva.

Ramban agrees, however, that some parts of the *Mikdash* are not to be counted as individual mitzvot. He writes that if a given item is needed as a prerequisite for the performance of a specific mitzva, then it should not be counted individually. Therefore, Ramban does not count the *Shulḥan* (Table) as an independent mitzva. Since a mitzva exists to place *leḥem hapanim* (show bread) on the *Shulḥan*, building the *Shulḥan* is merely a prerequisite (*hekhsher mitzva*), and not an independent mitzva.

The second mitzva enumerated by the *Ḥinnukh* is to arrange the *leḥem hapanim*. Here, too, he follows the view of Rambam in his listing of the mitzvot. In the brief version of Rambam's list printed at the beginning of *Mishneh Torah* (*Aseh* 27), Rambam writes, "To arrange the bread and frankincense before God every Shabbat, as it says, 'You shall place upon the Table *leḥem hapanim* before Me always.'" The Raavad (ad loc.) asks why Rambam did not count the sacrificial offering of the frankincense and the consumption of the *leḥem hapanim* as separate mitzvot.

Although the mitzva of *leḥem hapanim* is mentioned in *Parashat Teruma*, the details of this obligation appear only later, in *Parashat Emor*. The Torah (Vayikra 24:5–10) specifies that we are required to take fine flour and bake twelve loaves, place them in two piles of six loaves each, and put frankincense on each pile. This is to be done every Shabbat, continually (*tamid*). On Shabbat, the frankincense is to be burned on the Altar and the loaves (of the prior week) are to be eaten by Aharon and his sons (*kohanim*) in a "holy place."

The Raavad understood that the Torah actually presents three mitzvot related to the *leḥem hapanim*: (1) to arrange the *leḥem hapanim* on the *Shulḥan*; (2) to burn the accompanying frankincense; (3) to eat the loaves. To explain Rambam's position, Rabbi Yosef Karo (*Kesef Mishneh* ad loc.) notes that neither the burning of the frankincense nor the eating of the loaves was stated in the Torah as an imperative. Apparently, he felt that the offering of the frankincense was merely a prerequisite act (*mattir*) permitting the *leḥem hapanim* for consumption by the *kohanim*. The Torah then added that if the *kohanim* do eat the bread, they must do so "in a holy place."

Rambam elaborates upon this mitzva in his *Sefer HaMitzvot* (*Aseh* 27), where he writes, "We are commanded to continually place *leḥem hapanim* before God. As you know, the Torah's intent is that we must place warm bread [on the Table] every Shabbat; it must be accompanied by the frankincense and the *kohanim* must eat the bread of the previous Shabbat."

Rabbi Ḥayim Soloveitchik (*Novellae of the Graḥ*, Jerusalem, 1976) explains that the obligation to eat the *leḥem hapanim* stems from a different mitzva: it is an adjunct to the general requirement (*Aseh* 88) to eat the remainder of every *korban minḥa* (meal offering).

Of course, this approach is based on the assumption that *leḥem hapanim* belongs to the category of *menaḥot*. Indeed, there are several halakhot that can support this assumption. The Torah forbids preparing any *korban minḥa* as *ḥametz* (Vayikra 2:11), and the Gemara (Menaḥot 57a) applies this prohibition to the *leḥem hapanim*, as well, on the basis of the Torah's formulation of the prohibition: "*any minḥa* that you bring as an offering." The Gemara (8a) also determines that a *minḥa* is accepted even if it contains no oil in light of the fact that the *leḥem hapanim* does not contain any oil. Rashi there writes explicitly that *leḥem hapanim* is a *minḥa*.

Rav Ḥayim proceeds to explain why we should not consider the offering of the frankincense a separate mitzva. He proves that there is no specific obligation to offer the frankincense every Shabbat, but this requirement stems from the general obligation to offer every *korban* in its proper time. He cites the ruling of the Yerushalmi (Shekalim 6:2) that if no new bread was prepared for Shabbat, the frankincense was not offered and the twelve loaves remained on the Table for an additional week. If there was an independent mitzva to burn the frankincense, why would we not burn it even if there were no new loaves? Why does the *tamid* aspect of the *leḥem hapanim* take precedence over the mitzva of offering the frankincense? Apparently, he concludes, this is not a mitzva per se. Rather, when there are new loaves prepared, it is a mitzva to offer the frankincense, just as with any other *korban*. In this particular case, it is a prerequisite act (*mattir*) that allows the *kohanim* to eat the *leḥem hapanim*.

Although the *Ḥinnukh* and others have suggested various reasons for this mitzva, it is interesting to note that Rambam seemed perplexed about this issue. In his discussion of the rationale for various mitzvot, he writes (*Guide for the Perplexed*, III:45), "But the *Shulḥan* and the bread that is always on it... I do not know the reason for it." Likewise, in the poem *Asadder LiSe'udta*, written by the Ari and which many people recite or sing at the Shabbat morning meal, he writes, "He will reveal to us the reasons of the twelve loaves." The Ari, like Rambam, was unable to determine the underlying reason behind the mitzva of *leḥem hapanim*.

Parashat Tetzaveh

The Priestly Garments

After Benei Yisrael were commanded to build the *Mishkan*, they were informed of the laws concerning the *bigdei kehunna*, the priestly garments. The Torah tells us to prepare "vestments of sanctity" for Aharon and his sons. The *kohen gadol* generally wore eight garments, while a regular *kohen* wore four. However, on Yom Kippur, the *kohen gadol* wore only four garments. The Torah describes these special clothes as signs of "glory and splendor" (Shemot 28).

Rabbi Saadia Gaon's *Sefer HaMitzvot* contains several distinct sections. Of course, there is a section of *mitzvot aseh* and another of *mitzvot lo taaseh* (positive and negative commandments). In addition, Rabbi Saadia also wrote one section containing sixty-five mitzvot that he called *parashiyyot*. In his lengthy introduction to that section, Rabbi Yeruḥam Fishel Perlow (editor of and commentator on Rabbi Saadia's *Sefer HaMitzvot*) explained that this section contains requirements that are obligations of the community at large and are not mitzvot incumbent upon individuals. The sixty-second *parashiya* is "The Eight Garments of Splendor." Rabbi Perlow explained that Rabbi Saadia did not think that there is any mitzva, either positive or negative, for a *kohen* to wear *bigdei kehunna*. Rather, these garments form a prerequisite for any *avoda* (service) performed by the *kohanim*. If a *kohen* performs *avoda* without *bigdei kehunna*, his *avoda* is invalid, because a *kohen* without *bigdei kehunna* is not really a *kohen*. The Torah said, "They shall make the clothes of Aharon to sanctify him to serve as a *kohen* to Me" (Shemot 28:3). The Gemara (Zevaḥim 17b), citing additional sources, as well, explains this to mean that "when they are wearing their [special] garments, their priesthood is upon them; if they are not wearing their [special] garments, their priesthood is not upon them." Thus, the prohibition of performing *avoda* without *bigdei kehunna* is not a special prohibition: it flows naturally from the prohibition for any *zar* (non-*kohen*) to perform *avoda*.

According to Rabbi Saadia, the only specific mitzva concerning *bigdei kehunna* is the communal obligation to make these garments. These vestments are actually communal property. If an individual owns such a garment, he must donate it to the community, and only then can it be used (Rambam, *Hilkhot Kelei HaMikdash* 8:7). Therefore, Rabbi Saadia listed only one communal mitzva: to make the *bigdei kehunna*. In this mitzva Rabbi Saadia includes all eight garments, including the four standard garments and also the four additional garments worn by the *kohen gadol*. Rabbi Perlow explained that Rabbi Saadia included all eight garments in this mitzva because the *kohen gadol*'s four special garments were required in addition to, rather than in place of, the four standard *bigdei kehunna*. (Considerable controversy surrounds this last point, which is subject to a well-known debate among Rishonim cited by Rabbi Perlow.)

Rambam (*Sefer HaMitzvot, Aseh* 33), on the other hand, defines the mitzva somewhat differently: "The *kohanim* were commanded to wear special garments for glory and splendor." In his list of mitzvot at the beginning of *Hilkhot Kelei HaMikdash*, Rambam writes, "To wear *bigdei kehunna* for *avoda*." Although Rambam (*Hilkhot Kelei HaMikdash* 10:4) also writes, "There is a *mitzvat aseh* to make these clothes and have the *kohen* perform *avoda* while wearing them," he did not count the preparation of these garments as an individual mitzva. He apparently understood that making them constitutes only a *hekhsher mitzva* – a prerequisite for the mitzva of performing *avoda* while garbed in *bigdei kehunna*.

Ramban (*Sefer HaMitzvot* ad loc.) cited the *Behag*, who also did not enumerate wearing *bigdei kehunna* as a *mitzvat aseh*, because he considered it a *hekhsher avoda*. Ramban proceeds to challenge Rambam's view that wearing the *bigdei kehunna* constitutes a mitzva. If this is so, he asks, why did he not count three individual mitzvot: one mitzva for the *kohen gadol* to wear eight garments, a second for a regular *kohen* to wear four garments, and a third mitzva for the *kohen gadol* to wear four garments on Yom Kippur?

The Brisker Rav (Rabbi Yitzḥak Ze'ev Soloveitchik) explained that according to Rambam, there is one mitzva to wear *bigdei kehunna* in order to prepare oneself to perform *avoda*. Although there are three different types of *bigdei kehunna*, they all serve one generic purpose: they permit the *kohen* who wears them to perform *avoda*. Rambam (*Hilkhot Kelei HaMikdash*, introduction) is careful to describe this mitzva as a "*mitzvat aseh* to wear *bigdei kehunna* for *avoda*." Therefore, it is all to be considered one mitzva. Ramban, on the other hand, thought that wearing *bigdei kehunna* is an independent mitzva, as one thereby actually becomes a *kohen*. Inasmuch as there are, according to Ramban, three different types of *bigdei kehunna*, they should be considered three individual mitzvot (*Novellae of the Griz*, Zevaḥim 18; in *Novellae of Rabbi Efrayim Mordekhai*, Yevamot, section 9, the author elaborates upon this idea, which he heard directly from Rabbi Soloveitchik).

It should be noted that although Ramban left these questions against Rambam unanswered, he later said (in his animadversions to Rambam's *Sefer HaMitzvot*, positive commandment 33) that he felt that the opinion of Rambam is valid since a *kohen* who does *avoda* properly, i.e., while wearing the proper clothes, fulfills a mitzva. However, Ramban asked, in that case, Rambam should have added another mitzva: to perform *avoda* while standing. Based on the *pasuk* "Hashem, your God, chose him of all your tribes to stand and serve" (Devarim 18:5), the Gemara (Zevaḥim 23b) establishes a mitzva for the *kohen* to stand during *avoda*. Therefore, Ramban asks, if we count wearing *bigdei kehunna* as a mitzva, why should we not also enumerate standing? Ramban suggests a distinction between these two laws: the mitzva of *bigdei kehunna* was given in an imperative form – "You shall make *bigdei kodesh*" – while the law of standing was stated in narrative form, rather than as a command. He adds, however, that this issue nevertheless remains unclear.

Rabbi Menachem Genack (*Birkat Yitzḥak,* addenda to chapter 45) brings an interesting proof for the notion that wearing *bigdei kehunna* does not merely confer the formal status of *kohen* upon the wearer, but also serves as preparation for *avoda*. The *Shulḥan Arukh* (*Oraḥ Ḥayim* 98:4) writes that one should wear special clothes for *tefilla* "similar to *bigdei kehunna*." Rabbi Genack observed that if the entire reason behind wearing *bigdei kehunna* is to establish oneself as a *kohen,* one could not draw any comparison at all between *bigdei kehunna* and the regular laws of *tefilla*. If, however, there is an independent mitzva to wear *bigdei kehunna* for *avoda,* then at least some basis exists to compare the priestly garments and the special clothing worn during *tefilla*.

We have thus seen various possibilities as to the number of mitzvot involved with *bigdei kehunna*. Rabbi Saadia counted one communal *mitzvat aseh* to make the vestments. The *Behag* enumerated one individual *mitzvat lo taaseh*. Rambam counted a single *mitzvat aseh,* while Ramban suggested that conceivably, we might count three separate mitzvot.

Parashat Ki Tissa

The Half-Shekel

The Torah (Shemot 30:11–16) told us that when we count our nation, every man should give money as an atonement in order to prevent a plague, which could strike us during the census. This is followed by the instruction that everyone who is counted should give *maḥatzit hashekel* – a half-shekel. The Torah adds that a poor man may not give less and a rich man may not give more.

Although the introduction seems to imply that every person should give *maḥatzit hashekel*, the latter statement states quite clearly that only those who are counted must do so. Since the census included only people over twenty years of age, it would seem that anyone below that age is exempt from this mitzva.

In truth, however, this point is subject to a debate among the Rishonim. In this section the Torah actually alludes to three separate *terumot* (literally, "donations") that had to be collected from Benei Yisrael (see Rashi, v. 15). There was one donation to be used for the sockets of the *Mishkan* (Tabernacle), another for the general expenses of building the edifice itself, and a third that went towards the purchase of the necessary sacrifices.

Ramban (ad loc.) explains that the obligation to donate *maḥatzit hashekel* for the sacrifices – as opposed to the other terumot – is an annual mitzva and applies to everyone above the age of bar mitzva. He adds that this is implied by the Torah's reference to atonement as the purpose behind this donation, indicating that all those in need of atonement – presumably every bar mitzva – must give *maḥatzit hashekel.* Apparently, Ramban understood that the connection between the census and the *maḥatzit hashekel* obligation applies only to the money given for the *Mishkan* itself. The half-shekel donated for the purpose of purchasing sacrifices, however, does not depend upon the census, and thus applies even to those below the age of twenty.

The *Sefer HaḤinnukh* (105), by contrast, ruled that the obligation includes only men above the age of twenty. Interestingly, this position marks a deviation from the *Ḥinnukh*'s strong tendency to follow the opinion of Rambam. Rambam (*Hilkhot Shekalim* 1:1) obligates all adults to give *maḥatzit hashekel,* stating plainly that minors (below the age of bar mitzva) are excluded.

Regarding women's obligation in this mitzva, the commonly accepted view maintains – based on the Mishna in Shekalim (1:4) – that women do not have to give *maḥatzit hashekel.* Rambam (*Sefer HaMitzvot, Aseh* 171) deduced this exemption from the clause in the *pasuk* that says that everyone included in the census must give *maḥatzit hashekel.*

This rationale, however, appears to contradict the aforementioned ruling of Rambam in *Hilkhot Shekalim,* where he obligates everyone above the age of bar mitzva. This ruling implies that he understood the mitzva as Ramban did, that although only those included in the census were obligated in all three types of *teruma,* everyone was included in the *teruma* for the purchasing of sacrifices. It is therefore difficult to understand how Rambam used the connection between the census and the obligation of giving *teruma* for the *Mishkan* as a source to exclude women from the *teruma* for the sacrifices.

It has been suggested for other reasons that Rambam changed his views after writing *Sefer HaMitzvot* (see *Minḥat Asher:* Shemot, p. 384). If this is true, then perhaps in *Sefer HaMitzvot* he only obligated men above twenty. Therefore, in *Sefer HaMitzvot* he may have maintained (like the *Ḥinnukh*) that the entire obligation of *teruma* is only incumbent upon those involved in the census. By the time he wrote the *Mishneh Torah,* however, he had changed his mind and wrote that all male adults are obligated. If, indeed, the mitzva includes all adults, even those not included in the census, then we must find a different source to exempt women from *maḥatzit hashekel.*

The Me'iri (Shekalim 1:4) explains that women are exempt from this mitzva because it is a mitzva caused by time (*zeman gerama*). Rabbi A. Sofer, in his commentary on the Me'iri, remarks that this reason is difficult to understand, given that there does not exist any specific time to give *maḥatzit hashekel.* Perhaps the Me'iri felt that the obligation is to give it every year. Once the year has begun, the onset of the new year creates a new obligation, and we must therefore consider this a mitzva caused by time.

Rabbi Ovadya Bartenura (Shekalim 1:4) suggests a different source for the exemption of women from *maḥatzit hashekel*: the use of the word "*ish*" ("man") in the verse (Shemot 30:12), which would seem to exclude women from all three *terumot.*

The Mishna does not give any source for this exemption, but merely rules that we do not coerce women to give *maḥatzit hashekel.* This led Rabbi Moshe Sternbuch (*Mo'adim UZemanim,* II:119) to suggest a very novel theory: that women should, in fact, give *maḥatzit hashekel* because they are included in the atonement attained by the sacrifices. According to this approach, they may and should donate this money, but we would not force them to do so.

The Rema (*Oraḥ Ḥayim* 694:1) ruled that we should give one-half of the local coin (one half-dollar in the USA, half a pound in Britain, etc.) as a *zekher* (commemoration) of *maḥatzit hashekel.* He adds that inasmuch as there were three separate *terumot,* we should give three *maḥatziyyot hashekel.* He writes, however, that this obligation applies only to those twenty years of age and above.

The *Magen Avraham* (ad loc.) explains that this position of the Rema is based on the opinion of Bartenura (which we saw in the *Ḥinnukh*). However, many *posekim* (including, as we have seen, Rambam and Ramban) say that all benei mitzva must give *maḥatzit hashekel,* and therefore even those between the ages of thirteen and twenty should give the *zekher*. A novel idea of the *Matteh Yehuda* (cited in *Mikra'ei Kodesh,*

Purim, p. 70) maintains that the Rema limited the obligation to those twenty years of age and older only with regard to all three *terumot*. However, he suggests that the Rema would concede that a bar mitzva under the age of twenty should give a single *maḥatzit hashekel* as a reminder of the one that was given to buy the sacrifices.

The Rema makes no mention of the halakha concerning women's inclusion in or exemption from this obligation. The *Magen Avraham* (ad loc.), however, cites an opinion that they, too, should give the *zekher*. The *Magen Avraham* comments, though, that he knows no source for that opinion. Quite possibly, this opinion felt that women should give the *maḥatzit hashekel* for the purchase of the sacrifices, but that they are not coerced to do so. If so, it is proper for women to give the *zekher*, as well.

The *Kaf HaḤayim* writes that inasmuch as the purpose of this donation is to attain atonement, every person should be included. *Yalkut Yosef* (v:313) cites the controversy over whether men between the ages of thirteen and twenty are obligated, and recommends that the stringent opinion be followed. He then states categorically that women should also give the *zekher*. The *Torah Temima* (Shemot 30:13) writes that although the original *maḥatzit hashekel* was given only by those included in the census, everyone should give the *zekher*. He cites in this context the Gemara's comment that we give the *zekher* before Purim to remember that Haman offered *shekalim* as an incentive to murder all the Jews. We, therefore, give *shekalim* to avert disaster. The *zekher* should then be given on behalf of all those who were threatened by Haman, i.e., men, women, and children. The *Mishna Berura* (ad loc.) observes that the general custom is to give the *zekher lemaḥatzit hashekel* on behalf of all people, including unborn children.

Parashat Vayak'hel

Punishment on Shabbat

In reference to Shabbat, besides the general prohibition "you shall not do any work (*melakha*)" (Shemot 20:10), the Torah also writes specifically, "You shall not kindle a fire in any of your dwellings on the Shabbat day" (Shemot 35:3). The Talmud (Sanhedrin 35b) records a debate regarding the implication of this reiteration.

Some rabbis thought that the prohibition of lighting a fire was singled out in order to teach that violating this *melakha* incurs only lashes, whereas all other intentional violations of *melakha* carry either the death penalty or *karet* (spiritual excision). The Gemara refers to this position by the term "*havara lelav yatzat*" – burning was singled out to teach that it is merely a negative prohibition, as opposed to a capital offense.

Others thought that a single *melakha* was spelled out in order to teach that each *melakha* is an independent prohibition. The legal implication of this is that if one were to violate several *melakhot* unintentionally in one lapse of knowledge (i.e., without remembering in between violations that these acts were forbidden), he would be obligated to bring a *korban ḥattat* for each *melakha* he had violated. (However, in a case of an intentional violation there is no relevance to this principle, as one cannot be put to death twice.) The Gemara refers to this position as "*havara leḥallek yatzat*" – burning was singled out to teach that each *melakha* is a separate entity.

In addition to the above derivations, the Gemara propounds that the phrase "in any of your dwellings" indicates that the courts may not carry out capital punishment on Shabbat. The exact nature of this rule, though, is unclear. One possibility is that the Gemara was simply negating a possible assumption one might have made. One might have thought that the mitzva to "expunge the evil from your midst" (Devarim 13:6, inter alia; a general directive to rid society of criminals) overrides Shabbat, just as some other mitzvot do. For example, the Temple service is permitted on Shabbat despite the various acts of *melakha* that are involved. Therefore, it was necessary to teach that the mitzva to execute criminals does not take precedence over Shabbat.

According to this view, the verse does not introduce a new prohibition: it simply indicates that the original prohibition remains in effect. This is similar to the rule that building the Temple does not override Shabbat, derived from the verse "Guard My Sabbaths and fear My Temple" (Vayikra 19:30). There, the verse does not introduce a new prohibition: it just clarifies that the normal prohibitions of Shabbat remain in effect even in light of the mitzva to build the Temple.

However, the Yerushalmi (Sanhedrin 4:6) derives from this verse that courts may not adjudicate cases on Shabbat, implying that this is a more expansive prohibition, independent of whether *melakha* is performed. Yet many commentators assume that the general prohibition to judge on Shabbat is not biblical, but rather a rabbinic injunction meant to prevent people from writing.

Rambam in *Sefer HaMitzvot* (*Lo Taaseh* 322) enumerates an independent prohibition. He says that it is forbidden to punish sinners on Shabbat. He explains that the derivation from the verse about fire teaches that it is forbidden to administer the capital punishment of *sereifa*, burning, on Shabbat. From there we extrapolate that it also is prohibited to carry out any of the other capital punishments.

In *Hilkhot Shabbat* (24:7), Rambam expands this prohibition to include lashes, as well. The *Magen Avraham* (*Oraḥ Ḥayim* 339:3) asks why administering lashes should be forbidden: unlike capital punishment, this does not necessitate violating Shabbat. He suggests that perhaps lashes are forbidden because they might cause a wound, which is a *melakha*. Some suggest that inflicting a wound while administering lashes is inevitable (though not specifically intended), and thus forbidden as a *pesik reisha* – the rule that prohibits doing any action that will inevitably cause *melakha* to be violated. (The supercommentaries on the *Magen Avraham* offer other suggestions as to why administering lashes would or would not entail *melakha*.) In any case, the *Magen Avraham* clearly thought that there was no separate prohibition, but rather the derivation simply taught that the mitzva to punish criminals did not override Shabbat.

The *Minḥat Ḥinnukh* agrees with the *Magen Avraham* and asks why Rambam counted this as a separate mitzva. If only punishments that include *melakha* are forbidden, there should be no reason to count a separate prohibition. However, Rambam seems to have felt otherwise, assuming that the prohibition to administer punishment on Shabbat was independent of whether *melakha* was violated. As we have noted, this position can be seen in the Yerushalmi, as well.

While the above Aḥaronim rejected this position of Rambam, others accepted it. The *Avnei Nezer* (Responsa, *Oraḥ Ḥayim* 46, par. 5) rules in accordance with Rambam and expands on his position, claiming that it is biblically forbidden to excommunicate someone on Shabbat, as excommunication is a form of punishment. He also notes that Rambam's position emerges clearly from the Yerushalmi. However, in response to the question he was asked, he offers a fascinating limitation of this prohibition. He had been asked whether a scholar could excommunicate someone who had disgraced him. The *Avnei Nezer* claims that such a person is defined as a heretic, and is thus legally defined as lower than a non-Jew. The prohibition to punish on Shabbat seems to only apply to Jews. Thus, in such a case it would be permitted to excommunicate the person in question.

In addition to excommunication, there are other in-between cases where one must inquire whether they are included in Rambam's prohibition to administer punishment on Shabbat. For example, in many cases we are allowed to use force and administer lashes to someone who refuses to perform a mitzva he is obligated to perform. We are even allowed to hit him "until his soul departs" (Ketubbot 86a). The *Peri Megadim* (in his introduction to *Hilkhot Shabbat*) is unsure of whether this is considered a punishment, and therefore whether it would be permitted on Shabbat. (Obviously, if one believes that there is only a prohibition to carry out punishments that include *melakha*, the relevant issue will be whether these blows will cause a wound, not their possible status as punishment.) The *Shibbolei HaLeket* cites a responsum from Rabbi Sherira Gaon that forbids incarcerating a criminal on Shabbat, even in a holding cell, as this violates the above prohibition. (From context, this is clearly limited to cases where the criminal poses no danger to the public.)

The *Sefer HaḤinnukh* explains the reason for this prohibition:

> God wanted to give honor to the day, so that all people will find rest on it, even sinners and convicted criminals. It is like a king who invites all his subjects to a feast one day and does not prevent anyone from coming in. [Only] after the holiday will he exact justice. The same is true of God, who commanded us to sanctify and honor the day so it will be good for us and benefit us.

Parashat Pekudei

Washing Hands (and Feet) for Avoda

After describing the actual building of the *Mishkan* (Tabernacle), the Torah relates that the Laver (*Kiyyor*) was placed between the *Ohel Moed* (Tent of Meeting) and the Altar. Water was put in the Laver that was used to wash the hands and feet of Moshe and Aharon and his sons whenever they came to the *Ohel* or approached the Altar (Shemot 40:30–32). There are several significant differences between this discussion and the actual commandment regarding the Laver, which appears several chapters earlier.

In the beginning of *Parashat Ki Tissa* (Shemot 30:17–21), the Torah says that the purpose of the Laver was for Aharon and his sons to wash whenever they enter the *Ohel Moed* or approach the Altar to perform *avoda*. No mention is made at all of Moshe. The Torah there adds that they must wash their hands and feet "and [thus] not die," implying, of course, that entering the *Ohel* or doing *avoda* without such washing is punishable by death (to be administered by the heavenly court, as opposed to a *beit din*). Why is Moshe mentioned in conjunction with the Laver here, in *Parashat Pekudei*, but not in *Parashat Ki Tissa*?

The earlier *parasha* makes no reference to Moshe for the simple reason that he was not a *kohen* and therefore had no obligation to wash from the Laver. During the days of the *Mishkan*'s inauguration (*milluim*), however, Moshe in fact served as *kohen gadol*, and so the latter *parasha* mentions that Moshe also washed himself from the Laver.

Although the Torah told the *kohanim* to *wash* their hands and feet, the Gemara constantly refers to this mitzva as "*sanctification* (*kiddush*) of hands and feet." In fact, Targum Onkelos translated the word "*leroḥtza*" ("to wash") as "*lekiddush*."

Rambam (*Sefer HaMitzvot, Aseh* 24), *Sefer HaḤinnukh* (130), and Rabbi Saadia Gaon (*Aseh* 127) all count this *kiddush* as one of the 613 mitzvot. The *Behag* does not count it as a *mitzvat aseh*, but includes it in the list of sins for which the death penalty (by the heavenly court) is imposed. Ramban interprets this to mean that the *Behag* also views this as an independent mitzva but merely has a different system of enumerating the mitzvot. (See Rabbi Perlow's brief comment in his edition of Rabbi Saadia Gaon's *Sefer HaMitzvot* ad loc.)

Rabbi Aryeh Leib Malin raises the question of whether this *kiddush* is itself an *avoda* (act of divine service) or only a means of preparation (*hekhsher*) for the performance of *avoda*. He points out that although considerable controversy exists as to whether wearing *bigdei kehunna* (priestly vestments) constitutes a separate mitzva (see the chapter on *Parashat Tetzaveh*), everyone seems to agree that this *kiddush* is an independent mitzva. This implies that it is more than *hekhsher avoda*, but rather is considered an actual *avoda*. Also, Rambam (*Hilkhot Biat Mikdash* 5:16) codified that this *kiddush* must be performed standing because *kiddush* is like an *avoda*, and all *avoda* must be performed standing. (The Gemara [Zevaḥim 19b] derives the obligation to stand during washing from the Torah's reference to this *kiddush* as "*sheirut*" ["service"], and all *sheirut* must be done standing. Rambam, however, attributes this obligation to the *avoda* status of *kiddush*. Interestingly, it seems that the donning of *bigdei kehunna* can be done while seated [*Simḥat Olam* ad loc.] even according to Rambam, who considers wearing *bigdei kehunna* an independent mitzva.)

The *Sefat Emet* (Zevaḥim 23b) adds that it would therefore appear that the *kohen* must wear *bigdei kehunna* during this *kiddush*. Rambam indeed mentions that the *kohen gadol* should do *kiddush* on Yom Kippur while wearing *bigdei kehunna,* but he never mentions this point regarding the daily service. Nevertheless, the *Sefat Emet* maintains that this point is self-evident: if *kiddush* must be done while standing and is like an *avoda,* it obviously requires *bigdei kehunna,* as well.

Rabbi Malin adds that in addition to being an independent mitzva, *kiddush* must also be viewed as *hekhsher avoda*. This would explain why a new *kiddush* is required daily. Even if the *kohen* did the *kiddush* for an evening *avoda* and did not leave the *Beit HaMikdash,* in the morning he requires a new *kiddush* (Rambam, *Hilkhot Biat Mikdash* 5:8). There may also be specific instances where *kiddush* functions only as *hekhsher avoda* (perhaps after briefly leaving the *Mikdash*) and thus perhaps would not require all the technical laws of *kiddush* (*Novellae of Rabbi Arye Leib,* 11:11).

The Gemara (Sota 39a) says that nowadays, a *kohen* should wash his hands before *Birkat Kohanim* (the Priestly Blessing). Rashi and the *Tosafot* explain that this has nothing to do with ritual cleanliness. Rather, it is a special requirement to wash immediately prior to *Birkat Kohanim,* and apparently according to this view, a *berakha* should be recited over this washing. However, Rambam (*Hilkhot Tefilla* 15:8) rules that the *kohen* should wash just as one would wash for *avoda*. The *Kesef Mishneh* (ad loc.) explains that according to Rambam, if a *kohen* washed in the morning, he need not wash again immediately before *Birkat Kohanim*. The common practice today is that *kohanim* do wash immediately before *Birkat Kohanim,* but do not recite the *berakha*. This is because we accept the more stringent view of Rashi and the *Tosafot* and therefore require *kohanim* to wash, but omit the *berakha* out of concern for Rambam's view that no *berakha* is required. The *Mishna Berura* (128:6) writes that if for whatever reason a *kohen* finds it difficult to wash, he may rely on Rambam's position and need not wash again for *Birkat Kohanim,* since he already washed his hands in the morning.

The Rashba (Responsum 191) writes that the obligation instituted by the Rabbis to wash one's hands before *tefilla* parallels the requirement for a *kohen* to wash before beginning *avoda*. Rambam (*Hilkhot*

Tefilla 4:2) codifies that everyone must wash his hands before *tefilla,* adding that before Shaḥarit, one should wash both his hands and his feet. The Raavad (ad loc.) comments that he sees no reason to require washing of the feet. The *Torah Temima* (Shemot 30:19) suggested that Rambam (like the Rashba) thought that we should prepare ourselves for *tefilla* just as *kohanim* prepare themselves for *avoda*. This would logically require washing hands and feet for all three daily prayers. However, since Rambam maintains that prayer is biblically mandated only once daily, the Rabbis obligated us to wash our feet only for Shaḥarit (the first daily prayer). Since the other prayers are only of rabbinic origin, the Rabbis were not as stringent with regard to them and merely required hand washing for those prayers. The *Shulḥan Arukh,* however, does not mention any requirement of washing feet at all.

Sefer Vayikra

Parashat Vayikra

Asham Taluy

There are thirty-six mitzvot in the Torah punishable by *karet*. ("*Karet*" literally means "cutting off"; the meaning of this punishment and its relationship to *mita biyedei shamayim* [death at the hands of Heaven, as opposed to court-administered execution] is discussed by the *Tosafot*, Yevamot 2a.) Intentional violation of these prohibitions renders one liable for *karet*; when one commits one of these violations unintentionally, he must bring a *korban ḥattat* (a sin offering). If one is in doubt as to whether he has indeed committed such a sin, he must bring an *asham taluy* (Mishna Karetot 1:1). The Torah introduces this offering in *Parashat Vayikra* (5:17–19).

Ramban explains that the different names of the various sacrifices reflect fundamental differences in their respective natures. The *ḥattat* is etymologically related to the word *ḥet*, which literally means "to deviate," or "to miss the target." "*Asham*," however, is related to "*shemama*," meaning "desolation." This sacrifice is brought to atone for and protect one who deserves to be lost and desolate. Thus, the *asham taluy*, which one brings in situations of doubt, is, in one sense, more severe than the *ḥattat*. Ramban (Vayikra 5:15) explains that since the person involved thinks he does not actually deserve punishment, as he is unsure of whether he sinned, the Torah was even more stringent in his case.

Rabbenu Yona, a disciple of Ramban, quotes and amplifies his mentor's opinion. He writes that a person who knows he has sinned will be concerned and worried. He will regret his action and perform genuine teshuva (repentance). By contrast, a person who is unsure of whether he sinned will not find it necessary to perform teshuva, for perhaps he did nothing wrong at all. The *asham* is therefore costlier than the *ḥattat,* as the Torah wished him to be aware of the severity of the matter, and not to take it lightly. If he does not bring his *asham,* he will enter a state of *shemama,* desolation (Rabbenu Yona, Berakhot 1, cited by Rabbi Chavel in his notes to Ramban's commentary).

The word "*taluy*" literally means "hanging." Rambam (*Hilkhot Shegagot* 8:1) explains that this *korban* atones for the case in doubt and the matter is held "hanging" in abeyance until the issue is clarified. If it is later discovered that the individual did in fact sin, he must then bring a *korban ḥattat*. The *asham* did not earn him full atonement for his misdeed: it serves merely to temporarily allay his fears and doubts.

R. Eliezer holds that anyone may bring an *asham taluy* anytime he so desires. He feels that since this *korban* does not really attain atonement, but rather temporarily protects the individual, one may bring it whenever he wishes. In fact, it is recorded that Bava b. Buta brought an *asham taluy* every day of the year except for the day after Yom Kippur (since he undoubtedly achieved at least some level of atonement on Yom Kippur). The Sages, however, disagree, and hold that one may bring an *asham taluy* only in the specific instance where this type of doubt arises (Mishna Karetot 6:3). Rambam (*Peirush HaMishnayot* ad loc.) comments that according to the Sages, the obligation to bring an *asham taluy* stems from the severity of the issue involved. The *korban* serves to calm and allay the fears of the person plagued by the possibility that he may have committed a grave sin. Rambam codified the opinion of the Sages forbidding one from bringing a voluntary *asham taluy* (ibid.; *Hilkhot Shegagot* 8:1).

At first glance, this issue appears practically irrelevant nowadays, until the time when *korbanot* are restored. In truth, however, the issue has interesting, practical ramifications even nowadays. The *Tur* (*Oraḥ*

Ḥayim 1:7) writes that after the daily recitation of each of the sections of *korbanot*, one should say, "Master of the universe, may this be considered and accepted as if I brought this particular *korban*." However, one may not say this prayer after reciting the *ḥattat* section, since one never brings a *ḥattat* unless he committed a transgression requiring a *ḥattat*. Yet, he says one may recite this prayer after the *asham* section. The *Beit Yosef* (ad loc.) reasoned that the *Tur*'s ruling allowing the recitation of this prayer after the *asham* section demonstrates that he, like Bava b. Buta, followed the opinion of R. Eliezer. Of course, the *Beit Yosef* was then compelled to wrestle with the question of why this is not limited to the *asham taluy*. After all, a regular *asham*, like a *ḥattat*, certainly may not be brought voluntarily. The *Shulḥan Arukh* (*Yoreh De'ah* 1:7) raises another issue where this matter becomes relevant, and the *Shakh* suggests that the Rema was unsure of how to rule, and says we should therefore act stringently in this regard.

The *Sefer Yere'im* (441) mentions that there is only one mitzva involved, namely, to atone for sin through prayer and sacrifice. The commentary *To'afot Re'em* explains that this would include all *korbanot* brought as a result of sin: *ḥattat*, *asham*, and *asham taluy*. Rambam, however, enumerates each *korban* individually. In fact, he found it necessary to explain (in *Sefer HaMitzvot*, principle 14) why he did not list each individual sin that would require each *korban*, and instead listed one mitzva including those who must bring a *ḥattat*, another including everyone who must bring an *asham taluy*, and so on.

Rabbi Perlow finds this puzzling. Even if Rambam listed all those who must bring a *ḥattat* and all who must bring an *asham* as separate mitzvot, why does he count *ḥattat* and *asham taluy* separately? Why does he not count a single mitzva to atone for sins involving *karet* either through an *asham taluy* (when in doubt) or through a *ḥattat* (when he knows with certainty that he has sinned)?

We might suggest that a fundamental distinction exists between the atonement of the *ḥattat* and that achieved through the *asham taluy*. Whereas the *ḥattat* grants the sinner full atonement, the *asham taluy* merely "hangs" the situation in abeyance. Given that these two sacrifices yield such different results, Rambam counts them as two separate mitzvot.

The *Sefer HaḤinnukh* (128) writes that when it is discovered that the sin was in fact committed, the initial *asham taluy* is not sufficient and one must bring a *ḥattat* to complete the atonement. If it turns out that the individual did not commit the sin, this indicates that the *asham taluy* was sufficient, and thus no other *korban* is required.

This formulation would imply that even one who has not actually sinned requires the *asham taluy* (as the *Ḥinnukh* says this was "sufficient" if it turns out that no sin was committed). Quite reasonably then, the requirement to bring this *korban* to assuage feelings of guilt and allay fears may be considered an independent mitzva, as this obligation differs fundamentally from the obligation to earn atonement through a *ḥattat* when one knows with certainty that he has sinned.

Parashat Tzav

"A Mitzva Is Precious When Performed at Its Proper Time"

A general halakha mandates that all *korbanot* must be brought specifically during the daytime. The Gemara (Zevaḥim 98a) derives this halakha from a *pasuk* in *Parashat Tzav* (Vayikra 7:38): "on the *day* He commanded Benei Yisrael to bring their *korbanot* to Hashem." There is, however, one exception to this rule. After *avodot* (sacrificial offerings) involving the blood of *korbanot* are completed, we may place upon the Altar (a procedure known as "*hekter*") the *emurim* and *evarim* (the parts of the animal that are not to be eaten) throughout the night. *Ḥazal* derive this halakha from the *pasuk* (Vayikra 6:2) "This is the *olah* [*korban* that is completely burned on the Altar] on the flame on the Altar all night until morning." Rambam (*Hilkhot Maaseh HaKorbanot* 4:2) rules that the Sages enacted a provision requiring that these parts of the *korbanot* be placed upon the Altar before *ḥatzot* (halakhic midnight), so as to avoid negligence in this regard. Rashi (Mishna Berakhot 1:1) seems to disagree and does not apply this rabbinic provision to *hekter emurim ve'evarim*. Regardless, all agree that Torah law allows this ritual to take place throughout the night.

It would seem, therefore, that the *emurim* and *evarim* of *korbanot* brought on Shabbat should not be placed on the Altar on Shabbat, but held until *Motzaei Shabbat*. As is well known, *korbanot* brought on Shabbat necessitated performing certain *melakhot* (proscribed acts of work). These *melakhot* are permitted inasmuch as the Torah requires offering these *korbanot* (see Rashi, Shemot 20:8). However, it appears that there would be no justification for putting the *emurim* and *evarim* on the Altar before Shabbat ends, since it is possible to wait until nighttime, when the ritual can be performed without suspending the prohibitions of Shabbat.

Nevertheless, the Gemara (Menaḥot 72a) states that we may, and in fact should, place these items on the Altar before Shabbat ends. The Gemara quotes two opinions regarding the reason for this surprising ruling. R. Shimon says, "This shows that *ḥaviva mitzva bishe'atah* (a mitzva is precious when performed at its proper time)." According to R. Shimon, it is permitted to perform *hekter evarim* on Shabbat even though it may be done after Shabbat simply because of the immense value of performing mitzvot at their optimum time.

It should be noted that this concept of "*ḥaviva mitzva bishe'atah*" is not the same as the principle "*zerizim makdimim lemitzvot*" ("Those who are quick perform mitzvot earlier"). The principle of "*zerizin makdimim*" refers to mitzvot that can be performed either earlier or later, but some opt to do so at an earlier time. For example, there is a mitzva to perform a *brit mila* on the child's eighth day. Although the *brit* may be performed anytime during the day, *zerizim* fulfill the mitzva as early in the morning as possible. The concept of "*ḥaviva mitzva bishe'atah*," by contrast, involves mitzvot that should be performed at a *specific* time. The *Avnei Nezer* (*Oraḥ Ḥayim* 23) explains that there is an actual obligation to perform the *hekter* during the daytime. Although it may be done at night, "*ḥaviva mitzva bishe'atah*" tells us that we can and should do it in the daytime, even on Shabbat.

The Gemara also cites the view of R. Eliezer, who disagrees. He permits performing *hekter* on Shabbat and accepts the concept of "*ḥaviva mitzva bishe'atah*," but in his view, this principle is not the reason *hekter* may be performed on Shabbat. Rather, according to R. Eliezer, the Torah permits *hekter* on Shabbat because the *avoda* of the *korban* has already been performed on Shabbat. He presumably feels that the requirement to bring a given *korban* on Shabbat amounts to the suspension of all laws of Shabbat with respect to this *korban* (in halakhic terminology, this means he holds that Shabbat is *huttera*, rather than merely *deḥuya*, in this case).

In any event, all agree that "*ḥaviva mitzva bishe'atah*" exists as an important halakhic concept; they only argue whether the case of *hekter* demonstrates the power of this rule to override the prohibitions of Shabbat.

Another example of the concept of "*ḥaviva mitzva bishe'atah*" is found in connection with the *korban oleh veyored* (a type of *korban* requiring different standards for people of different financial status; see Vayikra 5:5–11). The Torah tells us that in certain cases, a person obligated to bring a *ḥattat* (sin offering) who can afford neither a sheep nor pigeons may bring a flour offering, which is less expensive (Vayikra 5:11). R. Yehuda (*Torat Kohanim* ad. loc.) comments, "*Ḥaviva mitzva bishe'atah*; the [poor] man should bring the flour offering immediately, rather than wait until he becomes more affluent and can afford a sheep."

Some Aḥaronim derive from this halakha that one should not delay the performance of a mitzva even if the mitzva can be performed in an enhanced fashion later. Others, however, disagree, and claim that in such a case, it is preferable to delay the mitzva and perform it later with *hiddur* (in a more beautiful and dignified manner). One practical example of this dilemma is raised by the *Terumat HaDeshen* (35), who discusses whether one should recite *Kiddush Levana* (the *berakha* upon seeing the new moon) at the first available opportunity, or wait until Motza'ei Shabbat, when we are still dressed in our Shabbat clothes. Another example, discussed by the Ḥakham Tzvi, is a case of a Jewish prisoner whom the authorities permit to leave jail once yearly. Should he leave as soon as possible, so that he can fulfill the first mitzva that comes his way, or should he wait until he can perform an important mitzva (such as hearing the Megilla on Purim, or going to shul on Yom Kippur)?

Some *posekim* distinguish between cases where the opportunity for a more enhanced performance will very likely arise, such as waiting until Motza'ei Shabbat, and cases where the arrival of this opportunity is far from certain or is a remote possibility (e.g., one is not always likely to become wealthy). One source for this view is the Raavad's comment (in his commentary to *Torat Kohanim, Tazria* 4) that if one has a good chance of receiving a loan or gainful employment, he should delay bringing his *korban oleh veyored* until he can afford the more expensive *korban*. (Many sources relevant to this issue can be found in *Torah Temima*, Shemot 12:17, and *Encyclopedia Talmudit*, XII:504.)

There is another category of "*ḥaviva mitzva bishe'atah*" that is not really related to the halakhic concepts mentioned and discussed above. There is a concept of honoring people who are involved in fulfilling mitzvot. For example, the Gemara (Kiddushin 33a) states that although halakha forbids laborers from interrupting their work to stand for a Torah scholar, all the tradesmen in Jerusalem would stand to honor those who were bringing *bikkurim* (first fruits) to the *Beit HaMikdash*. The Gemara explains this distinction based on the principle of "*ḥaviva mitzva bishe'atah*." The actual performance of the mitzva of *bikkurim* is of such value that it demands disrupting one's work as a display of honor, something that the presence of a Torah scholar would not mandate. Of course, this application of the term "*ḥaviva mitzva bishe'atah*" differs from that discussed above.

This concept was also employed by the *Taz* to explain another halakha. In the *Shulḥan Arukh* (*Yoreh De'ah* 361:4), there is a requirement to stand when a funeral procession passes. The *Taz* (ad loc.) explains that this is in order to show respect for those who are involved in the mitzva of *halvayat hamet* (accompanying the dead).

In this context, we should briefly discuss the widespread custom to stand when we reach *Vayevarekh David* in the *Pesukei DeZimra* section of the Shaḥarit service. Some claim that this was the custom of the Ari and hypothesize that he stood up at this point in order to give tzedaka (*Yesodei Yeshurun*, I:256). On this basis, some speculate that the custom of standing for *Vayevarekh David* actually resulted from the desire to honor the *gabbai* who went around collecting tzedaka at that point in the service, due to the notion that *ḥaviva mitzva bishe'atah*.

Parashat Shemini

Consuming Human Flesh

There is a prohibition against eating the meat of non-kosher animals, several specific species of which are listed by the Torah (Vayikra 11:4 ff.). Rambam, who counts this as one of the 613 mitzvot (*Sefer HaMitzvot, Lo Taaseh* 172), adds that although other animals were not specified in these *pesukim*, the Torah described the signs of kosher animals and emphasized, "This is what you may eat" (v. 3). This constitutes a *lav haba mikelal aseh* (a negative prohibition derived from a positive statement), which is treated as a *mitzvat aseh*. Rambam goes on to explain that other animals are also included in the prohibition. Therefore, one who eats non-kosher animals violates both a positive commandment and a prohibition.

However, Rambam points out in the *Mishneh Torah* (*Hilkhot Maakhalot Asurot* 2:7) that although the Torah (Bereshit 2:7) refers to humans using the same term, "*nefesh ḥaya,*" used to describe animals, there is no Torah prohibition against eating human flesh. Therefore, one who eats human flesh is not liable for *malkot*. On the other hand, eating human flesh would transgress the *lav haba mikelal aseh* of "These are the living things that you may eat" (Vayikra 11:2).

It has been pointed out that the source of this ruling may be the *Torat Kohanim*, which states explicitly that there is no prohibition to eat human flesh or drink human milk. It emphasizes that there is no *lav* and implies that there is, however, a *mitzvat aseh* not to do so.

It should be noted that Rabbi Aharon HaLevi (Raah on Ketubbot 60a) cites a variant text that does not exclude human flesh from the *lav*. The Rashba feels that there is a rabbinic injunction against eating human flesh. Ramban (Vayikra 11:3) disagrees with Rambam, and says there is no law at all against eating human flesh, as there is no prohibition against human blood or milk. If human flesh were prohibited, the law would be that anything that comes from it, like blood or milk, would also be prohibited.

The *Maggid Mishneh* quotes all of these sources and explains that Rambam thinks that if human flesh were forbidden by a *lav*, it would be prohibited, as Ramban says. However, since there is only an *aseh* involved, this rule does not apply. Conversely, Rabbi Aharon HaLevi would have to say that although there is a *lav* to eat human flesh, the *Torat Kohanim* nevertheless permits human blood and milk despite the general rule that something that comes from a prohibited creature also is prohibited.

Ramban adds that this discussion revolves only around flesh from a live person, since a dead body is *asur behanaa* (i.e., all benefit from it is forbidden).

Although the Rema (*Shulḥan Arukh, Yoreh De'ah* 79:1) rules that it is biblically forbidden to eat human flesh, the commentators (Gra, *Shakh, Taz,* etc.) say that this reflects the opinion of Rambam and not Rabbi Aharon HaLevi.

In a well-known discussion at Yeshivat Har Etzion, the following issue was raised: what should a person do in a situation where his only two choices are to eat meat from a non-kosher animal or to eat human flesh – which is preferable halakhically? To a pure halakhist, it may seem that human flesh would be preferable, as there is no *lav* involved. However, Rabbi Yehuda Amital cited the opinion of the *Dor Revi'i* (Rabbi Moshe Glasner, a great-grandson of the *Ḥatam Sofer*) in his introduction to his commentary on Ḥullin: "With regard to every disgusting object that the human spirit despises, even if there is no specific biblical law forbidding it, if someone would eat it, this would be worse than eating something specifically forbidden. Therefore, it is better to eat non-kosher meat than to eat human flesh, as universal natural law, accepted by all civilized humanity, is to reject anyone who would eat human flesh." It is not possible that a wise, intelligent nation that was commanded to be holy would permit something that is anathema to the enlightened world. (This story has been related orally many times and is printed in Rabbi Amital's book *Resisei Tal,* Alon Shevut, 2005.)

Parashat Tazria

Performing a Brit Mila on Shabbat

The Torah (Vayikra 12:2–3) teaches us that a woman who gives birth to a male child becomes *teme'ah* (impure) for seven days, and that on the eighth day her son must be circumcised. The Gemara (Shabbat 132a) derives from the phrase "on the eighth day" that the *mila* can and must be done on the eighth day, even if it is Shabbat.

The Gemara also quotes R. Asi, who derives from the same verse that we wait only eight days for the circumcision in cases where the mother becomes impure as a result of childbirth (Shabbat 135a). According to R. Asi, in cases where the mother does not become impure, the child is to be circumcised immediately. Rashi explains that these cases include instances where the child is born by caesarean section, or is born to a non-Jewish woman who converts immediately after giving birth. Abaye questions R. Asi's assertion by pointing to the circumcisions that took place from the time of Avraham's children through the giving of the Torah. Starting with Yitzḥak, our forefathers were commanded to circumcise their children on the eighth day, even though the laws of impurity did not come into effect until the giving of the Torah. R. Asi (135a–b) responds that the giving of the Torah changed the nature of this law, and of all others. While it is true that originally the law of *brit mila* being performed on the eighth day was not dependent on the impurity of the mother, once the laws were re-commanded in our *parasha*, the details changed and this aspect was included.

Rambam (*Hilkhot Mila* 1:10) rules that a child born by caesarean section is to be circumcised on the eighth day. At first glance, it would seem that Rambam adopts the position of Abaye, as opposed to that of R. Asi. However, he also rules (1:11) that in such a case, if the eighth day falls out on Shabbat, the *brit mila* must be postponed, as it does not override Shabbat. This accords with the position of R. Asi that only when the mother becomes impure does the obligation to perform the circumcision override Shabbat. How did Rambam arrive at this hybrid position?

Rabbi Ḥayim Soloveitchik, in his comments to the above halakha, explains that Rambam accepts the fundamental model suggested by Abaye, that the mitzva of *brit mila* is modeled after the mitzva given to our forefathers. Thus, all things being equal, a circumcision must always take place on the eighth day, as derived from the commandment given to Avraham. In addition, the mitzva was commanded again after the giving of Torah, this time uniquely to the Jewish people. The rule that a *brit mila* is performed even on Shabbat is derived from the third verse at the beginning of our *parasha*. Thus, if the mother does not become impure, the child will be circumcised on the eighth day unless the eighth day is on Shabbat, in which case the rule allowing the circumcision to override Shabbat does not apply.

This model also can be used to explain the position of another Rishon. The Gemara (Bava Batra 127a) quotes R. Sheizevi, who argues that a *tumtum* (a child who was born with covered genitals) who was operated upon and found to be a male is not to be circumcised on the eighth day. He derives this from the end of the above-mentioned verse, which emphasizes "*veyaleda zakhar*," "and gives birth to a male." He understands this to limit the application of that verse to children who were born in a state that made it immediately clear that they were male. Ramban (*Milḥamot Hashem*, Shabbat 55a in Rif) explains that according to R. Sheizevi, the *mila* can be done on the first day of the child's life.

However, the Rashbam argues that R. Sheizevi does not dispute that such a child ideally is to be circumcised on the eighth day: he argues only that such a circumcision does not override Shabbat.

We can suggest that his source is the same as that of Rambam as understood by Rabbi Ḥayim Soloveitchik. While all circumcisions are ideally to be performed on the eighth day, as derived from the command to Avraham, only children who fit the strict criteria derived from the verse in *Parashat Tazria* may be circumcised on Shabbat. Thus, whether the child was a *tumtum,* born to a new convert, or born by caesarean section, he will be circumcised on the eighth day unless that day happens to be Shabbat.

Parashat Metzora

Tumat Metzora

The laws of *nega'im* (various forms of afflictions) are written in the Torah immediately following the laws of childbirth. These laws are unusual: whereas most laws were told only to Moshe, who then conveyed them to the entire community, these laws were presented to both Moshe and Aharon. Ramban (Vayikra 13:1) explains that God included Aharon in the initial presentation of these laws because *kohanim* are assigned the responsibility of examining *nega'im* and determining their status. The *kohanim* were the ones in charge of examining *nega'im* and exhorting the people to observe these laws. Ramban adds that the laws concerning *taharat hametzora* (process of purification) were told only to Moshe because it was not necessary to issue a command regarding these laws to Benei Yisrael, given the innate desire to attain purity.

It emerges from these laws that the *kohen* served as a spiritual guide who assisted the new mother in attaining *kappara* (atonement; see Vayikra 12:8) and was also involved at times of crisis, when a *nega* appeared.

Rambam enumerates thirteen different types of *tuma* (ritual impurity) and explains why he considers them thirteen separate mitzvot.

Although there is obviously no prohibition against becoming *tameh*, the very fact that one becomes *tameh* as a result of touching a *nevela* (animal carcass) or any other type of *tuma* constitutes a *mitzvat aseh* (*Sefer HaMitzvot, Aseh* 96–108).

Ramban, in his comments to *Sefer HaMitzvot*, disagrees, claiming that these types of *tuma* should not be counted as separate mitzvot. Rather, the various specific laws regarding *tuma* should themselves be counted as mitzvot. One prohibition forbids a *tameh* from entering the *Mikdash*, and another prohibition forbids him from eating *kodashim* (*Mitzvot Lo Taaseh* 77, 129). Given these prohibitions, the Torah had to instruct us regarding the various types of *tuma* and therefore enumerated these thirteen types; they should not, however, be considered individual mitzvot.

Ramban cites another example to prove his point. There is a general halakha that forbids us from offering an animal with a *mum* (blemish) as a *korban* (sacrifice). This general prohibition constitutes an independent mitzva (*Lo Taaseh* 91), but the various *mumim* mentioned in the Torah are not individual mitzvot. The Torah lists them simply in order to teach us what qualifies as a *mum* with respect to this prohibition. Similarly, Ramban argues, in our case, the general prohibitions for a *tameh* to enter the *Mikdash* or eat *kodashim* are specific mitzvot, but the various types of *tuma* do not constitute individual mitzvot.

The *Megillat Esther* (ad loc.) draws a distinction between these two cases in justifying Rambam's position. An animal with a blemish cannot be considered a mitzva per se. By contrast, a person who is *tameh* must conduct himself in a manner of *tuma* – he must strictly observe the halakhic ramifications of his status – and herein lies the actual mitzva.

In the specific case of *tzaraat* (leprosy), we can establish a more precise definition of the mitzva. Rambam (*Sefer HaMitzvot*, end of principle 7) cites from the *Torat Kohanim* that there is a mitzva to declare the person afflicted by a *nega* as pure or impure. Rambam spells out this mitzva very clearly in the introduction to *Hilkhot Tumat Tzaraat*, where he enumerates eight mitzvot relevant to this section, the first one being "to instruct regarding the laws of human leprosy according to the law written in the Torah." Rambam appears to refer to a mitzva incumbent upon *kohanim* to examine *nega'im* and determine their status.

The *Sefer HaḤinnukh* approvingly cites the opinion of Ramban, who does not count the different types of *teme'im* as individual mitzvot. Nevertheless, in discussing these laws he follows Rambam's system, as he usually does, and counts each *tameh* individually (Mitzvot 159, 169). It appears, however, that he understands the law of *tumat metzora* somewhat differently from Ramban. He writes that the mitzva requires anyone who sees a sign of leprosy to approach a *kohen* to inquire about his situation. The individual must then conduct himself according to the law of the Torah as instructed by the *kohen*. The individual should not look upon this as merely an incidental illness, but must rather engage in serious introspection and understand that the affliction resulted from a grave sin.

It seems that according to the *Ḥinnukh*, the mitzva is directed towards the afflicted individual, rather than the *kohen*. Later, the *Ḥinnukh* reiterates, "Anyone who became a leper and did not conduct himself according to the law of the Torah concerning leprosy, but rather took it casually and did not approach the *kohen* to show him, negated this mitzva." A comment in the notes to the Machon Yerushalayim edition of the *Ḥinnukh* is notable. Inasmuch as a person who sees a sign of leprosy is not *tameh* until the *kohen* so decides, the person would not want to approach a *kohen* at all. Therefore, the Torah placed an obligation upon him to approach the *kohen*, even if he is not inclined to do so.

One could argue that according to this reasoning, there might exist two separate mitzvot: one that is incumbent upon the *kohen*, and another obligating a person who sees a sign of leprosy to approach the *kohen*.

Yet another definition of this mitzva is found in the *Zohar* (section 3, chapter 45, cited in *Torah Shelema*, Vayikra 13:23), which takes note of the Torah's formulation that the leper "shall be brought" to the *kohen* (14:2). This term indicates that the Torah obligates anyone who sees someone else with signs of leprosy to bring him before a *kohen*. Ibn Ezra (Vayikra 13:2) similarly comments that a person who develops symptoms of *tzaraat* must be brought, willingly or under coercion, before a *kohen*.

The *Minḥat Ḥinnukh* (171) raises the question of whether this mitzva applies to minors. He explains that according to the *Ḥinnukh*'s view that the mitzva obligates the leper himself, it would not apply to a minor. He suggests, however, that the obligation instituted by *Ḥazal* of *ḥinnukh* (training one's child in the performance of mitzvot – see Rashi and *Tosafot,* Berakhot 48a) might create an obligation with regard to this mitzva, as well. We should add that according to the reasoning of Rambam that the mitzva rests upon the *kohen,* or the *Zohar*'s view that the mitzva obligates the general public, it seems likely that this mitzva would apply in the case of minors as well.

Parashat Aḥarei Mot

Affliction on Yom Kippur

The prohibitions of Yom Kippur are formulated in positive terms, e.g., "you shall afflict your souls" (Vayikra 16:31), rather than in negative terms, e.g., "you shall not eat." For this reason, Rambam (*Sefer HaMitzvot, Aseh* 164) counts the prohibitions of Yom Kippur among the positive commandments: "He commanded us to fast on the tenth of Tishrei." Rambam also records a negative commandment (*Lo Taaseh* 196): "He prohibited us to eat on the fast of Kippur," but there is no explicit source for such a prohibition in the Torah. Rather, the prohibition against eating on Yom Kippur is inferred from the fact that one who eats on Yom Kippur is liable to the punishment of *karet* (excision), as the Mishna at the beginning of Karetot implies that only negative commandments can be subject to that punishment (with the exception of two specific positive commandments, circumcision and the Paschal offering).

In contrast to Rambam, Rabbi Saadia Gaon does not recognize a prohibition against eating on Yom Kippur, but only the positive commandment to afflict one's soul. Rabbi Yeruḥam Fishel Perlow (in his notes to Rabbi Saadia Gaon's *Sefer HaMitzvot, Aseh* 55) rejects Rambam's proof from the Mishna in Karetot. He argues that it is possible that circumcision and the Paschal lamb are the only positive commandments mentioned there because only in those cases is *karet* imposed even though the transgression is committed by passively refraining from doing something that the Torah requires. The positive commandment banning eating on Yom Kippur may also be punishable by *karet*, but it is not mentioned in the Mishna because this transgression involves an actual action.

In light of the fact that the prohibition against eating on Yom Kippur is not explicitly mentioned in the Torah, it is possible to contemplate whether that prohibition is similar to other prohibitions against eating, or is merely a fulfillment of the positive commandment. For example, the *Shaagat Arye* (76) considers the possibility that even though eating in an unusual manner is not considered eating in other realms of the Torah, it could be that one who eats in an unusual manner on Yom Kippur is liable, since by doing so he avoided afflicting himself. The *Binyan Tziyyon* (34) even raises the possibility that one who already ate on Yom Kippur can no longer fulfill the obligation of affliction, and as such would not be liable for *karet* for any additional eating. Ultimately, though, he rejects this possibility, because he could not find a Rishon who accepts it.

How does one fulfill the obligation of "affliction"? All the Rishonim understand that it includes a prohibition against eating and drinking, for which the punishment of *karet* is imposed, but they disagree about whether the other afflictions, such as wearing leather shoes, are prohibited by Torah law or by rabbinic decree.

According to the Rosh, the other afflictions are forbidden only by rabbinic decree. He explains that this is why there are certain leniencies in these laws, such as that the king and queen are permitted to wash their faces. However, the Ran believes these prohibitions are also mandated by Torah law, as part of the commandment "you shall afflict your souls" or based on the word "sabbath." He maintains that the Torah nevertheless delegated to the Sages the authority to determine which specific actions are forbidden and which are permitted, and explains that this accounts for the various leniencies.

According to Rambam (*Sefer HaMitzvot, Aseh* 164), all of the afflictions are required by Torah law: "It has come down to us by way of tradition that washing, anointing, wearing [leather] shoes, and sexual relations are forbidden [by Torah law], and that one is obligated to desist from all of these activities." The Aḥaronim have suggested various explanations for the leniency regarding washing, according to the Rambam's understanding that the prohibition is required by Torah law. For example, some say that Torah law only forbids a person to wash his entire body, and therefore washing one's face is forbidden by rabbinic decree, and is therefore permitted in the case of a king and a queen. There is also room to consider whether the principle of "half the legal quantity" applies to washing. However, that requires a more lengthy analysis.

Parashat Kedoshim

Awe of Parents, Awe of the Temple, and Awe of Shabbat

Ramban (Vayikra 19:30) explains that the Torah mentions the obligation to observe Shabbat many times due to the fact that Shabbat is equal to all other mitzvot. In *Parashat Kedoshim,* the phrase "*et shabbetotai tishmoru*" ("You shall observe My Shabbatot") is mentioned twice, once in connection with *mora av va'em* (awe of parents; Vayikra 19:3) and once in connection with *mora Mikdash* (awe of the Temple; 19:30). *Ḥazal* derived from these juxtapositions that one must observe Shabbat even if his parents ask him to desecrate it, and that it is forbidden to build the *Mikdash* on Shabbat.

There are thus two obligations of *mora* (displaying reverence) in this *parasha*. *Mora* of parents forbids standing or sitting in their designated places, contradicting them, and taking any position when they have an argument with someone else (Kiddushin 31b). The laws of *mora Mikdash* include the prohibitions against going to the Temple Mount carrying a cane or wearing shoes, taking a shortcut through it, and other laws (Berakhot 54a). In his discussion of *mora Mikdash*, Rambam, as usual, culled many halakhot found in various sources and codified them in a single chapter (*Hilkhot Beit HaBeḥira* 7). He includes a prohibition against sitting anywhere in the *azara* (Temple courtyard; Halakha 6) and a prohibition against producing an exact replica of the *heikhal* or its appurtenances (Halakha 10). The Radvaz (ad loc.) points out that this final halakha likewise stems from the law of *mora Mikdash*, as it is based on the fact that "we should not use the King's scepter." This point appears to be obvious, given that Rambam placed this halakha in the chapter devoted to *mora Mikdash*. The *Sefer HaḤinnukh* (254) also cites these laws in his discussion of *mora Mikdash* and explicitly writes, "and all this is due to the awe of the place."

Besides these two mitzvot of *mora*, there is an astonishing mitzva enumerated in *Sefer Yere'im*: *mora Shabbat* (awe of Shabbat, Mitzva 410). He explained that inasmuch as the Torah connected *shemirat Shabbat* to *mora Mikdash*, these two laws are intertwined. Just as there are two separate laws relating to *Mikdash* – *shemirat Mikdash* (protecting the Temple; *Sefer HaMitzvot, Aseh* 22; *Ḥinnukh* 388) and *mora Mikdash* (awe of the Temple; ibid.) – so are there two laws relating to Shabbat: *shemirat Shabbat* and *mora Shabbat*. The *Yere'im* defines this mitzva to mean that "a person should reflect [on how] to honor and observe and to fear it."

The *Yere'im*, who generally follows the enumeration of mitzvot of the *Behag*, appears to be the only Rishon who counted or even recognized a mitzva of *mora Shabbat*. In fact, the Gemara (Yevamot 6a) seems to explicitly negate such a notion. It points out that two different verbs are employed in connection with Shabbat and *Mikdash*: "It says *shemira* regarding Shabbat and *mora* regarding *Mikdash*" (Rashi, 6b: it does not say *mora* in the context of Shabbat). This remark appears to clearly deny any obligation of *mora* in connection with Shabbat. Shabbat requires only *shemira*, which does not mean that one must be in awe of Shabbat.

The *To'afot Re'em*, the commentary on *Sefer Yere'im*, cites a variant text of this gemara that he found in the *Sefer Mitzvot Katan*. (The standard editions have the text as quoted above.) That edition reads, "It says *shemira* and *mora* regarding Shabbat and it says *shemira* and *mora* regarding *Mikdash*." Of course, if indeed this was the text of the Gemara that the *Yere'im* used, it can be readily understood why he counted *mora Shabbat* as a separate mitzva.

If we do not accept the opinion of the *Yere'im* that this *pasuk* introduces the concept of *mora Shabbat,* why did the Torah indeed associate Shabbat with *Mikdash*? We have already noted that this juxtaposition teaches that building the *Mikdash* does not override Shabbat. In truth, however, this law had already been taught earlier in the Torah, when it prefaced the laws of building the *Mishkan* with a discussion of Shabbat (Shemot 35:1–3). Rashi (ad loc.) explains that through this juxtaposition, the Torah alludes to the prohibition against building the *Mishkan* on Shabbat. The *Or HaḤayim* and others offer explanations for this seeming redundancy, but in any event the Gemara deduces another halakha from this juxtaposition in *Parashat Kedoshim*. The Gemara (Yevamot 6b) comments that just as Shabbat is eternally binding, so does the obligation of *mora Mikdash* apply for all time. Rambam quotes this gemara but adds one important point: "Even though the Temple is desolate today due to our sins, we are still obligated in its *mora*.... Just as *shemirat Shabbat* is eternal, so is *mora Mikdash* eternal, since its holiness is still intact despite its desolation" (*Hilkhot Beit HaBeḥira* 7:7). Rambam clearly refers here to his own opinion (6:15) that while the *kedusha* of the Land of Israel can dissipate, the *kedusha* of Jerusalem and the *Mikdash* is everlasting. One can only speculate what the Raavad, who disagrees with Rambam's view of the eternal *kedusha* of the *Mikdash,* would say about the law of *mora Mikdash* today. The *Sefer Mafte'aḥ* in the Frankel edition of Rambam presents an impressive list of writers who debated this issue.

Let us return to the opinion of the *Yere'im*. What exactly would be included in *mora Shabbat*? Could the awe or fear of Shabbat warrant adopting very stringent standards of observance, beyond the regular, obligatory laws, in an attempt to avoid desecrating Shabbat in any situation? Many have noted in this context the Yerushalmi's comment (Demai 4) that on Shabbat we assume everyone tells the truth, including those whom we generally would not trust, since they feel the awe of Shabbat.

Rabbi Perlow, in his commentary to Rabbi Saadia Gaon's *Sefer HaMitzvot* (1:234), suggests that we infer what may be included in *mora Shabbat* from various aspects of *mora Mikdash*. Just as *mora Mikdash* forbids making an exact replica of the *Mikdash,* perhaps there is a law (in addition to the general prohibition of *bal tosif,* which precludes adding anything to the Torah) forbidding one from observing Shabbat on a different day of the week. He further speculates that this might be the reason for standing while reciting Kiddush. The obligation of *mora Mikdash* forbids sitting in the *Mikdash,* and thus sitting should, perhaps, be forbidden on Shabbat. Obviously, halakha could not possibly require us to stand throughout Shabbat, especially given the concept of *oneg Shabbat.* On the other hand, there is a need to show that *mora Shabbat* should imply that we stand out of *mora.* Quite possibly, therefore, we stand during Kiddush to reflect the idea of *mora.* Of course, there are various customs relating to Kiddush, and some people sit for the entire Kiddush.

We have seen that there are two mitzvot involving *mora,* one relating to *Mikdash* and another relating to parents. There is one opinion that acknowledges a mitzva of *mora Shabbat,* as well, and this view may yield several fascinating ramifications.

Parashat Emor

Ḥol HaMoed

The Torah contains a number of sections dealing with the laws of Yom Tov. In *Parashat Bo* (Shemot 12:15–16), in connection with the Exodus narrative, the Torah presents the laws of Pesaḥ for the first time. It establishes the requirement to observe a seven-day festival, the first and last days of which are to be observed as *mikra kodesh* (a holy assembly), on which no *melakha* (labor) may be performed (Shemot 12:15–16). In *Parashat Emor* (Vayikra 23:37), however, the Torah describes all the holidays with the term "*mikra'ei kodesh*." The *Mekhilta* (*Bo* 9) deduces from this description that even the period of Ḥol HaMoed is considered *mikra kodesh*. Accordingly, Rambam (*Hilkhot Yom Tov* 7:1) mentions that although Ḥol HaMoed is not called *shabbaton*, it is nevertheless a *mikra kodesh*.

In light of this principle, some Rishonim maintain (based on Moed Katan 18a) that *melakha* is biblically forbidden on Ḥol HaMoed. This position, however, must explain why some *melakha* is permitted on Ḥol HaMoed. True, even on Yom Tov itself one may perform *melakha* for purposes of preparing food. On Ḥol HaMoed, however, halakha permits other categories as well, such as *davar haaved* (work that must be done to avoid financial loss) and work involving public welfare. This led the Rosh and others to conclude that Torah law permits all *melakha* on Ḥol HaMoed, but *Ḥazal* later forbade certain types of *melakha* while permitting others. By contrast, Ramban and Rashba held that all *melakha* that is neither necessary for Yom Tov nor would incur a financial loss is biblically forbidden. The Rabbis then added other *melakha* prohibitions on Ḥol HaMoed, such as *maaseh omman* (skilled work).

The *Yere'im* (417, 418) goes so far as to include all eight days of Sukkot in the biblical mitzvot of sanctifying Yom Tov and refraining from *melakha*. Although he expresses some doubt about this matter, he nevertheless enumerates these two mitzvot and claims that they apply to all eight days of Sukkot.

The *Beit Yosef* (*Oraḥ Ḥayim* 530) cites all these sources and then advances a theory of his own. He explains that the Torah itself prohibits performing *melakha* on Ḥol HaMoed, but it left it to our Sages to determine which types of *melakha* should be included under this biblical prohibition. Apparently, according to the *Beit Yosef*, there is a biblical requirement that Ḥol HaMoed must have the character of a Yom Tov, but not be identical to Yom Tov. The very term "Ḥol HaMoed" (literally, "the weekdays of the festival") implies this dual characteristic of being simultaneously a Yom Tov and a weekday. Therefore, while the Torah required us to abstain from some *melakha* on Ḥol HaMoed, it was desirable to have other *melakha* permitted. It left the exact parameters for the Sages to establish.

The *Beit Yosef* brings a precedent for the concept that the Torah assigns the Sages the task of determining the parameters of a given law from the opinion of the Ran regarding the laws of Yom Kippur. The Ran maintains that the Torah requires experiencing *innui* (some type of affliction) on Yom Kippur, and empowered the Sages to delineate the activities from which we must refrain to achieve *innui*. It should be stressed that whatever our Sages included under this prohibition is considered biblically forbidden. Interestingly, Rabbi Dovid Cohen published a pamphlet (*Gevul Yaavetz*, Brooklyn, 1986) with over fifty possible examples of this type of biblical law, where the Torah leaves it for the Sages to determine its details.

Does the concept of *mikra kodesh* apply to other issues, as well, besides the prohibition of *melakha*? The *Mekhilta* (*Bo* 9) explains that this status requires us to sanctify Ḥol HaMoed (as well as Yom Tov) through food, drink, and special clothing. Rambam (*Hilkhot Yom Tov* 6:16) writes that the requirements of *kavod* (honor) and *oneg* (enjoyment) apply to Ḥol HaMoed, just as they do to Shabbat, because Yom Tov also is called *mikra kodesh*. Given Rambam's later remark (7:1) that Ḥol HaMoed also is called *mikra kodesh*, it follows that the mitzvot of *kavod* and *oneg* apply then, as well. Accordingly, we are required to eat a meal on Ḥol HaMoed just as on Yom Tov.

There is a general rule that whenever halakha requires eating a meal (such as Shabbat and Yom Tov), one must repeat *Birkat HaMazon* if he inadvertently omitted the appropriate addition (*Retzeh* on Shabbat and *Yaaleh VeYavo* on Yom Tov). It would follow, therefore, that even on Ḥol HaMoed someone who omitted *Yaaleh VeYavo* in *Birkat HaMazon* must recite it again. The *Shulḥan Arukh* (*Oraḥ Ḥayim* 188:7), however, ruled that Ḥol HaMoed resembles Rosh Ḥodesh in this respect, and one need not repeat *Birkat HaMazon* if he omitted *Yaaleh VeYavo*. Rabbi Akiva Eiger (Responsum 1; addendum at end of volume) understood this as proving our premise wrong. He claims that although Rambam (*Hilkhot Yom Tov* 6:17, 22) writes that the obligation of *simḥa* (rejoicing) applies to Ḥol HaMoed, he does not require *kavod va'oneg* on Ḥol HaMoed. He ignores Rambam's comments that Ḥol HaMoed is considered *mikra kodesh* and that all days of *mikra kodesh* require *kavod va'oneg*.

The *Ḥafetz Ḥayim* (*Shaar HaTziyyun* 530a) suggests a middle position to resolve this difficulty. He writes that although there indeed exists an obligation of *kavod va'oneg* on Ḥol HaMoed, as stated in the *Mekhilta*, this *kavod va'oneg* requires merely treating Ḥol HaMoed as a day more special than a regular weekday. It does not mean that we must treat it as an actual Yom Tov. Thus, for example, there is no obligation to eat a meal on Ḥol HaMoed, despite the fact that such an obligation applies on Yom Tov. Therefore, if one omitted *Yaaleh VeYavo* in *Birkat HaMazon*, he need not repeat it.

The Mishna (Avot 3:11) says in the name of R. Elazar HaModa'i that whoever disgraces the "*mo'adot*" has no share in the World to Come. Rashi explains that "*mo'adot*" refers to Ḥol HaMoed. Anyone who performs (forbidden) labor or treats Ḥol HaMoed as a regular weekday with regards to food and drink has no share in the World to

Come. According to Rashi, this mishna does not refer to Yom Tov at all. Since Ḥol HaMoed is not to be treated as an actual Yom Tov, a person may be inclined to take it lightly. Therefore, R. Elazar included Ḥol HaMoed in the mishna to impress upon us the importance of treating Ḥol HaMoed as something more than an ordinary weekday. Rabbenu Yona (ad loc.) adds that the verb used in the mishna is "disgrace," rather than "desecrate." A person who *disgraces* Ḥol HaMoed treats it as a regular weekday and does not demonstrate that it is a day of *mikra kodesh*. With this in mind, we can understand the position of the *Yere'im* cited towards the beginning of the *shiur*. The Torah requires observing the days of Ḥol HaMoed by treating them in some way as days of *mikra kodesh*. Although we are not to treat them in precisely the same manner as we do Yom Tov, they are nevertheless included under the same *mikra kodesh* obligation as Yom Tov itself.

Parashat Behar

Fraud and Aggravation

Two separate verses in *Parashat Behar* address the prohibition known as *ona'a*. The first (Vayikra 25:14), which refers to cases of selling and buying, tells us that neither the buyer nor the seller may indulge in *ona'a*. Although this is often translated as "do not aggrieve one another," or "you shall not oppress one another," it seems that "*ona'a*" here translates more precisely as "fraud." The Gemara in the fourth chapter of Bava Metzia details the exact parameters of fraud, and includes in this prohibition dishonest practices such as gouging a buyer and overcharging.

Three verses later (25:17), the Torah again warns against committing *ona'a* against one's fellow man and adds in this context that one must fear God. The Gemara (Bava Metzia 58b) explains this verse as referring to *ona'at devarim* (verbal *ona'a*) and gives various examples of such improper behavior. For example, one may not remind a *baal teshuva* or a convert of his previous lifestyle. Additionally, if someone wishes to buy a certain product, one may not refer him to a store if he knows that it does not stock such merchandise. R. Yehuda added that a person may not pretend he is a potential customer if he has no intention of buying.

Although the same word is employed in both verses, it seems that the second instance, which deals with *ona'at devarim*, refers to aggravation rather than fraud. It appears to forbid causing grief, rather than fraudulent practices. Thus, Rambam (*Sefer HaMitzvot, Lo Taaseh* 251) defines this prohibition as follows: "We are enjoined... not to say things that hurt and anger another person."

Accordingly, Rambam (250–251) enumerated two separate mitzvot – monetary *ona'a* (fraud) and verbal *ona'a* (aggravation). Rambam juxtaposed these two prohibitions in his list of mitzvot, whereas the *Yere'im* separated them completely. One section of the *Yere'im* is entitled, "Monetary Prohibitions Etc.," and another section is entitled, "Prohibitions Involving Someone Who Does Evil to God and Mankind Without Stealing or Deriving Monetary Benefit." The prohibition of fraud is included in the former category (127), while the prohibition against causing aggravation is included in the latter group (180).

Although some Rishonim combine both of these prohibitions together into a single mitzva, this very likely stems from their different method of counting mitzvot, rather than from any similarity in definition between them. Rabbi Perlow (Rabbi Saadia Gaon's *Sefer HaMitzvot*, II:111a) points out that two separate mitzvot of *ona'a* are enumerated in connection with fraud and aggrievance of a convert.

The Mishna states in Bava Metzia (58b), "Just as there is *ona'a* in business, there is verbal *ona'a*." Inasmuch as these are two separate independent laws, what does the Mishna seek to convey through this equation? The *Baḥ* (*Tur, Ḥoshen Mishpat* 228a) explains that one might think that *ona'at devarim* need not be treated as severely as cases of monetary fraud, and the Mishna therefore emphasizes the similarity between these two prohibitions. In fact, the Gemara gives a number of reasons why *ona'at devarim* constitutes a more severe prohibition than fraud. Monetary gain from fraud can always be returned, whereas grievances caused by words can never be undone. Fraud involves money, but *ona'at devarim* affects one's physical being. Also, the phrase "you must fear God" is written in connection with aggravation, and not with respect to fraud.

The *Ḥasdei David* (Tosefta Bava Metzia 3:13) points out that the severity of *ona'at devarim* might have led one to apply the punishment of *makkot* (lashes) to such cases. Fraud, like any other monetary crime, can be repaid, and thus the perpetrator does not receive *makkot*. But since one cannot repay a victim for his aggravation, one might think that *ona'at devarim* entails a punishment of *makkot*. The Mishna therefore compared the two prohibitions, thereby indicating that *makkot* applies in neither case, since only prohibitions involving physical action are punishable by *makkot*, whereas *ona'at devarim* is violated verbally.

Surprisingly, the Maharam of Rothenburg (Responsum 785) ruled that one is indeed liable to *makkot* for this prohibition, since it cannot be repaid. The *Beit Yosef* (*Ḥoshen Mishpat* 1) suggested that perhaps the Maharam meant only that the Sages instituted *makkot* for this prohibition, while biblical law would not call for a punishment of *makkot*, as no action is involved.

The Gemara (Bava Metzia 59a) cites R. Ḥanina b. R. Idi as commenting that since the Torah forbids aggrieving "your fellow," it follows that this prohibition applies only to people who observe the mitzvot. The *Baḥ* (*Tur*, *Ḥoshen Mishpat* 228a) cites the Mordekhai's position that since the Torah employs the word "fellow" only in connection with *ona'at devarim*, but not regarding monetary fraud, we might conclude that the Gemara limits only *ona'at devarim* to observant Jews, whereas the prohibition against monetary fraud applies to all Jews. However, if this were true, fraud would turn out to be more stringent than *ona'at devarim*, and we have already seen that the prohibition of causing aggravation is at least as strict as, and possibly stricter than, that of fraud.

Obviously, this problem leads us to one of two conclusions. We may either disregard R. Ḥanina's statement and include all Jews in both prohibitions, or accept his position and apply it to fraud, as well, and thus neither defrauding nor aggravating an unobservant Jew would violate a Torah prohibition.

Both Rambam and Rabbi Yosef Karo omit the opinion of R. Ḥanina, and apparently adopted the first approach. However, the Rema (*Ḥoshen Mishpat* 228:1) rules, "There are those who say that the prohibition against causing aggravation applies only [when doing so] to God-fearing people." The *Arukh HaShulḥan* modifies this position and comments that one may commit *ona'at devarim* against a sinner, as this may cause him to perform teshuva. If a person's intent is totally honorable, he may aggravate someone in order to cause him to improve his ways. If so, then perhaps we could defraud him, as well, if our intention is to bring him to greater observance of Torah and mitzvot. The *Baḥ* (ibid.) quotes an opinion that holds that since it is obvious that the laws of fraud are less stringent than the laws of *ona'at devarim*, one may defraud a sinner, as well. However, the *Baḥ* himself is quick to point out that he presents this thesis only theoretically, and is reluctant to allow following this position as a practical matter.

The Ritva advances a particularly novel interpretation of R. Ḥanina's statement, claiming that it refers specifically to causing aggravation to one's wife. While this approach may not seem compatible with the text of the Gemara, and the editor of the Mossad HaRav Kook edition in fact suggested that the Ritva had a different version of the text, the Gemara does continue with details about the importance of not causing aggravation to one's wife. Of course, everyone agrees that this law applies to others as well, but we must exercise particular care with regard to our spouses.

Parashat Beḥukkotai

Valuations

The last chapter of the Sefer Vayikra (26) deals with a person who wishes to contribute a sum of money to the Temple treasury, calculated as the "value" of a human being, an animal, a house, or a field, where the sum to be paid is established according to specific amounts set by the Torah.

Rambam, in his *Sefer HaMitzvot* (*Mitzvot Aseh* 114–117), counts four separate commandments: "That which our Torah has instructed us *regarding the valuations* of a human being," "of an unclean animal," "of houses," and "of fields." In the heading of *Hilkhot Arakhin VaḤaramim* in his *Mishneh Torah,* he formulates the obligation in a slightly different manner: "*To render judgment concerning the valuations* of a human being," etc.

Who is bound by this commandment? Certainly, as Rambam writes at the beginning of *Hilkhot Arakhin,* a person who pledges a value thereby makes a vow to the Temple treasury, and is obligated to fulfill his vow, in keeping with what is stated, "He shall do all that proceeds from his mouth" (Bemidbar 30:3). If he fails to fulfill the vow, he is liable for the violation of the prohibitions "you shall not delay paying it"

(Devarim 23:22), and "he shall not break his word" (Bemidbar, ibid.). However, Rambam's wording (1:2), "*to render judgment* concerning valuations," implies that there also is a mitzva incumbent upon the kohanim to establish the valuation in accordance with Torah law.

The *Sefer HaḤinnukh* (350) writes, "One who transgresses, and vows a valuation at a time that the Temple is standing, but does not pay the value set by the Torah... has neglected this positive commandment, and his punishment is exceedingly great, as he has committed a trespass against Hashem." His words imply that the commandment applies specifically to the person who took the vow and is thus obligated to fulfill it. The *Ḥinnukh* goes on to explain that one who does not honor his vow within the prescribed time violates the prohibition of "you shall not delay paying it," but he does not say that he also violates the prohibition of "he shall not break his word." It is therefore possible that he disagrees with Rambam, and in his opinion the obligation to pay the valuation is based exclusively on the section dealing with valuations, and not on the general laws governing vows.

If a person pledged his value but is unable to pay the full amount set by the Torah ("But if he be too poor for the valuation"; Vayikra 27:8), he pays in accordance with his means, as assessed by a priest. This is understandable according to the *Sefer HaḤinnukh,* who maintains that valuations are governed not by the laws of vows, but by a separate set of laws unique to valuations. However, according to Rambam, who understands that vows of valuation fall into the general category of vows made to the Temple treasury, it is difficult to understand how it is possible to reduce the obligation. The *Ḥazon Ish* suggests that, according to Rambam, when a person takes a vow to pay a value, he conditions it on the laws set down in the Torah, and therefore his actual obligation is determined in accordance with his ability to pay.

There is a disagreement in the Talmud (Arakhin 5b) regarding whether a gentile can take a vow of valuation. Rambam rules that if a gentile promises to pay his own value or the value of another person, he must pay according to his vow (*Hilkhot Arakhin* 1:11). The *Mishneh LaMelekh* (*Hilkhot Melakhim* 10:7) asks, given that the law "he shall not break his word" is not one of the seven Noahide laws, and hence a gentile is not obligated to fulfill his vow, what does it mean that a gentile can take a vow of valuation? He suggests that this merely means that if a gentile took a vow of valuation and set aside the proscribed sum, the money becomes consecrated, so that it requires interment, and is subject to the laws governing misuse of consecrated property, similar to other money or objects donated to the Temple.

However, according to the *Sefer HaḤinnukh*, who seems to hold that the law of valuations itself makes the vow binding, it is possible to say that if a gentile takes a vow of valuation, he is included under that law, and therefore obligated to fulfill his vow.

The *Minḥat Ḥinnukh* maintains that a minor who has reached the age at which he understands the meaning of vows can take a vow of valuation and the money becomes consecrated, even though he is not bound by the prohibition of "he shall not break his word." Might it be possible to say that since such a minor is mentioned in the biblical *parasha* of valuations, he is automatically obligated to fulfill his vow even though he is still a minor?

Sefer Bemidbar

Parashat Bemidbar

Giving Pidyon HaBen to a Woman or Minor

In *Parashat Bo* (Shemot 13:13), the Torah mentioned the mitzva of *pidyon haben,* the obligation to "redeem" one's firstborn son, in general terms: "you must redeem every *bekhor* (oldest son)." However, the specific details of this mitzva are not presented until Sefer Bemidbar. In our *parasha* (Bemidbar 3:48), we are instructed to give the money to Aharon and his sons, and in *Parashat Koraḥ* (18:16) we are told that the obligation is to give five *shekalim* when the son is one month old.

Inasmuch as there are also other sections in the Torah that relate to this mitzva, it is interesting to note which verses the Rishonim cite as the source in their listings of the mitzvot. The *Sefer Yere'im* (140) writes that the mitzva is to fulfill the Torah's command in *Parashat Koraḥ*. He apparently felt that the section of *pidyon haben* in our *parasha* deals only with the mitzva's performance in the desert. The eternally binding mitzva, however, is expressed most clearly in *Parashat Koraḥ*. In his *Sefer HaMitzvot* (*Aseh* 80), Rambam cites the Torah's general statement in *Parashat Mishpatim* (Shemot 22), but adds that the details of the mitzva were stated in *Parashat Koraḥ*. Elsewhere, however, in *Hilkhot Bikkurim* (1:10), Rambam cites our *parasha* as the halakhic source regarding the details of *pidyon haben*. He writes, "The *pidyon haben* is to be given to male *kohanim*, as it says [in our *parasha*], 'You shall give the money to Aharon and his sons.'" The *Yere'im* did not cite this verse, which requires giving the *pidyon haben* money specifically to male *kohanim*, perhaps indicating that in his view, *pidyon haben* may be given to a female *kohenet*, just as other gifts to the kohanim, such as *teruma*, may be given to females.

While the opinion of the *Yere'im* is open to speculation, there are two explicit opinions of the *Tosafot* regarding this issue. The Gemara tells that R. Kahana accepted a turban as payment for *pidyon haben* (Kiddushin 8a). The *Tosafot* note that R. Kahana was not a *kohen* but was married to a *kohenet*. How, then, did he receive the turban as *pidyon haben*? One answer suggested by the *Tosafot* is that there were two different people named R. Kahana, and the one who received the turban was indeed a *kohen*. But the *Tosafot* then suggest a different answer, namely, that R. Kahana acted as an agent for his wife, who was a *kohenet*, and received the turban on her behalf. This explanation is based on two novel assumptions: that a *kohenet* can accept *pidyon haben*, and that she may even appoint a *shaliaḥ* (agent) to receive it on her behalf.

The *Ḥatam Sofer* was once "accused" of allowing a *kohenet* to receive money for *pidyon haben*, but he denied ever having done so. He said that he had merely mentioned in casual conversation the theoretical possibility of conducting a *pidyon haben* without a male *kohen*, but then rejected such a notion. Inasmuch as the *kohenet*'s husband – who is not a *kohen* – enjoys rights to his wife's monetary assets (*kinyan peirot*), giving *pidyon haben* to his wife would, presumably, deprive the clan of *kohanim* of money rightfully owed to them.

Despite this objection and other reservations, the *Ḥatam Sofer* (Responsa, *Yoreh De'ah* 301) ruled that if no *kohen* is readily available, one may give the *pidyon* to a *kohenet*. However, since there is an opinion (Rambam and others) that a *kohenet* may not receive the *pidyon*, this should be done without a *berakha*. And when the opportunity arises at some later point to give the money to a *kohen*, the father should repeat the ceremony with a *kohen*.

Optimally, a father is obligated to give the *pidyon* to a *kohen* who can trace his lineage all the way to Aharon. Since today most *kohanim* cannot do so, we rely on the presumption that people recognized as *kohanim* are indeed *kohanim* (*kohanei ḥazaka*). The *Ḥatan Sofer*, a grandson of the *Ḥatam Sofer*, recommended giving the *pidyon* to a *kohen* who is married to a *kohenet*. This would increase the probability of having a proper recipient, as either spouse may be a legitimate recipient (*Responsa Ḥatan Sofer* 25).

According to Rambam (*Hilkhot Bikkurim* 1:10), the *pidyon* must be given to "Aharon and his sons." Does this refer specifically to adults, or may the *pidyon* be given to a minor? The *Peri Ḥadash* pointed out that the Gemara implies that other priestly gifts may be given to minors. The Gemara in Yevamot (99b) comments that one should not allot *teruma* from the granary to a *katan*. Rashi explains that it is inappropriate to treat *teruma* so casually in a public place: proper respect would entail giving it more formally to an adult. It therefore appears that according to strict halakha, a *katan* may receive *teruma* if it is done in a respectful manner, and so perhaps a *katan* may receive *pidyon haben*, as well. However, the *Peri Ḥadash* pointed out that there are some halakhic complications involved in a *katan*'s performance of a *kinyan* (formal act of acquisition). This engendered a long halakhic debate regarding the *kinyan* of a *katan* in general (Rabbi Akiva Eger, *Yoreh De'ah* 305, cited the *Peri Ḥadash*; the *Ketzot* and *Netivot*, inter alia, debate these points in *Ḥoshen Mishpat* 343). The *Ḥatam Sofer*, however, felt that the entire problem may not be relevant. The Torah merely told us to "place" ("*venatan*") the *pidyon* in the *kohen*'s hands, perhaps referring simply to the physical act of placing, rather than a formal *kinyan* (*Ḥatam Sofer, Yoreh De'ah* 292). This brings to mind the opinion of the *Ketzot* (200:5) that a *get* (divorce document) must merely be placed in the woman's hands, and need not be legally acquired by the woman, since regarding a *get*, as well, the Torah says "*venatan*."

What remains for us to determine is the extent of the *kohen*'s involvement in the mitzva. If the *kohen* is viewed as playing an active role in the process of *pidyon*, beyond simply receiving the money and fulfilling the halakhic obligation for the child, then clearly it would not be allowed to give the *pidyon* to a minor. The *Ḥatam Sofer* pointed out that the various statements made by the *kohen* during the *pidyon* ceremony (although they are not found in the Gemara at all and were enacted by the *Geonim*) imply that the *kohen* has an active role in the *pidyon*, which therefore may not be done by a *katan*.

Moreover, there is a general principle that requires performing a mitzva in as dignified a manner as possible. One should try to find a *kohen* who is a *talmid ḥakham* (Mahari Assad, Responsum 55), and one should stand as a sign of respect towards the *kohen*, who should be seated during the ceremony (*Yam shel Shlomo*, Kiddushin 1:54). It would thus seem more appropriate to have an adult involved in this mitzva (*Arukh HaShulḥan* 305:12). However, if it is impossible to find an adult, it seems preferable to perform the mitzva on time with a *kohen katan*.

Parashat Naso

Birkat Kohanim

In *Parashat Naso* (Bemidbar 6:22–27), God commands Moshe to instruct Aharon and his sons with regard to the prescribed *Birkat Kohanim*. Although this mitzva is ideally to be performed by the *kohanim* in the *Beit HaMikdash,* the same mitzva (with minor variations) is obligatory today, as well. In fact, Rambam lists this mitzva as one of the sixty mitzvot that remain obligatory in all times under normal conditions (*Sefer HaMitzvot, Aseh* 26; end of *mitzvot aseh* section). It should be noted that Rabbi Yaakov Emden (*Mor UKetzia* 128) maintains that the biblical obligation of *Birkat Kohanim* applies only in the *Beit HaMikdash* when the *avoda* (Temple service) is performed. However, the *Sifrei* (Devarim 12:5) says explicitly, "I know [the source of *Birkat Kohanim* in the *Mikdash*]; from where do we know that it applies outside the *Beit HaMikdash,* as well? From the verse 'wherever I permit My name to be mentioned, I shall come to you and bless you.'" Similarly, the *Shulḥan Arukh* (*Oraḥ Ḥayim* 128:12) states plainly, "A *kohen* who does not bestow the *berakha* negates the mitzva," implying that he, too, considers this a Torah obligation even nowadays.

The *Behag* enumerated two separate mitzvot regarding *Birkat Kohanim*. He listed it in his general list of individual mitzvot, and counted it again under the heading of general mitzvot (*parashiyyot*). Some have taken this to mean that the *Behag* considers *Birkat Kohanim* in and outside the *Mikdash* to be two separate mitzvot. It seems more likely, however, that the two listings reflect the idea that one mitzva is a personal obligation upon the *kohanim*, while the other is a communal responsibility of the Jewish people to hear and receive the *berakhot*. In fact, a well-known view of the *Sefer Ḥaredim* (quoted in *Mishna Berura* 128, introduction) maintains that when Am Yisrael stand opposite the *kohanim* face-to-face and silently have the intention to receive the *berakha* according to the will of God, they are included in the mitzva.

The Gemara (Rosh HaShana 28b) says that a *kohen* who has already said *Birkat Kohanim* may go to another synagogue and recite it again there. The *Tosafot* explain that the prohibition of *bal tosif* (adding mitzvot) never applies to performing the same mitzva twice. The *Ḥatam Sofer* (Responsa, *Oraḥ Ḥayim* 22), however, suggests a different explanation, claiming that the *kohen* may give the *berakha* again because the second congregation still bears an obligation to hear the *berakha*. He cites the *Yere'im* as the source for the idea of a communal obligation to hear the *berakha*, but this position is not found in the standard editions of the *Yere'im*.

There is a well-known custom for the community to close or cover their eyes during *Birkat Kohanim*. The Gemara (Ḥagiga 16a) says that we should avoid looking at the *kohanim* when they pronounce the ineffable name of God during *Birkat Kohanim* in the *Beit HaMikdash*. Rashi (Megilla 24b) writes that looking at the *kohanim* during *Birkat Kohanim* anywhere, even outside the *Mikdash*, causes dimness of the eyes. The *Tosafot* (in Ḥagiga), however, reject this reason, and explain that we should not look at the *kohanim* in order to focus our concentration on the *berakha*. The *Tosafot* quote a passage in the Yerushalmi citing R. Ḥaggai as saying that he, unlike most people, may look at the *kohanim*. Since he felt assured of his ability to concentrate on the *berakha*, in his case looking was permitted. The *Devar Avraham* notes that this would lend support to the aforementioned view of the *Sefer Ḥaredim*. If there were no mitzva upon the community, why would they need to concentrate and receive the *berakha*? Apparently, they must concentrate to fulfill their own obligation of *Birkat Kohanim*.

Regarding the prohibition against looking at the *kohanim*, the *Mishna Berura* (128:89) distinguishes between the blessing as it is performed in the *Mikdash* and outside the *Mikdash*. Since the *Shekhina* rests on the *kohanim* in the *Mikdash*, it is forbidden to look at them at all. However, outside the *Beit HaMikdash* one should not look at the *kohanim* in order to maintain one's concentration. Therefore, a brief glance, which would not hinder concentration, would be permitted.

The *Minḥat Ḥinnukh* (378) adds that women should also be included in this mitzva, since it does not depend upon any particular time frame (*mitzvat aseh shelo hazeman gerama*). Therefore, it is obvious that women, as well as men, should face the *kohanim* but avoid looking at them during the *berakha*.

The Gemara (Sota 38a) says that the *kohanim* and the community should face each other during the *berakha*. The Torah instructed the *kohanim* to "say to them" (Bemidbar 6:23), which implies that this should be done in the normal manner of conversation, namely, with the two parties facing each other.

An interesting practice has evolved regarding the blessing recited by the *kohanim* before they recite the actual *Birkat Kohanim*. The *kohanim* face the *aron kodesh* with their backs to the community and begin that *berakha*. In the middle of the *berakha*, they turn to face the community and remain in that position until the end of *Birkat Kohanim*.

The Gemara did not describe the proper position for the recitation of the *berakha* before *Birkat Kohanim*. The Me'iri (Sota 3a) said that the *kohanim* should face the people while they say that *berakha* as well as when they say the entire *Birkat Kohanim*. On the other hand, Rambam (*Hilkhot Tefilla* 14:12) ruled that the *kohanim* should recite the introductory *berakha* facing the *aron kodesh*, and then, when they conclude that *berakha*, they should turn to face the community and say *Birkat Kohanim*. The *Tur* and *Shulḥan Arukh* (*Oraḥ Ḥayim* 128:11) codify the opinion of the Me'iri. The *Mishna Berura* (ad loc.) comments that meticulous people try to satisfy both opinions and turn in the middle of the *berakha*. Although the *Ḥafetz Ḥayim* seems to endorse this compromise solution, the *Arukh HaShulḥan* finds this practice very surprising and thinks that we should follow the opinion of the Me'iri, as stated in the *Shulḥan Arukh*.

This debate between Rambam and the Me'iri hinges upon the fundamental relationship between the introductory *berakha* and *Birkat Kohanim* itself. Rambam apparently felt that given the impropriety of turning one's back to the *aron kodesh,* the *kohanim* should do so to face the congregation only when absolutely necessary, meaning for *Birkat Kohanim* itself. However, the Me'iri felt that the *berakha* is inherently related to *Birkat Kohanim* and therefore must be said as the *kohanim* face the people, similar to *Birkat Kohanim* itself. In fact, the Me'iri thinks that this *berakha* is a form of enhancing *Birkat Kohanim* (*hiddur mitzva*) and therefore is directly related to it.

In conclusion, we may suggest a homiletical approach to explain the prevalent custom. Inasmuch as God commanded *kohanim* with regard to this mitzva, should it be considered a mitzva between man and God (*bein adam laMakom*) or between man and man (*bein adam laḥavero*)? Perhaps the *kohanim*'s practice is intended to demonstrate that this mitzva actually contains both elements. They begin the *berakha* as a mitzva *bein adam laMakom,* by facing the *aron,* but they also wish to demonstrate that it is a *mitzva bein adam laḥavero,* and therefore face the people for the end of the *berakha.*

We have seen that there is a mitzva for *kohanim* to recite *Birkat Kohanim* and that there may be a mitzva upon the community, as well. There is a third partner in this mitzva, as well, and that is, of course, God Himself: "Do not wonder, 'What benefit is there in a human *berakha*?' The acceptance of the *berakha* depends not on the *kohanim,* but on God.... The *kohanim* fulfill the mitzva that they were commanded, and God, in His mercy, blesses Israel as He wishes" (Rambam, *Hilkhot Nesiat Kappayim* 15:7).

Parashat Behaalotekha

Simḥa on Shabbat

There are four things that were said in connection with Shabbat – two of biblical origin, and two *midivrei soferim* (described by the prophets). The Torah said "*zakhor*" (remember) and "*shamor*" (observe), while *kavod* (honor) and *oneg* (enjoyment) were described by the prophets" (Rambam, *Hilkhot Shabbat* 30:1).

The two rabbinic laws of *kavod* and *oneg* apply not only to Shabbat, but to Yom Tov, as well (see Rambam, *Hilkhot Yom Tov* 6:16). However, on Yom Tov there also is a biblical obligation of *simḥa*: "You shall rejoice on your holiday" (Devarim 16:14). Is there a mitzva of *simḥa* on Shabbat, as well?

In *Parashat Behaalotekha*, the Torah lists the days on which the *ḥatzotzerot* (trumpets) must be sounded in the Temple, including "on your days of joy, on your designated holidays, and on your New Moons" (Bemidbar 10:10). Inasmuch as the "designated holidays" also are days of *simḥa*, what does the Torah add with the phrase "days of joy"? Ibn Ezra (ad loc.) explained that this refers to days of celebration that we must declare when we emerge victorious from war. It seems that in his view, days such as Ḥanukka and Purim, though halakhically treated as rabbinic obligations, actually have a biblical source. (One may conjecture as to how this might apply to Yom HaAtzmaut and Yom Yerushalayim.) In any event, the *Sifrei*, according to the standard edition, presents a different explanation of the phrase "days of joy," claiming that this refers to Shabbat. The variant text of the Vilna Gaon, as cited in the Netziv's edition of the *Sifrei*, says that "the day" – rather than the complete phrase, "days of joy" – refers to Shabbat. Quite possibly, these two versions differ as to the question of whether there is an obligation of *simḥa* on Shabbat.

Many other sources indeed indicate that such an obligation in fact exists. The *Behag* enumerates the mitzva of Shabbat as "the *simḥa* and *oneg* of Shabbat." It should be noted that the *Behag* most likely refers here to rabbinic obligations of *kavod* and *oneg*, as he is wont to count rabbinic laws in his list of mitzvot.

The *Sefer HaManhig* records that the custom in France and Spain was to omit *Taḥanun* every Friday afternoon, despite the fact that Spanish communities had the practice of reciting *Taḥanun* on the afternoon before Rosh Ḥodesh. He explains this custom on the basis of the fact that Shabbat, unlike Rosh Ḥodesh, is a day of "feast and *simḥa*," and cites the aforementioned comment in the *Sifrei* that the phrase "days of joy" refers to Shabbat. The *Shibbolei HaLeket* (82) also cites the *Sifrei* and mentions that Rabbi Avigdor Kohen Tzedek viewed this *Sifrei* as the source for the recitation of *Yismeḥu BeMalkhutekha* ("They Will Rejoice in Your Kingship") on Shabbat. He also makes reference to a text that says, "All the lovers of Your name will rejoice," which some recite on Shabbat.

The Yerushalmi (Megilla 1:4) establishes that if Purim falls on Shabbat, the Purim feast should not be held on that day. It explains that the Megilla (9:21) instructs us to "make" Purim a day of *simḥa* and feasting. Inasmuch as Shabbat is automatically a day of *simḥa*, there is no way or need to "make" it a day of *simḥa*.

The *Tosafot* (Ketubbot 7b) rule that although generally we recite *Sheva Berakhot* at a meal during the first week of marriage only in the presence of *panim ḥadashot* (someone who has not yet taken part in the wedding celebration), this condition does not apply on Shabbat. They explain that Shabbat itself constitutes *panim ḥadashot*, as we always observe Shabbat as a more festive day through *simḥa* and feast. One might claim that the *Tosafot* do not refer to a halakhic obligation of *simḥa,* but merely observe common practice. On the other hand, this might indicate that an obligation of *simḥa* does exist.

A well-known halakha establishes that although a mourner does not observe mourning practices on Shabbat, the day of Shabbat nevertheless counts towards the seven days of mourning. Yom Tov, by contrast, cancels mourning altogether, and if a person passes away on Yom Tov, mourning does not begin until after Yom Tov. The Yerushalmi (Moed Katan 3:5) discusses the reason for this distinction and says that if Shabbat would cancel mourning, there would never be a seven-day week of mourning. The Yerushalmi appears to hold that fundamentally, both Shabbat and Yom Tov are days of *simḥa* and should cancel mourning. It is only due to a technical problem that Shabbat counts as a day of mourning.

On the other hand, other sources seem to indicate that no obligation of *simḥa* at all applies on Shabbat. The *Tosafot* (Moed Katan 23b), for example, state explicitly that Shabbat counts towards the seven days of mourning because *simḥa* is not mentioned in connection with Shabbat. Only Yom Tov, which features an obligation of *simḥa,* cancels mourning entirely.

The *Shita Mekubbetzet* (Ketubbot 7) quotes an opinion that one may not get married on Shabbat because doing so violates the prohibition against mixing together two types of *simḥa* (*ein me'arevin simḥa besimḥa*). However, this opinion was rejected by the argument that there is no requirement of *simḥa* on Shabbat.

The Maharil (end of *Hilkhot Yom Tov*) forbids fasting on Yom Tov, as it is a day of *simḥa,* but permits fasting on Shabbat, on which there is no obligation of *simḥa.*

The *Shulḥan Arukh* (*Oraḥ Ḥayim* 529:4) writes that we should wear nicer clothing on Yom Tov than on Shabbat, and the *Magen Avraham* (ad loc.) explains this ruling based on the fact that Yom Tov, unlike Shabbat, is a day of *simḥa.*

The *Tashbetz* (298:2) goes so far as to suggest the possibility of allowing eulogies on Shabbat. He says that inasmuch as Shabbat is not called a day of *simḥa* and one observes some mourning laws (in private, though not in public) on Shabbat, perhaps eulogies could be permitted, as well.

It is possible that traces of this discussion can be found in variant texts of the siddur. On Friday night, we say (or sing) *Lekha Dodi* as we welcome Shabbat. The last stanza of this poem reads, "Come in peace, crown of her husband, in *simḥa* and good cheer." The Ari substituted the word "*rinna*" ("song") in place of "*simḥa*." When, however, Shabbat and Yom Tov coincided, the Ari recited "*simḥa*" instead of "*rinna*." Apparently, he felt that the idea of *simḥa* applies only to Yom Tov, and not to Shabbat.

On the other hand, the Ari had the practice of reciting *Yismeḥu* during all the Shabbat prayers, as opposed to the practice of *Nusaḥ Ashkenaz*, to recite it only at Musaf. Including this paragraph in every prayer would imply that *simḥa* applies to Shabbat, whereas limiting it to Musaf would suggest that there is no law of *simḥa* per se on Shabbat. Rabbi Soloveitchik explained that the verse in our *parasha* cited by the *Sifrei* as the source for an obligation of *simḥa* on Shabbat refers only to the actual time when they brought the Shabbat offering (*musaf*). There is an obligation of song and *simḥa* when the sacrifice was brought, and therefore the custom of *Nusaḥ Ashkenaz* is to recite *Yismeḥu* only at Musaf.

Regardless of the dispute concerning this issue, it is worth recalling the last words of *Shulḥan Arukh, Oraḥ Ḥayim*. In a different context, the Rema writes, "One should fulfill all opinions by making a greater feast and a good-hearted person will always feast."

Parashat Shelaḥ

The Obligation to Wear Tzitzit

There are seven mitzvot that *Ḥazal* considered equivalent to the entire gamut of mitzvot. Interestingly, three of them directly relate to *Parashat Shelaḥ*. Rashi (Bemidbar 15:41) cites Rabbi Moshe HaDarshan as explaining that the Torah in this parasha juxtaposed the story of the *mekoshesh* (the person who desecrated Shabbat; see Shabbat 96b) with the laws of inadvertent idolatrous worship because both Shabbat and idolatry are equivalent to the entire Torah. He adds that the laws of tzitzit follow the story of the *mekoshesh* as that, too, is a mitzva that is equivalent to the entire Torah.

But whereas it is obvious that we must observe Shabbat and refrain from idolatry, wearing tzitzit does not, at first glance, appear to be a complete obligation. After all, halakha requires one to wear tzitzit only if he is wearing a four-cornered garment. In fact, the Gemara (Menaḥot 41a) asks rhetorically, "Is it possible that one who does not wear a four-cornered garment is obligated in tzitzit?" The Gemara there relates that R. Kattina wore special clothes in order to avoid wearing a four-cornered garment and was harshly rebuked for this practice. When he responded, "Is there a punishment for not fulfilling a *mitzvat aseh*?" he was told that it is improper to maneuver in such a way so as not to perform a mitzva. Moreover, in a period of divine anger, one would be punished for intentionally avoiding a *mitzvat aseh*.

The *Tosafot* (Arakhin 2b) maintain that this punishment applied only at the time when most people wore four-cornered garments. A person would then have to obtain special clothes in order to avoid wearing tzitzit. However, in a culture such as ours, when people do not generally wear four-cornered garments, there is no punishment for not fulfilling this mitzva. The *Tosafot* did not say that no obligation at all would exist at such a time; they merely said that not wearing tzitzit would not incur punishment.

The Gemara (Pesaḥim 113b) included a person who does not wear tzitzit in the list of people who are excommunicated by God. The *Tosafot* there comment that this refers only to a person who wore a four-cornered garment and did not put tzitzit on them. They then proceed to cite a second view: that a person must always make an effort to involve himself in mitzvot. This list would therefore include every person who could buy a four-cornered garment and wear tzitzit, but fails to do so.

We have seen that at severe times, during periods of divine anger, one may be punished for not wearing tzitzit. Additionally, someone who does not fulfill mitzvot in general may be excommunicated by God. There does not, however, seem to be an absolute obligation to wear tzitzit.

The *Or Zarua* (*Hilkhot Birkat HaMotzi* 140) attempted to explain the reason for the different formulations used in the *berakhot* recited over mitzvot. He claimed that the "*le-*" form (e.g., "*lehaniaḥ tefillin*") is used when there is an absolute obligation to fulfill the mitzva. By contrast, we employ the "*al*" form (such as "*al netilat yadayim*") when performing mitzvot that are not necessarily obligatory. The *Or Zarua* therefore asks why we recite the *berakha* of "*lehitattef batzitzit*" over tzitzit, given that there is no obligation to wear tzitzit. He answers that *Ḥazal* indeed instituted an obligation to fulfill this mitzva. He also suggests another answer: that once it became the custom to make a point of wearing a four-cornered garment in order to obligate ourselves in tzitzit, it automatically became an obligation. He compares this to the Arvit service, which the Gemara considered a "*reshut*" (optional) but became an outright obligation once it was accepted as such.

Rambam's position on this issue is somewhat unclear. After his list of the *mitzvot aseh* in his *Sefer HaMitzvot*, Rambam lists sixty mitzvot that ordinary people, i.e., those who live in a city, do business, marry, and have children, must perform. In this list he includes the mitzva of tzitzit. True, Rambam also includes mezuza on this list, and one can absolve himself from this obligation by living in a boat or tent (see *Hilkhot Berakhot* 11:2). However, a clear distinction exists between tzitzit and mezuza. An ordinary person under normal circumstances lives in a house and is therefore obligated to place a mezuza on his doorframe. But a person could lead an entirely normal life (especially given today's style of clothing) without ever wearing a four-cornered garment. If Rambam included tzitzit as a mitzva that must be performed under normal circumstances in daily life, he apparently felt that there is an absolute obligation to fulfill this mitzva.

We may draw further proof from a ruling of Rambam in *Hilkhot Shevuot* (1:6), where he addresses the situation of a person who swears to abrogate a mitzva. He gives a number of examples: "If a person swore not to wear tzitzit or put on tefillin, not to sit in a sukka on Sukkot, not to eat matza on Pesaḥ." This list includes mitzvot that are incumbent upon every person – as well as the mitzva of tzitzit. Seemingly, then, Rambam viewed this mitzva as an absolute obligation that one must perform.

On the other hand, Rambam writes in *Hilkhot Tzitzit* (3:11):

> Even though it is not obligatory to buy a *tallit* and wear it in order to fulfill the mitzva of tzitzit, it is not appropriate for a pious person to exempt himself from this mitzva. He should try to wear a garment obligated in tzitzit, in order to fulfill the mitzva. During the time of prayer, one should be especially meticulous (to wear tzitzit). It is a terrible disgrace for a *talmid ḥakham* to pray while not wearing tzitzit.

Rambam then concludes this section by commenting, "Everyone should be careful to perform this mitzva, since the Torah said that all mitzvot are equal to and dependent upon it."

This section seemingly contradicts the thesis that Rambam elucidated in *Sefer HaMitzvot* and *Hilkhot Shevuot*. In fact, Rabbi Yosef Kapaḥ felt that Rambam had changed his mind about this issue, as these conflicting passages cannot be reconciled at all.

The *Shulḥan Arukh* (*Oraḥ Ḥayim* 8:1) writes that one must stand while reciting the *berakha* over tzitzit. The *Magen Avraham* asks why halakha requires standing for this *berakha* but allows one to sit while reciting the *berakha* over *hafrashat ḥalla* (removing some dough while baking bread). He suggests that taking *ḥalla* is a less important mitzva since one takes *ḥalla* only so that he may eat the bread. The Vilna Gaon refuted this opinion, arguing that *ḥalla* is of no less importance than any other mitzva. The *Yeshuot Yaakov* also disagrees with the *Magen Avraham* and argues that *ḥalla* is certainly similar to tzitzit. Just as a person who bakes with a certain quantity of dough and wishes to eat must take *ḥalla*, similarly, one who wears a four-cornered garment must wear tzitzit. There is no obligation either to give *ḥalla* or to wear tzitzit: both are required only once a person chooses to place himself in a certain situation. The *Yeshuot Yaakov* therefore resorts to other answers to explain why the *berakha* on tzitzit must be recited while standing.

Apparently, the *Magen Avraham* understood that there indeed exists an absolute obligation to wear tzitzit, perhaps by force of rabbinic enactment, as suggested by the *Or Zarua*.

Although the precise nature of the tzitzit obligation, as we have seen, is subject to debate, it is nevertheless considered equivalent to all other mitzvot. One who wears tzitzit reminds himself of all the mitzvot (see Bemidbar 15:39; Rashi, Ramban, and Sforno ad loc.). In fact, Ibn Ezra commented that although men wear a *tallit* specifically while praying, it would seem more appropriate to wear a *tallit* outside of shul. A person praying in shul is automatically involved in the spiritual world. It is specifically outside the context of prayer that a person needs tzitzit to remind him of the entire gamut of Torah and mitzvot.

Parashat Koraḥ

Maḥaloket

The story of Koraḥ and his group is seen as the epitome of a *maḥaloket* with improper motives. At the opposite extreme, the constant disagreements between the schools of Shammai and Hillel serve as the paragons of *maḥaloket* waged for sublime purposes. The Mishna (Avot 5:17) states, "A *maḥaloket* for the sake of Heaven [such as exhibited by Hillel and Shammai] will endure; a *maḥaloket* that is not for the sake of Heaven [such as the story of Koraḥ and his group] will not endure." Rabbenu Yona (ad loc.) comments that the *maḥaloket* between the schools of Shammai and Hillel will extend to many issues and they will constantly discuss these issues. They will also be granted a long and extended life. On the other hand, a *maḥaloket* conducted for ulterior motives will not endure, since the disputants will perish, as we see in the story of Koraḥ.

It has been pointed out that the Mishna contrasted the *maḥaloket* between Shammai and Hillel with the *maḥaloket* of "Koraḥ and his group." In the former case, the Mishna mentioned the two adversaries, Shammai and Hillel. However, in the latter case, the opposing side (apparently Moshe) was not mentioned at all. It has been suggested that the Mishna deliberately omitted the name of Moshe in order to avoid mentioning his name with regard to *maḥaloket*. Others have suggested that Koraḥ and his group actually represented two conflicting parties. When the *maḥaloket* is for ulterior motives, each participant has his own specific agenda. Although Koraḥ and his group joined forces to oppose Moshe, they were themselves at odds over their ultimate goals.

While this mishna undoubtedly disapproves of an improper *maḥaloket*, it remains to be seen whether the Torah forbids such a *maḥaloket*, and if such a prohibition should be codified as one of the 613 mitzvot.

The Gemara (Sanhedrin 110a) says in the name of Rav that we should not allow any *maḥaloket* to take root, and in fact anyone who does initiate *maḥaloket* transgresses a prohibition, as it says (Bemidbar 17:5), "One should not be like Koraḥ and his group." R. Ashi added that anyone who transgresses this prohibition deserves to be afflicted with leprosy.

Many Rishonim (*Semag* 156–157; *Semak* 132; and others) seemingly take this gemara at face value and include a prohibition of *maḥaloket* in their list of the 613 mitzvot.

Rambam (*Sefer HaMitzvot*, principle 8), however, interprets the Torah's intention quite differently. He explains this verse to mean that anyone who disputes the issue of *kehunna*, as Koraḥ did, "will not be like Koraḥ," meaning that he will not be swallowed by the earth and burned. Instead, his punishment will be "as God spoke to Moshe." The actual words of the Torah are "as God spoke, with the hand of Moshe." Therefore, Rambam explained that the punishment for *maḥaloket* surrounding the *kehunna* will henceforth be leprosy, just as Moshe's hand was afflicted when he made somewhat derogatory remarks about the Jewish people. Rambam understood the Gemara in Sanhedrin as an *asmakhta* (a rabbinic law, whose proof text is not meant literally). However, Rambam himself added that the prohibition of *maḥaloket* is included in another prohibition, to be explained in its proper place. In the Frankel edition of *Sefer HaMitzvot*, we are referred to *Mitzvat Lo Taaseh* 45, the prohibition of *lo titgodedu* (Devarim 14:1). There, Rambam explains that the primary intention of this verse is the prohibition against slashing one's skin during mourning, as was the custom among the pagans. However, he adds, the Rabbis included in this a prohibition against breaking off into conflicting sects, and Rambam here also mentions the prohibition of *maḥaloket*. However, he makes it clear that this is an additional meaning expounded upon by the Rabbis, and is not the real biblical meaning of this prohibition.

Rabbi Aḥai Gaon (*She'iltot* 131) states categorically that the People of Israel are forbidden to cause any *maḥaloket*. Although he does not specify that this is a biblical law, he says that participating in *maḥaloket* may cause people to detest one another, in violation of the prohibition (Vayikra 19) "Do not hate your brother in your heart." Rabbi Aḥai Gaon perhaps viewed this prohibition as a *seyag* (fence, or safeguard) and acknowledged the existence of a Torah-mandated *seyag*. (There is a well-known discussion among talmudic scholars as to whether the Torah itself imposed specific safeguards against certain violations.) The *Tashbetz* (*Zohar HaRakia* 114) quotes the *She'iltot* but proceeds to seek another source for the prohibition of *maḥaloket*. He suggests that this prohibition might be included in the obligation to follow the majority. If we always follow majority rule, all disputes will be resolved. He also suggests that it might be included in *lo tasur* (Devarim 17:11), the prohibition against deviating from the words of our Sages, which also serves as a means of avoiding *maḥaloket*.

We have thus encountered two different interpretations of the verse "He should (will) not be like Koraḥ." The *Semag* et al. think that this verse introduces a direct prohibition against participating in *maḥaloket*, while Rambam claims that it is meant as a threat, warning of the punishment that will befall a person who disputes the *kehunna*.

Ramban (*Sefer HaMitzvot*, principle 8) suggests a third explanation. In his view, this is a specific prohibition forbidding anyone from disagreeing with the idea of Aharon's God-given right to the *kehunna*. The *Yere'im* also follows this opinion, but adds that this prohibition also includes questioning or protesting any God-given appointment or honor. Therefore, anyone who rebels or questions Moshe's authority has also violated this prohibition. In any event, it seems that both Ramban and the *Yere'im* agree with Rambam that this source does not involve the general issue of *maḥaloket*.

Even those authorities who did not include *maḥaloket* in the list of biblical mitzvot certainly feel that it should be abhorred and avoided at all costs. A typical comment to this effect is found in the Me'iri

(Sanhedrin ad loc.): "Even though all *maḥaloket*, in general, is despicable and repulsive, and it was mentioned parenthetically that it is considered a prohibition, nevertheless, one who disagrees with his rabbi or anyone else to whom he should acquiesce, is even more despised."

Of course, as indicated in the above-mentioned mishna in Avot, a *maḥaloket* with proper motivation is permitted and even commendable. It is only in regard to an improperly motivated *maḥaloket* that Rabbi Yeḥezkel Landau (*Responsa Noda BiYehuda, Yoreh De'ah* 1) comments, "There is nothing worse than *maḥaloket*. In our generation it is not common to have a *maḥaloket* with purely noble intentions."

Many times people heatedly dispute issues concerning religious custom, such as whether *Av HaRaḥamim* should be recited on a given Shabbat. We must keep things in perspective and realize that *maḥaloket* should be avoided at all costs, and may even entail an actual biblical prohibition.

The *Sifrei* (Bemidbar 42), commenting on the blessing of peace with which *Birkat Kohanim* concludes, cites the remark of R. Elazar b. R. Elazar HaKappar that *shalom* is so great that it even protects idol worshipers, adding, "Peace is great, and *maḥaloket* is despised."

Parashat Ḥukkat

Tahara and Tuma

The first section of *Parashat Ḥukkat* presents the laws of *tumat meit* (ritual impurity caused by contact with a dead body). Rambam (*Sefer HaMitzvot, Aseh* 107) and *Sefer HaḤinnukh* (398) count the law of *tumat meit* as a separate mitzva. In fact, Rambam enumerates thirteen individual mitzvot (no. 96–109) relating to *tuma*. Ramban disagrees and argues that all of these mitzvot are not obligations or prohibitions, but rather optional laws. Of course, we are forbidden from any involvement with the *Mikdash* and eating *kodashim* while in a state of impurity. However, there is no prohibition at all against becoming *tameh*, and if one indeed becomes *tameh*, he bears no obligation to become *tahor*. He may remain in his state of *tuma*, as long as he refrains from the prohibitions involved. In Rambam's rather lengthy introduction to this section, he appears to basically agree with Ramban. He writes, "The mitzva is what is stated in this law, namely, that someone who contacts this [*tuma*] is *tameh*," and he then proceeds to explain the halakhic ramifications of *tuma*.

This controversy seems to revolve around the general methodology of enumerating mitzvot. There are certain mitzvot that are obligatory, such as Shabbat, and there are other mitzvot that merely tell us how to deal with certain given situations. For example, Rambam counted the laws of *shomerim* (people entrusted with the property of another) as three separate mitzvot. There is certainly no obligation to appoint or become a *shomer*. Rather, the mitzva is to follow the Torah's dictates when a case of *shomerim* arises. Similarly, Rambam counts the mitzva of *tumat meit* (and others) even though this mitzva seems to involve merely the definition of *tuma* and *tahara*, rather than an outright commandment. Indeed, in his introduction to *Hilkhot Tumat Meit* in the *Mishneh Torah*, Rambam states clearly that the mitzva consists of the law of *tumat meit*.

Ramban apparently disagrees and maintains that only mitzvot that are obligatory should be counted in the list of mitzvot. However, Rabbi Perlow (Rabbi Saadia Gaon's *Sefer HaMitzvot*, 1:703) questions the consistency of Ramban's position in this matter. Rambam counts *kiddushin* (halakhic engagement) and *geirushin* (divorce) as mitzvot, and Ramban raises no objection against the inclusion of these laws among the 613 mitzvot. Rabbi Perlow asked, why did Ramban agree that these are to be counted as mitzvot? After all, they involve no absolute obligation, and serve merely to determine marital status for purposes of halakha. One could argue with Rabbi Perlow about these specific examples, and the laws of *shomerim* would have been a better example to show that there are laws of this type that Ramban agrees count as mitzvot. Nevertheless, Rabbi Perlow's point is well taken.

In any event, one verse in the Torah appears, at least at first glance, to indicate that there is an absolute prohibition against becoming *tameh*. In regards to rabbits, pigs, etc., the Torah (Vayikra 11:8) writes, "Do not eat their meat and do not touch their carcass." Rabbi Avraham ibn Ezra (ad loc.) interpreted this statement literally, as introducing a prohibition against touching the meat or carcass of these animals, and even claims that one who does so would receive *makkot* (lashes). However, in his book *Yesod Mora*, Ibn Ezra counts this as one of the 613 mitzvot but writes that no *makkot* are involved.

The Gemara (Rosh HaShana 16b), by contrast, quotes R. Yitzḥak, who interprets this prohibition very differently, and a *baraita* that argues that it is inconceivable that the Torah forbade Jews from becoming *tameh*. The *baraita* draws proof to this effect from the fact that the Torah specifically forbids *kohanim* from becoming *teme'ei meit*, clearly implying that other Jews may become *teme'ei meit*. If an ordinary Israelite may become *temeh meit*, which represents the highest form of *tuma*, then certainly he may contract a lower form of *tuma*, by coming in contact with the carcass of a non-kosher animal. The Gemara therefore arrives at a much different interpretation of this verse, and says that it introduces a specific prohibition against becoming *tameh* on Yom Tov.

Rambam (*Hilkhot Tumat Okhalin* 16:10) codifies this law in accordance with the Gemara's explanation. He writes, "All Israelites are commanded to be *tehorim* on the festivals, since they must be prepared to enter the Temple and eat *kodashim*. The statement in the Torah, 'Do not touch their carcass' refers only to the festivals. If one did become *tameh*, he does not receive *makkot*. However, there is no such prohibition during the rest of the year."

Rambam appears to have understood that the biblical prohibition against being *tameh* on Yom Tov stems from the mitzvot of Yom Tov, which involve the Temple and sacrifices, and thus necessitate a state of ritual purity. This point may help resolve a difficulty raised by many commentators: why does Rambam say that no *makkot* are involved? If this indeed constitutes a biblical prohibition, we would expect that a punishment would be administered to the transgressor. It has been written in the name of Rabbi Soloveitchik (*Mesorah* 8, p. 29) that this prohibition does not involve *makkot* because its underlying purpose is to enable us to fulfill the requirements of the mitzvot of Yom Tov. Someone who does not fulfill those requirements would not receive *makkot*. Therefore, the prohibition that serves to ensure the fulfillment of the obligation cannot be more severe than the obligation itself. If a person who does not visit the *Mikdash* on a festival does not receive *makkot*, then a person who becomes *tameh* on a festival also does not receive *makkot*. This prohibition thus becomes akin to a *lav she'ein bo maaseh* (a prohibition whose violation entails no concrete action), which is not punishable by *makkot*.

The *Shaagat Arye* (67) writes that since Rambam views the law of *tahara* on Yom Tov as merely a means of facilitating the fulfillment of the mitzvot involving *Mikdash* and *kodashim*, these laws do not apply today, in the absence of the *Beit HaMikdash*. He adds that this law would not ever apply on Rosh HaShana and Yom Kippur – even during Temple times – since the obligation of *aliya laregel* (going to the *Beit HaMikdash*) and related mitzvot apply only on Pesaḥ, Shavuot, and Sukkot, and not on Rosh HaShana and Yom Kippur.

The *Noda BiYehuda* (*Tziyyun LeNefesh Ḥaya,* Beitza 18b), however, disagrees with this interpretation and maintains that the Torah issued a general prohibition against becoming *tameh.* The logic employed by the Gemara in Rosh HaShana teaches us that the prohibition does not apply all year round. If we would search for a time when it would be appropriate to be *tahor,* we would naturally come up with the days of Yom Tov, when we should attempt to reach a higher spiritual level. Once, however, the Torah forbids us from being *tameh* on Yom Tov, this prohibition extends beyond the specific purpose of facilitating our entry into the *Mikdash.* On the basis of this argument, the *Noda BiYehuda* postulates that this prohibition applies to Rosh HaShana and Yom Kippur, as well. It also follows that it would apply even today, without a *Beit HaMikdash.*

The Me'iri (Rosh HaShana 16b) advances a different explanation for this halakha. Every person must purify himself on festivals in order to eat his regular food – not the sacrificial meat – in a state of purity. Rabbi A. Sofer (in his notes on the Me'iri) notes the novelty of this approach and its far-reaching ramifications. For example, once a person comes to the *Mikdash* and partakes of *kodashim,* the halakha as understood by Rambam would, presumably, no longer apply. According to the Me'iri, however, even after one completes his consumption of the *korbanot,* he must still eat the rest of his food in a state of purity.

Another practical difference between Rambam and the Me'iri involves a person who, for one reason or another, is exempt from *aliya laregel.* Whereas Rambam would likely exempt this individual, too, from becoming *tahor* on the festival, the Me'iri would apply the obligation even in such a case.

It would also follow that the Me'iri would apply this halakha even to Rosh HaShana and Yom Kippur. The *Tur* (*Oraḥ Ḥayim* 603) cites a tradition from *Avi HaEzri* that one should try to eat all his food in a state of purity during the seven days between Rosh HaShana and Yom Kippur. He explains that this tradition speaks of only seven days (rather than all ten days of repentance, including Rosh HaShana and Yom Kippur) because it is superfluous on Rosh HaShana. Since a person must be pure on the festivals (including Rosh HaShana), there is no need for a special tradition to require eating in a state of *tahara* on Rosh HaShana and Yom Kippur. Clearly, the *Tur* here follows the opinion of the Me'iri, which applies the obligation to all festivals. In fact, according to the Me'iri, it would apply to Rosh HaShana and Yom Kippur even more than to the other festivals. The solemnity of the Ten Days of Repentance would obviously require (or at least render worthwhile) the observance of additional measures of stringency. (The *Tur*, ibid., in fact suggests a different law, or custom, that one should observe during the Ten Days of Repentance.)

Likewise, the *Shibbolei HaLeket* (283) quotes the law of R. Yitzḥak and adds that this law applies to every festival, "and even more to Rosh HaShana and Yom Kippur, which are days of judgment." He goes so far as to require the recitation of a *berakha* when one immerses in a *mikve* before Rosh HaShana and Yom Kippur as part of his process of teshuva (repentance). The *Tur* (606) records Rabbi Saadia Gaon's ruling that one recites a *berakha* when immersing in the *mikve* before Yom Kippur. The Rosh, however, strongly disagreed, arguing that there is no basis at all in the Talmud for this custom. If the custom is based on R. Yitzḥak's halakha, it certainly does not apply today, for R. Yitzḥak refers only to a situation where a person could totally purify himself. Nowadays, however, when we are all *teme'ei meit* and do not have the *para adumma* (red heifer) to rid ourselves of this status, this law certainly does not apply. Therefore, immersing in a *mikve* before Yom Kippur constitutes only a *minhag*, and no *berakha* should be recited.

The *Baḥ* (ad loc.) attempts to justify Rabbi Saadia's view, claiming that R. Yitzḥak's halakha resembles any other law instituted by *Ḥazal*, and thus indeed warrants the recitation of a *berakha*. Although one cannot achieve complete *tahara* nowadays, the *Baḥ* argues, one should purify himself as much as possible, and a *berakha* may be recited even on partial purification. The *Baḥ* advances these arguments to defend the opinion of Rabbi Saadia, but concedes that as a practical matter, in light of the *maḥaloket* involved, one should not recite a *berakha* when immersing before Yom Kippur.

We have seen that in the time of the *Mikdash*, there was an obligation on Yom Tov to refrain from *tuma* and become *tahor*, and the

Aḥaronim debated whether this applies on Rosh HaShana and Yom Kippur, and whether it applies nowadays. The generally accepted view is that of Rambam and Ramban, namely, that no such prohibition applies during the year. The *Sefer HaḤinnukh* (159) likewise writes, "There is no sin to become *tameh* even if one does so intentionally. One may not touch *kodashim* until he becomes *tahor*. In any case, every understanding person should distance himself from *tuma,* for the soul rises in a state of *tahara.*"

Parashat Balak

Cursing

In this week's *parasha,* we read that Balak, king of Moab, called upon Bilam to curse Am Yisrael. Bilam responded that he must wait and follow God's instructions. After Bilam was told not to curse this nation, "for it is blessed," he exclaimed (Bemidbar 23:8), "How can I curse whom God has not cursed," and thereby incurred the wrath of Balak. It seems that Bilam realized that cursing people has no real physical effect at all, while Balak thought that curses could be effective and enable him to overcome Am Yisrael.

The Torah (Shemot 22:27) forbade us to curse judges and princes, and elsewhere prohibits cursing parents, a prohibition punishable by death (Shemot 21:17). Another prohibition forbids cursing a deaf person (Vayikra 19:14). Commenting on this prohibition, Rashi (ad loc.) cites the *midrash halakha* that says this verse actually forbids cursing any living person. Ramban (ad loc.) explains that the Torah found it necessary to specify that one may not curse even a deaf person, who does not hear the curse and is therefore not angered or upset by it. *A fortiori,* it is forbidden to curse a person who can hear and may thus suffer humiliation and distress upon hearing someone curse him.

The *Sefer HaḤinnukh* (231) acknowledges that he does not fully understand how curses affect the victim, but does state quite clearly that a curse can cause harm. He therefore writes, "The root of the mitzva is that we should not verbally harm others, just as we may not harm them through actions."

The *Ḥinnukh* then cites Rambam's opinion that the reason for this mitzva is to eliminate the emotions of anger and vengeance from people's hearts. The *Ḥinnukh* deduces from this explanation that Rambam does not agree with his view, and maintains that curses have no effect at all. Therefore, this prohibition is merely an educational device to improve our character. The *Ḥinnukh* concludes that he is more comfortable with his own position, but nevertheless accepts the opinion of Rambam.

Rambam (*Guide for the Perplexed,* III:41) also writes that the masses consider verbal damage more severe than physical damage. He implies that although the masses indeed entertain such a notion, it is not true, and only due to this general impression is this prohibition unusually severe. Cursing is one of the only three instances of a transgression that involves no action but is nevertheless punishable by *makkot* (lashes).

Rambam (*Hilkhot Sanhedrin* 26:1) writes, "It appears to me" that one violates this prohibition even if he curses a minor. Had Rambam agreed with the *Ḥinnukh* that cursing causes actual damage, this halakha would be readily obvious, and Rambam would have no need to write "it appears to me." However, since in Rambam's view no actual damage is involved, and this transgression is due only to the humiliation suffered by the victim, one might have discounted the shame suffered by a minor and limited the prohibition to curses uttered against adults. Rambam therefore clarifies that in his opinion, the Torah forbids even cursing a minor. The reason for this law could be that the educational element of this mitzva applies to the sinner, and does not involve the victim at all. Alternatively, perhaps Rambam feels that a minor also experiences shame. The practical difference between these two explanations would arise in a case of a very small child too young to even be aware of his having been cursed. In the standard editions of Rambam, the text reads, "He who curses a minor who is shamed," whereas in the Frankel edition, the text merely says, "He who curses a minor." It seems that the variant texts revolve around our two possible interpretations.

Instinctively, we might prove that one is liable for cursing even a very small child from the fact that the prohibition applies to cursing a deaf person. In both cases the victim will not suffer humiliation as a result of the curse. Furthermore, if the law is educational in nature, it should not depend at all upon the identity of the "victim." On the other hand, Rambam codifies that one who curses a dead person is not liable (*Hilkhot Sanhedrin* 26:2). If the purpose of the law is to educate, what difference should it make whether the "victim" is alive or dead? Perhaps the answer is that when a person curses the dead, there is really no victim at all. Or, perhaps, Rambam felt that cursing a dead person is also forbidden, but there is a technical exemption from punishment in such a case.

We generally divide mitzvot into two categories: mitzvot between man and God, and mitzvot between man and his fellow man. The Vilna Gaon (*Aderet Eliyahu, Yeshayahu 1:2*) explains that there is also a third category: between man and himself. These are mitzvot whose purpose is to develop positive character traits. It seems that the *Ḥinnukh* classified the *kelala* prohibition as a mitzva between man and his fellow man, while according to Rambam, it is a mitzva between man and himself, geared to help refine our character.

The Mishna (Shevuot 35a) establishes that one may not curse even himself. The Gemara (36a) bases this halakha on the verse "Beware for yourself and guard your soul" (Devarim 4:9). According to the *Ḥinnukh*, it can be explained that since cursing may cause harm, halakha forbids even cursing oneself, as a person is not permitted to cause himself harm. However, according to Rambam, why should a person not be allowed to curse himself? After all, no damage is done. And if we assume that in terms of developing character traits, the "victim's" identity is of no consequence, then why do we need that verse in Sefer Devarim to introduce this prohibition? This source strongly implies that one may not curse himself because it may cause him physical harm.

Rabbi Moshe Feinstein (*Iggerot Moshe, Oraḥ Ḥayim,* III:390) explains that generally speaking, cursing does not really hurt anyone. Words are certainly capable of hurting people, but God would not heed the curse of someone who curses needlessly and thereby transgresses this prohibition. Rav Moshe therefore explained that the prohibition is intended to avoid humiliation and disgrace. However, Rav Moshe writes, a person who curses himself may indeed cause himself harm and will thus be punished by God for transgressing and cursing himself. The Torah forbade us from cursing ourselves because of the obligation to maintain our physical well-being, as indicated by the commandment "Beware for yourself and guard your soul."

If we accept Rav Moshe's reasoning, we should actually count the prohibition against cursing oneself as a separate mitzva, independent of the prohibition against cursing others. Rabbi Perlow (Rabbi Saadia Gaon's *Sefer HaMitzvot*, 11:81) cites a number of Rishonim who indeed count cursing oneself as a separate mitzva. In fact, as he mentions, the *Tashbetz* questions why Rambam did not do so. The *Tashbetz* (*Zohar HaRakia* 218) comments that although Rambam seemingly tried to avert this question by saying, "Cursing oneself is included in [the prohibition against] cursing others" (*Hilkhot Sanhedrin* 26:2), nevertheless, it seems from the Gemara that this constitutes a separate prohibition.

The *Or HaḤayim* (Bemidbar 23:8) adopts a median position, in between Rambam and the *Ḥinnukh*. He explains that under normal conditions, a curse is totally ineffective. Presumably, he would, therefore, explain the prohibition according to Rambam. He adds, however, that if a person is deserving of punishment, sometimes God, in His mercy, will postpone or even cancel the punishment. In that particular case, a human curse could incite God, as it were, to punish the cursed person in accordance with what he deserves.

Bilam could not curse the People of Israel at all according to Rambam, since no one can actually curse anyone. According to the *Ḥinnukh*, the explanation would be that even if a man's curse is effective, God's *berakha* overcomes everything.

Parashat Pinḥas

Inheritance

The last mitzva in Rambam's list of *mitzvot aseh* is the mitzva of inheritance. At first glance, this mitzva appears to belong to the group of procedural laws that Rambam counts as mitzvot even though there is no actual commandment involved. In previous chapters we have encountered examples of these mitzvot, such as the mitzvot of *shomerim* (*Sefer HaMitzvot, Aseh* 242–245) and of *tahara* and *tuma* (96–108).

Whether inheritance indeed belongs to this group would seem to depend on Rambam's two different formulations in defining this mitzva. In *Sefer HaMitzvot* and the introduction to *Hilkhot Naḥalot,* Rambam defines the mitzva as "the law of the order of inheritance." This would suggest that the mitzva is not an actual commandment, but rather a statement of fact, clarifying who owns a person's estate after his death. However, in the abbreviated list of mitzvot printed in the beginning of the *Mishneh Torah,* Rambam says that the mitzva is "to adjudicate the laws of inheritance." This formulation seems to refer to an obligation incumbent upon the courts to judge these laws according to the Torah's laws. Indeed, Rabbi Saadia Gaon enumerated inheritance in his list of mitzvot that are incumbent upon the community and *beit din* (rabbinical court). By contrast, the *Sefer HaḤinnukh* (400) held that there is a mitzva incumbent upon every person, male or female, to adhere to the laws of inheritance as specified by the Torah. If a person stipulates that someone other than his legal heir should inherit his property, he has violated this mitzva. While it is true that such a stipulation has no legal validity, the statement itself constitutes a transgression of this mitzva.

The *Ḥinnukh* emphasizes that the Torah did not intend to forbid disposing of one's possessions any way he sees fit. In truth, one may give away all his assets to anyone. The only limitation imposed by the Torah is that no one else may be designated as heir.

We read in *Parashat Pinḥas* that the daughters of Tzelofḥad claimed the inheritance of their father, since he had died without leaving sons. Apparently, it was self-understood and practiced that a son inherits his father's estate. Moshe brought their case before God, who then detailed all the laws of inheritance: "If a man should die and have no sons, his inheritance should be transferred to his daughter" (Bemidbar 17:8). Ramban (ad loc.) points out that fathers are not included at all in this list of inheritors. Ramban explains that all relationships are reciprocal, and it is therefore understood that if a son inherits his father, a father would likewise inherit his son.

It is interesting to note that the Torah never explicitly states that a son inherits his father's property. The fact that a daughter inherits when there are no sons naturally implies that the son is the primary heir. This led the Gaon of Rogatchov, Rabbi Yosef Rozen, and others to propose a theory suggesting that a son is not merely an heir. Rather, he actually fills his father's shoes and takes over in his stead. In his characteristic, succinct style, Rabbi Rozen (*Responsa Tzafenat Pane'aḥ* 313) cites many sources to prove this point. One of his proofs comes from the laws concerning the *eved ivri* (Jewish servant). The Gemara (Kiddushin 17b) explains that if the owner dies, ownership over the *eved* is not transferred to his heirs. If, however, the owner leaves behind a son, the *eved* continues to work as the son's servant. This clearly demonstrates a fundamental distinction between a son and other heirs, namely, that the son somehow assumes his father's status.

The Rogatchover uses this theory to explain the difference between the Jewish laws of inheritance and those that apply to non-Jews.

The Gemara (Yevamot 62a) says that inheritance laws do not apply to non-Jews. Rashi (ad loc.) explains that there is indeed a biblical law of inheritance for non-Jews, but the specific laws of inheritance given in our *parasha* do not apply to non-Jews. Therefore, there is no distinction between sons and daughters with respect to the inheritance of a gentile's estate: they inherit equally. Rabbi Rozen explained that the concept of the father and son merging into one identity can apply only to Jews, and not to non-Jews, since a Jew's relationship or identity with his father can never be changed. As we explained, a son is not merely a relative: he takes over in place of his father. A non-Jew, by contrast, is only related to his father, and in fact, this relationship can be terminated. If a non-Jew converts to Judaism, biological father and son are no longer related. In terms of relationship, sons and daughters are equal, and they therefore inherit their non-Jewish father equally.

The laws of inheritance extend beyond the issue of finances and estates. Rambam (*Hilkhot Kelei HaMikdash* 4:20) rules that if a king or *kohen gadol* dies, his heirs take his place if they are suitable for the position. This process follows the normal order of precedence, so naturally the son comes first. In the case of kingship, however, there is an unusual law that may relate to the theory advanced by Rabbi Rozen. A king of Davidic lineage need not be anointed, as the original appointment and anointing of King David continues forever from father to son (Rambam, *Hilkhot Melakhim* 1:7). Rambam (1:12) adds that in situations of political contention or war, we do anoint the son of a king, in order to settle the dispute. Thus, Shlomo was anointed due to the dispute that arose with Adoniya's attempt to claim the throne.

The Brisker Rav, Rabbi Y. Z. Soloveitchik, deduced from this that Shlomo really did not need anointing, as he was David's heir and the natural inheritor of the kingship. Since he received rights to the throne through the laws of inheritance, no anointing would have been necessary had it not been for Adoniya's challenge. Seemingly, however, Shlomo's appointment as David's successor was not a normal case of inheritance, given that Shlomo took over the monarchy while David was still alive. How could this situation be applied to the laws of inheritance, which obviously cannot take effect until after the relative's death? We might suggest that the laws of kingship are unique and not actually based on the laws of inheritance. However, the Rashba (Responsa, 1:300) ruled that an aging *ḥazan* may appoint his son to replace him, even if the community objects. Inasmuch as the laws of inheritance cannot be applied until death, the Rashba's ruling may be understood as a unique provision that a son fills his father's place even before the father's death, when he becomes incapacitated. Since, as we have seen, a son differs from other relatives and inherits by virtue of his assuming his father's position, this particular form of inheritance may, indeed, take effect even before the father's death. (This reading of the Rashba assumes that he applies this law only in the case of sons, and not in the situation of other heirs.)

After the laws of inheritance were given, the Torah relates that God told Moshe that he may see but not enter the Land of Israel, at which point Moshe asked God to appoint a leader in his stead. The Midrash, cited by Rashi (Bemidbar 27:16), explains the juxtaposition of these events. Once Moshe saw that daughters also inherit, he requested that his own children take his place. God replied, however, that Yehoshua, Moshe's loyal and diligent attendant, would succeed him, rather than one of his children.

The *Ḥatam Sofer* (Responsa, *Oraḥ Ḥayim* 12) derives from this midrash that the rabbinate is not automatically transferred from father to son. He assumes that Moshe's children were worthy and could succeed Moshe, but *keter Torah* (the crown of Torah) is not passed on to one's children. Rabbi Meir Dan Plotzki (*Keli Ḥemda, Parashat Pinḥas*), however, holds that Moshe's children could not take their father's place since they were born as non-Jews and then converted to Judaism. We have already seen that according to the Rogatchover, this special father–son relationship applies only in the case of Jews, and not to non-Jews or converts. Therefore, the fact that Moshe's children did not inherit his leadership does not prove that a son born to a Jewish father and mother does not automatically succeed his father's pulpit if he is worthy of that position. Many disputes have arisen and much literature has been written with regard to this issue.

Parashat Mattot

Annulment of Vows

All *nedarim* (vows) may be dissolved (*hattarat nedarim*) by a *beit din* (court) if it finds that the *neder* was made in error or ignorance. The Mishna (Ḥagiga 10a) states that annulment of vows is "floating in the air," meaning, as Rashi explains, that the biblical text contains only an allusion to this institution, as its laws and details were transmitted through the oral tradition.

The Torah did, however, state explicitly that a husband can annul the *nedarim* of his wife, a concept called *hafara* (Bemidbar 30:4–30). A husband may perform *hafara* only regarding *nedarim* that affect their marital relationship or may cause great anguish.

A father may likewise perform *hafara* on the *nedarim* of his daughter. Rambam (*Hilkhot Nedarim* 12:1) rules that there is no limitation at all on this halakha, and the father may revoke any *neder* taken by his daughter. Others (*Kesef Mishneh* and other commentators ad loc.) disagree and maintain that the father may revoke only *nedarim* that may cause great anguish.

Whereas *hattarat nedarim* completely revokes the neder as if it were never made, the effect of *hafara* is not as clear. There is considerable discussion as to whether *hafarat nedarim* annuls the *neder* retroactively, or merely cancels it from the moment of *hafara* on. According to the second perspective, the *neder* was valid until the actual moment of *hafara*. (See the discussion in Nazir 21b; the ruling of Rambam in *Hilkhot Nedarim* 13:2, 15; *Kesef Mishneh* ad loc.)

Rambam lists as one of the 613 mitzvot the mitzva "to judge cases of *hafarat nedarim*" (*Sefer HaMitzvot, Aseh* 95). He emphasizes that this does not mean that there is a commandment to annul vows. Rather, it simply means that there is a law that is to be implemented in such cases. Rambam also mentions the law of *hattarat nedarim*, in addition to *hafara*, but does not count it as a separate mitzva. Perhaps he feels that only mitzvot that are firmly rooted in the biblical text may be classified as mitzvot. *Hattara*, which, as we saw, has little textual basis in the Torah, cannot be counted.

Ramban (96) disagrees with Rambam and refuses to count *hafarat nedarim* as a mitzva. In the chapter on *Parashat Ḥukkat* we saw that Ramban consistently disputes Rambam's inclusion of this type of mitzva. Rambam counts mitzvot such as the laws of *tuma* and *tahara* (ritual purity), and Ramban argues that these are merely laws determining personal status, rather than mitzvot. He feels that only obligations and restrictions should be counted. Ramban writes that there is a positive obligation (*Aseh* 94) to fulfill *nedarim*, as well as a mitzva (*Lo Taaseh* 197) not to transgress a *neder*, and *hattara* and *hafara* are simply laws instructing us how to avoid the issue of *nedarim*, rather than mitzvot.

A different picture arises from Rambam's formulation in his *Mishneh Torah*. In his introduction to *Hilkhot Nedarim*, he describes the third mitzva of this section as follows: "To annul a vow or oath, and this is the law of *hafarat nedarim* explicated in the biblical text." This seems to suggest that there is a mitzva incumbent upon a father and husband to do *hafara*. If this is the case, would there also be a mitzva upon *beit din* to do *hattarat nedarim*? Rambam very possibly held that there is, indeed, such a mitzva, and for this reason emphasized that *hafara* "is explicit in the biblical text." He perhaps sought to indicate that *hattara*, too, constitutes an actual obligation, only it could not be counted among the 613 mitzvot because it has no explicit scriptural basis.

Interestingly, a variant text in the Frankel edition of Rambam adds a single letter to this passage, so that it reads, "the vow or oath shall be revoked." This reading would be more consistent with Rambam's comments in *Sefer HaMitzvot,* according to which this mitzva is not an actual obligation, but merely a law.

The *Semak* (107) seems to maintain that there is an actual mitzva and obligation to perform *hafara.* He quotes the verse "and her husband shall revoke it" (Bemidbar 30:14), which suggests an imperative quality to *hafara.* He also cites the comment of Bar Kappara recorded in the Gemara (Yevamot 109a) that a person should always "adhere" to three things: *ḥalitza* (the ritual for refusal of a levirate marriage), creating peace, and *hafarat nedarim.* We should note, however, that the *Semak* at times lists rabbinic laws in his list of mitzvot, and we therefore cannot conclude that he considers *hafara* a biblical obligation. However, his citation of the biblical text does suggest that he follows the literal meaning of the verse, namely, that a husband or father actual bears an obligation of *hafara.*

Rabbi Saadia Gaon takes the basic approach expressed in the *Semak* and develops it further. He lists two separate mitzvot of *hafara* (*Mitzvot Aseh* 103, 104): an obligation upon a husband, and a mitzva incumbent upon a father. It is noteworthy that Rabbi Saadia chooses not to include *hafarat nedarim* in his list of communal and court obligations. The fact that he instead includes it in his list of standard *mitzvot aseh* clearly shows that he disagrees with Rambam and Ramban, and views it as a personal obligation. Furthermore, if the mitzva were to deal with the laws of *hafara,* it would be counted as one mitzva. By counting two separate mitzvot of *hafara,* Rabbi Saadia makes it clear that he considers *hafara* to be an outright, personal obligation.

The *Shibbolei HaLeket* (317) records the practice to recite a *berakha* over *hattarat nedarim.* He strongly disagrees with this custom and writes, "The source of this custom is unknown. How did this custom arise? The person who vows is obligated to fulfill the *neder.* The fact that it can be annulled is not a positive mitzva that requires a *berakha;* it is not even a rabbinic obligation. It is merely a remedy prescribed by the Torah."

The *Shibbolei HaLeket* obviously agrees with the position of Rambam and Ramban and therefore sees no possibility of a *berakha.*

The custom of reciting a *berakha* would be far more compatible with the approach of Rabbi Saadia and the *Semak*: that there is a biblical, or at least a rabbinic, mitzva to perform *hafara* (and presumably *hattara*, as well).

We have thus seen at least four opinions as to the nature of the mitzva of *hafara* and *hattara*. Ramban feels that *hafara* and *hattara* should not be counted as mitzvot at all. Rambam (in *Sefer HaMitzvot*) views them as procedural laws, which he counts as one mitzva. The *Semak* holds that there is a mitzva, but it may be only rabbinic in origin. Finally, Rabbi Saadia feels that two separate mitzvot are to be counted, and we may reasonably assume that this view prompted the custom recorded by the *Shibbolei HaLeket* to recite a *berakha* over *hattarat nedarim*.

Parashat Masei

Living in the Land of Israel

This week's *parasha* includes the statement (Bemidbar 33:53) "You shall inherit the land and live within it." In addition to the inherent value of learning about any mitzva, there is an additional reason to study the mitzvot relating to the Land of Israel: doing so is a fulfillment of the requirement of *derishat Tziyyon,* seeking out Zion. The Gemara (Rosh HaShana 30a; Sukka 41a) derives this obligation from a verse: "She is Zion, there is none who seeks her out" (Yirmiyahu 30:17).

At the end of *Sefer HaMitzvot,* Ramban lists the mitzvot that he believes Rambam omitted from his list. The fourth of these is *yishuv Eretz Yisrael* (the mitzva to live in the Land of Israel): "The fourth mitzva is that we are commanded to inherit the land that God gave to our fathers, Avraham, Yitzḥak, and Yaakov, and not leave it in the hands of other nations or in desolation." Apparently, Ramban holds that there are two aspects to this mitzva. The first is the obligation to conquer the land and inherent it, and the second is to develop it and to live there. Strikingly, he quotes the rabbinic adage that "anyone who leaves the Land of Israel, it is considered as if he worshiped idolatry." He also says that living in Israel is equivalent to all the mitzvot. (This statement requires elaboration, as the Rabbis also make similar statements about several other mitzvot.)

There are halakhic implications to the statement that it is a mitzva to live in the Land of Israel. The Gemara (Gittin 8b) says that if one wants to buy land in Israel, he can ask a gentile to sign the deed on his behalf on Shabbat. The simplest understanding of the Gemara is that due to the importance of the mitzva of *yishuv Eretz Yisrael*, the Sages granted an exemption to the rabbinic ordinance of *amira lenokhri*, which prohibits asking gentiles to perform prohibited labor on Shabbat on behalf of Jews. However, the *Or Zarua* (Shabbat 2:84), argues that the dispensation was provided only because the particular situation discussed in the Gemara involves an additional leniency beyond *amira lenokhri*. He suggests that the Gemara was dealing with a case where the gentile would write in a manner prohibited only by rabbinic law. Therefore, this would be a case of a prohibition removed from a biblical violation by two separate rabbinic decrees (known by the term *shevut dishevut*). However, it would not be permitted to violate an actually rabbinic prohibition. Rabbi Avraham Yitzḥak HaKohen Kook (*Responsa Mishpat Kohen* 146) felt it was important to point out these limitations to someone who believed that the mitzva of *yishuv Eretz Yisrael* overrides biblical prohibitions.

Whatever the extent of the dispensation, for Ramban, one cannot extrapolate to other mitzvot that are not necessarily as important as *yishuv Eretz Yisrael*.

Many have questioned why Rambam did not include *yishuv Eretz Yisrael*, which Ramban thinks is one of the most important mitzvot, in his list. It should be pointed out that while he does not count it as one of the 613 mitzvot, in several places he does reflect on the importance of living in the Land of Israel. For example, he cites the principle, discussed above, that the Sages waived the prohibition of *amira lenokhri* for the sake of enabling *yishuv Eretz Yisrael*. Additionally, he quotes the gemara (Ketubbot 110b) that says one should choose to live in the Land of Israel, even in a town populated mainly by gentiles, rather than live in the Diaspora, even in a city populated primarily by Jews (*Hilkhot Melakhim* 5:12). These references strengthen the question greatly.

Fascinatingly, the answers offered range from those who argue that Rambam holds living in the Land of Israel is not important enough to be counted as a mitzva to those who think he left it off the list precisely because of its supreme importance. Some think that the mitzva applied only during the time when Yehoshua led the nation of Israel into the land. At that time, there was a mitzva to enter the land, conquer it, and endow it with holiness. As a mitzva that applied only in a particular generation, it would not be counted in the list of 613 eternal mitzvot. Others have suggested that there is indeed a mitzva to live in the Land of Israel nowadays, but it applies on the level of rabbinic, and not biblical, law. These two opinions are not mutually exclusive: it is possible to suggest that there was a biblical mitzva in the time of Yehoshua, and a rabbinic mitzva nowadays.

The extreme position on the other side is quoted by Rabbi Goren in the name of Rabbi Kook (see *Torat HaShabbat VeHaMoed*, pp. 149–154). Rabbi Kook claims that it was not counted as a mitzva because it is included in, and is the basis of, all the other mitzvot. Hence, it cannot be counted as a separate mitzva. This explanation is related to Rambam's position that a *lav shebikhlalot*, a mitzva that reflects a general principle and not a specific law, cannot be counted as a mitzva, as doing so would be like commanding us to be religious or holy: such a mitzva would have no specific content.

However, Rabbi Goren points out that it is difficult to apply that issue to this discussion. It is true that *yishuv Eretz Yisrael* is a foundation for all the mitzvot, to the point where Ramban (Vayikra 18:25) claims that mitzvot count fully only in Israel, and that they are observed in the Diaspora in order that we remember them when we return to the Land of Israel. Nevertheless, this fact alone doesn't make *yishuv Eretz Yisrael* into a *lav shebikhlalot*. After all, it would seem that belief in God is an even more fundamental prerequisite to the mitzvot, and nevertheless Rambam counts it as the first mitzva. Furthermore, the commandment to conquer and live in *Eretz Yisrael* has specific content, and thus should be counted. This is the critique Rabbi Goren raises against Rabbi Kook's explanation.

Rabbi Goren therefore advances another theory. He notes that Rambam (Ḥullin 7:6) claims that we are commanded to perform mitzvot only because they were given at Sinai, but not because of the commandments given to our forefathers. This is true even though some mitzvot are mentioned in the Sefer Bereshit, such as the commandment of procreation given to Adam, and circumcision, given to Avraham. In order for these mitzvot to remain binding upon the Jewish people, they had to be given again at Sinai. Therefore, in the introductory principles to *Sefer HaMitzvot,* Rambam writes that only mitzvot given at Sinai are counted in the 613. However, Rabbi Goren claims that there is one exception to this rule, one mitzva that remains obligatory because it was commanded to the forefathers prior to Sinai and yet remains in force to this day: *yishuv Eretz Yisrael.* The reason for this is that the Torah enjoins us numerous times to inherit the land that was given to Avraham, Yitzḥak, and Yaakov: that is the very nature of the obligation. Therefore, it is in fact a biblical obligation, but since this mitzva was not commanded at Sinai, it does not count in the list of 613. It therefore turns out that according to Rabbi Goren's interpretation of Rambam, there are actually a total of 614 mitzvot!

However, this position is difficult to accept. According to Rambam, the idea that no commandments given prior to Sinai remain binding afterwards is a fundamental principle. Additionally, as is clear from the verse quoted at the beginning of this chapter, the command was repeated after the giving of the Torah at Sinai, and therefore it seems it should be considered a formal mitzva.

Let us therefore explore another theory, suggested by Rabbi Yehuda Gershuni, a student of Rabbi Kook, in his book *Kol Tzofayikh* (pp. 126–29). He explains that there are values that the Torah strongly endorses, and that are nonetheless not considered formal mitzvot. For example, the prohibition to cause pain to animals (*tzaar baalei ḥayim*) is certainly a value that the Torah endorses, although according to the Radbaz (Responsa, V:168) there is no formal positive or negative commandment related to it. Rabbi Gershuni makes a similar argument about living in the Land of Israel: it is a Torah value, but not a formal mitzva.

The reason for this, according to Rabbi Gershuni, is that there are things that are so basic to the human psyche that the Torah does not need to legislate them. For example, the Torah never commands us to eat or drink. The *Meshekh Ḥokhma* (Bereshit 9:7) remarks similarly about the mitzva of procreation (*peru urevu*). The accepted halakha, based on Yevamot 65b, is that women are exempt from this obligation.

This is certainly an oddity, given that men cannot fulfill their obligation without the participation of women. The *Meshekh Ḥokhma* suggests that the Torah did not need to command women to have children, because they have an instinctive desire to do so (this idea is apparently based on his estimation that the maternal instinct is stronger than the paternal one). In yet another example, Ramban (Shemot 21:9) claims that the primary obligation of a husband to take care of his wife is not a formal mitzva because it is a natural instinct to do so (nevertheless, Ramban acknowledges that there is a rabbinic ordinance obligating a husband to provide for his wife because there are some people who, unfortunately, do not abide by this fundamental instinct). Similarly, Rabbi Gershuni argues that it is a natural instinct for all nations to want a homeland. It is an inalienable right of a nation to have a country of its own, and thus natural for the Jews to want to live in their homeland, the Land of Israel. Therefore, although it is undeniably a Torah value, to the point where certain rabbinic prohibitions can be suspended in order to fulfill it, Rambam did not count it as a mitzva.

Sefer Devarim

Parashat Devarim

"You Shall Not Fear Any Man"

At the beginning of the Sefer Devarim, Moshe recounts how he set up a court system during the Jewish people's travels through the wilderness. Later, in *Parashat Shofetim*, Moshe introduces the actual mitzva of appointing judges and the unique status of the courts in the Land of Israel. However, certain requirements and obligations with which judges are charged are already conveyed in our *parasha*. The judges were instructed to listen carefully and judge righteously, and Moshe forbade them to show favoritism or to be afraid of any person (Devarim 1:16–17).

Rambam lists a *mitzvat lo taaseh* (276) in connection with the court system based on these verses in *Parashat Devarim*: a judge may not be fearful of anyone during the process of judicial decision-making. He must judge the particular case and reach his conclusion based purely on legal considerations, paying no attention to any possible danger he or his family may incur as a result of an honest ruling.

Rambam quotes the *Sifrei*'s statement that a judge may not express any fear that a litigant might kill him or his son, or burn his produce or uproot his plants.

In general, it is difficult to understand how the Torah could ever command someone not to be afraid. We might explain this prohibition by drawing a parallel to another mitzva (*Lo Taaseh* 58) listed by Rambam that seemingly forbids the experience of fear: we must not be afraid of infidels and must not flee from them during wartime. The Steipler Rav (*Birkat Peretz*, p. 80) writes that the Torah did not actually forbid someone to be afraid. Rather, the Torah simply mandated that a person should not dwell upon his fears and cause himself to panic. He further notes that a person who experiences fear may go home before the war begins and thereby avoid transgressing this prohibition.

Similarly, in our case, Rambam (*Hilkhot Sanhedrin* 22:1) rules that if one of the litigants is a particularly difficult person, a judge may refuse to preside over the case. Even if the court has heard the case but has yet to reach a conclusion, a judge may refuse to continue in the case. It is only in a situation where the judge has decided but has not yet announced his decision that he is forbidden to abandon the case.

Why doesn't this prohibition apply before the case begins? The *Taz* (*Ḥoshen Mishpat* 12:2) explains that this prohibition applies only to judges, and a person cannot be considered a judge until he has heard and decided the particular case. The *Taz* apparently feels that there is no direct obligation on any person to serve as a judge, even if he is a great *talmid ḥakham*. Although the Gemara (Avoda Zara 19b) sharply castigates those capable of deciding Jewish law who refrain from doing so, the *Taz* perhaps limits that passage to cases of ritual law. The obligation of appointing judges and serving in court is a communal, rather than personal, responsibility, and thus no one individual bears a personal obligation to serve in this capacity. Hence, the prohibition against fearing a litigant does not apply until an individual accepts upon himself the status of judge.

Rambam (*Hilkhot Sanhedrin* 22:1) adds that a communally appointed judge may not under any circumstances decline to hear a case. According to the logic of the *Taz*, it is clear that his appointment automatically yields the formal halakhic status of a judge even before the particular case has begun. It is therefore forbidden for him to refuse to hear a case due to fear.

Alternatively, we might explain that fear is forbidden only if it could cause the judge to decide the case unfairly. If he has yet to hear the arguments or has not determined his ruling, he is still entitled to excuse himself. Once, however, he has reached a conclusion, his refusal to render a decision due to fear amounts to dishonest handling of the case, and he thus violates this prohibition. When it comes to a communally appointed judge, he has already obligated himself to adjudicate all cases and thus does not reserve the right to refuse to hear any case.

One important question, however, remains: why must a judge be prepared to risk his life, or even his property, to preside over a case? The *Imrei Bina* (*Ḥoshen Mishpat* 19) discusses at length the broader issue of how much money a person must be prepared to forfeit in order to avoid transgressing a biblical prohibition. In this context, he cites the *Baḥ*'s ruling that when a judge faces the actual threat of financial loss, he is not required to hear the case. The prohibition refers only to a case where the litigant is difficult to control, but would not actually cause damage. On the other hand, as the *Imrei Bina* cites, the *Shevut Yaakov* disagreed with the *Baḥ* and claimed that this mitzva requires a judge to hear a case even if he might incur actual financial loss.

Needless to say, according to the *Baḥ*, in a situation of potential mortal danger this prohibition would be suspended, as the interest in preserving life overrides all Torah laws with the exception of the three cardinal sins (idolatry, adultery, and murder). The Rema (ibid.) records the custom in his day to ignore court cases involving sinners who might besmirch the judge before the local authorities and thus endanger his life.

Others, however, appear to maintain that this particular law overrides physical and even mortal danger. Rabbi Aharon Wolkin (*Zekan Aharon* 126) argues that the Torah here clearly intends to require a judge to risk potential danger. There are certain mitzvot, such as *brit mila*, that by their nature entail some physical danger, and thus the fact that the Torah commanded them clearly shows that we must accept some risk to perform these mitzvot. Rabbi Zalman Sorotzkin (*Mozenayim LaMishpat*, *Ḥoshen Mishpat* 12) likewise implies that a judge would actually have to sacrifice his life to avoid this transgression. He claims that if a violent person forces a judge to rule in his favor, the judge's acquiescence would constitute a falsification of Torah, which is akin to uprooting the principles of Judaism. The *Yam shel Shlomo* (Bava Kamma 6), in a different context, rules that falsification of the Torah is subject to the rule of *yehareg ve'al yaavor* (one must give up his life rather than commit the sin). Therefore, a judge may not distort his ruling under any circumstances, even to save his life.

Of course, majority opinion follows the view of the *Baḥ* and Rema, namely, that this law is suspended in cases of an actual threat or danger to life.

A subsidiary of this law involves a student who observes his teacher judging a case and has a relevant point to make. If he remains silent out of fear of his teacher, he transgresses this prohibition. In this case, the prohibition is not restricted to judges, but rather includes everyone. Although a student is ordinarily not allowed to disagree with his teacher (Rambam, *Hilkhot Talmud Torah* 5:6), he must, nevertheless, express his opinion. It appears that presenting his viewpoint in a tactful, respectful manner does not violate the prohibition against contradicting one's teacher. Indeed, the Gemara (Kiddushin 32a) prescribes the method by which a child may and should inform his parents of Torah laws of which they are ignorant. Presumably, one may, and in fact should, state his view to his teacher, provided that this is done with proper respect and reverence.

Parashat Va'etḥanan

Writing and Affixing a Mezuza

The first *parasha* of *Keriat Shema,* which appears in *Parashat Va'etḥanan,* contains the mitzvot of tefillin and mezuza. The Torah does not mention explicitly that we must write tefillin, but rather states that we must tie "these words" (of *Shema*) on our arms and have them on our heads (literally, "between our eyes"). Thereafter, the Torah requires that we write a mezuza on our doorposts. As opposed to tefillin, regarding which the Torah never specifies the obligation of writing, when it comes to mezuza the Torah says, "You shall write them." The Gemara (Menaḥot 34a) raises the possibility that the mitzva requires actually writing the mezuza on the stones of the house. The Gemara proceeds to present two proofs that a mezuza should be written on parchment, and not directly on the house. First, writing a mezuza parallels the mitzva to write a *sefer Torah,* which obviously requires parchment. Second, the fine art of writing a mezuza practically cannot be done on wood or stone.

Now that we have ascertained that a mezuza should be written on parchment, let us examine why the Torah specified that we write a mezuza, while in the context of tefillin it speaks only of tying and placing. One approach might be to deny this assumption altogether. The Gemara (Gittin 45b) indicates that the laws of writing tefillin correspond to the halakhot concerning writing mezuzot. If so, then it would seem that the clause "you shall write them" (Devarim 6:9) refers to both tefillin and mezuzot. According to this, there is no distinction between the Torah's formulation of the mitzva of tefillin and that of mezuza.

Alternatively, however, one might suggest that the specific mention of writing in the context of mezuza bears particular halakhic significance. In describing the mitzva of sukka, the *She'iltot* of Rabbi Aḥai Gaon (169) writes, "The Jewish people must make a sukka and dwell in it for seven days." The Netziv (*Haamek She'ala* ad loc.) pointed out that these two verbs ("make" and "dwell") imply a dual aspect to this mitzva – a requirement to build a sukka and to dwell in the sukka. Indeed, the Torah writes, "You shall make *Ḥag HaSukkot* for yourself" (Devarim 16:13) – which likely refers to an obligation to "make" (build) a sukka. Although the mitzva of dwelling in the sukka is obviously the primary aspect of this mitzva, nevertheless, making the sukka also constitutes a mitzva.

The Netziv adds that this principle applies anytime the Torah makes specific mention of the preparatory stages of a given mitzva. The Gemara (Menaḥot 42a) discusses the issue of reciting a *berakha* when making tzitzit. The Gemara says that just as there is no *berakha* on writing tefillin and mezuzot, so is there no *berakha* recited when making tzitzit. The Netziv points out that nowhere does the Gemara even raise the possibility of reciting a *berakha* when preparing a lulav or making a shofar. The Gemara discusses such a possibility only regarding mitzvot whose preparation also involves a biblical command. The Torah writes, "They shall make tzitzit for themselves" (Bemidbar 15:38), but never does it say, "Make a lulav." The Gemara therefore reasoned that where there is a specific commandment to "make" the mitzva, one recites a *berakha* on the preparation of the mitzva. The Gemara concludes, however, that the fact that there is no *berakha* recited over the preparation of tefillin and mezuza indicates that even when the Torah mentions the preparation, no *berakha* is required over the preparatory stages. The *Tosafot* (ad loc.) note that the Yerushalmi disagrees with the

Bavli and indeed requires a *berakha* on making tzitzit, building a sukka, and writing tefillin. However, no one entertains the notion of reciting a *berakha* on the preparation of a mitzva unless the Torah specifically mentions the preparation.

This principle could explain why the Torah uses the verb "you shall write them" in the context of mezuzah: in order to indicate that there is a mitzva – albeit not the main mitzva – to write a mezuza. Although clearly the primary obligation is to place the mezuza on the doorpost, the preparatory stage of writing a mezuza may also constitute a mitzva act.

We should note, however, that this analogy between tefillin, mezuza, and sukka becomes somewhat questionable in light of the *She'iltot*'s (145) own description of the mitzva of mezuza. He writes, "The People of Israel are required to affix a mezuza to their doors." He describes the obligation solely in terms of affixing mezuzot, not writing mezuzot, seemingly implying that there is not, in fact, any mitzva involved in writing a mezuza. Rambam (in his list of mitzvot printed in the introduction to *Mishneh Torah*) similarly writes that the mitzva is to "affix a mezuza on the doors of our gates." He mentions nothing at all of an obligation to write the mezuza. Rambam (*Hilkhot Mezuza* 5:7) also writes that "one recites the *berakha* before affixing it to the door… one does not recite a *berakha* at the time of writing it, as the placing of the mezuza is the mitzva." Thus, both the *She'iltot* and Rambam do not speak at all of any mitzva involved in the writing of the mezuza. It therefore seems difficult to explain why the Torah specifically says, "You shall write them," seemingly requiring that we write a mezuza.

Other Rishonim, however, clearly held that there is a mitzva to write the mezuza. *Targum Onkelos* and the *Targum* of Yonatan b. Uzziel both translate the verse as, "You shall write the mezuza and affix it." The *Tur* and *Shulḥan Arukh* both codified the halakha in accordance with the *targumim*. And although the *Tur* and *Shulḥan Arukh* agree with Rambam's view that no *berakha* is recited on writing the mezuza, they omit Rambam's explanation that "the placing of the mezuza is the mitzva." They seem to hold that although there is indeed a mitzva to write a mezuza, a *berakha* is recited only on the primary component of the mitzva, namely, affixing it to the doorpost.

One practical difference between these two opinions would seem to be whether it is better for a person to write the mezuza himself or appoint a *shaliaḥ* (agent) to write it for him. If writing the mezuza constitutes its own mitzva, then it would be preferable to write the mezuza personally, rather than commission a *sofer* (scribe) to write one on his behalf.

Rabbi Elimelekh Vinter (*Minḥat Elimelekh*, p. 152) raises another possible intriguing ramification of this issue. A woman is exempt from tefillin (Kiddushin 34a) and therefore may not write tefillin (Rambam, *Hilkhot Tefillin* 1:13; *Tur* and *Shulḥan Arukh, Oraḥ Ḥayim* 39:1). There is considerable controversy concerning the issue of a woman's obligation to write a *sefer Torah* (see *Minḥat Ḥinnukh* 613; *The 613th Commandment* by Rabbi J. Simcha Cohen, Northvale, NJ, 1994, chapter 4 and the sources quoted there).

Rambam (ibid.) rules that a woman may not write a *sefer Torah*, and the *Shulḥan Arukh* (*Yoreh De'ah* 281:3) rules accordingly. The *Tur*, however, omits this halakha, an omission interpreted by the *Derisha* (a commentary on the Tur, ad loc.) as indicating that the *Tur* allows having a *sefer Torah* written by a woman. When it comes to mezuza, the Gemara (Berakhot 20a) establishes that women are included in this obligation. Nevertheless, Rambam (ibid.) disqualifies women from writing a mezuza. In his view, a woman's obligation is simply to affix the mezuza; writing it, however, is not part of the mitzva. But the *Tur* and *Shulḥan Arukh*, as we saw, maintain that writing the mezuza also constitutes a mitzva. It would follow, then, that according to the *Tur* and *Shulḥan Arukh*, a woman may write a mezuza. Indeed, neither the *Tur* nor the *Shulḥan Arukh* makes any mention of a woman's disqualification from writing mezuzot.

We should note, however, that nowhere in the standard halakhic works on mezuza (e.g., *Ḥovat HaDar* by Y. Y. Blau) or in the books written specifically on women's role in halakha (e.g., *Halikhot Beitah* by D. Orbach, *Otzar Dinim* by Y. Yosef) do we find any allusion to such a notion. In fact, these works raise the issue of whether a woman may even affix a mezuza on her own house, and Rabbi D. Orbach rules that it is preferable for a man to do so (*Halikhot Beitah*, p. 401 and note 32). Others (cited in *Halikhot Beitah*, ibid.; cf. letter of approbation by Rabbi

Vozner for *Ḥovat HaDar*) disagree, arguing that it is inconceivable that a woman is obligated in this mitzva but may not perform it. In any event, this entire discussion appears to negate the possibility of allowing a woman to write a mezuza, as the question focuses entirely on her affixing the mezuza.

In conclusion, it is worth citing the comments of the *Tur* (*Yoreh De'ah* 285) concerning the particular importance of the mitzva of mezuza:

> One should be very meticulous about this…as the mezuza contains the unity of God and whenever one enters or leaves he will remember that unity.… Moreover, the house is protected by it.… Nevertheless, one's intent should be only to fulfill the commandment of the Creator as we were commanded.

Parashat Ekev

Birkat HaMazon

B*irkat HaMazon* (Grace After Meals) is counted as a mitzva by all the Rishonim who listed the mitzvot. The biblical origin of the obligation to recite *Birkat HaMazon* emerges clearly from the Torah's comment in *Parashat Ekev* (Devarim 8:10) "You will eat and be satiated, and you shall say a blessing to Hashem, your God, for the good land that He has given you." Of course, the specific text of the *berakhot* is not ordained by the Torah, but the general content is, apparently, biblically mandated. A *baraita* (Berakhot 48b) establishes that the various clauses of this verse refer to the different components of *Birkat HaMazon*. The phrase "You will eat and be satiated" refers to *Birkat HaZan*, the first *berakha* of *Birkat HaMazon*; "to Hashem, your God" refers to *zimmun* (*Birkat HaMazon* as said by a group); "land" alludes to the second *berakha*, known as *Birkat HaAretz*; "good" refers to *Boneh Yerushalayim* (the third *berakha*); and "that He has given you" refers to *HaTov VeHaMetiv* (the fourth *berakha*). However, the Gemara (ibid.) then cites R. Naḥman's view that Moshe instituted *Birkat HaZan* when the Jewish people ate manna, Yehoshua enacted *Birkat HaAretz* when they entered the land, David and Shlomo instituted *Boneh Yerushalayim*, and *HaTov VeHaMetiv* was instituted by the scholars of Yavne.

There is a similar discussion with regard to the obligation of daily prayer. Rambam (*Hilkhot Tefilla* 1:1) considers daily prayer a Torah obligation. While it is true that it was the *Anshei Keneset HaGedola* who formulated the text of our prayers, the structure of prayer, according to Rambam, is biblically ordained. Rambam (1:2) writes, "The obligation of this mitzva is as follows: A person must supplicate and pray daily. He should describe the praise of God and then ask [God] for his needs.... Afterwards he should praise and thank God for the bounty." The *Or Same'aḥ* (ad loc.) and others have attempted to show the biblical source of this required structure of praise, supplication, and thanksgiving.

We might, therefore, explain the obligation of *Birkat HaMazon* along similar lines. The basic thematic structure of food, Land of Israel, Jerusalem, and the Davidic monarchy is required by the Torah, and Moshe, Yehoshua, David, Shlomo, and the scholars of Yavne merely formulated the exact text. Of course, this would assume that *Birkat HaZimmun* and *HaTov VeHaMetiv* also are of biblical origin, but the Gemara (Berakhot 46b) ultimately comes to the conclusion that *HaTov VeHaMetiv* was added by the Rabbis. We still could argue that the three first *berakhot,* based on the verse in the Torah, constitute a biblical requirement, but the Gemara speaks of a biblical source of the other *berakhot* as an *asmakhta* (subtle allusion in the text, rather than an outright source).

Indeed, the Ritva, Rabbi Aharon HaLevi, and other Rishonim seem to take this approach. They note the problem that whereas the syntax of the verse implies that the *berakhot* are biblically required, they were instituted much later. The Ritva (Berakhot 48b) explains, "*Birkat HaMazon* has some biblically mandated text, as one must recite a *berakha* on food and mention the land and Jerusalem. It thus turns out that all are based on the Torah. However, if one recites those components in a different manner from that prescribed by Moshe, Yehoshua, etc., he still fulfills the biblical command." It is noteworthy that the Ritva omits any mention of *zimmun* or *HaTov VeHaMetiv,* even though the Gemara includes them, as well, in the biblical source. He likely held that these *berakhot* are entirely rabbinic in origin, as suggested above.

The three components mentioned earlier are therefore biblically mandated, and must be included in *Birkat HaMazon* in order for one to fulfill the Torah obligation. It is possible that the biblical command would also include a requirement to mention these three themes in three separate *berakhot*. The Gemara (Berakhot 16a) formulates an abbreviated form of *Birkat HaMazon* for salaried workers, so that they would not have to take too much time from work to recite *Birkat HaMazon*. This abbreviated form incorporates the same three themes into two *berakhot*, rather than three. The *Tosafot* (ad loc.) ask how the Gemara permits workers to dispense with a biblical requirement, and they answer, quite simply, that the Sages indeed have the power to abrogate a law of the Torah. The *Tosafot* clearly felt that the three *berakhot* themselves, and not merely their content, are required by Torah law.

Although this opinion holds that the mitzva requires three *berakhot*, it still constitutes only a single mitzva. This may be compared to the mitzva of taking a lulav, which actually consists of four components – the lulav, hadasim, aravot, and etrog – but is still considered one mitzva. Rambam (*Sefer HaMitzvot*, principle 9) gives other examples of mitzvot that consist of several elements (such as tzitzit on the four corners of a garment) but are nevertheless counted as a single mitzva.

Rabbi Yosef Karo (*Beit Yosef, Oraḥ Ḥayim* 191) argues with the *Tosafot* and claims that the Torah does not require any specific number of *berakhot*. He understands Rambam's definition of the mitzva as requiring only that one recite a *berakha* after eating. He apparently felt that the entire section of the Gemara that shows the source for each component is an *asmakhta*, rather than an actual biblical source for each of the *berakhot*. According to this, any form of *berakha* recited would actually fulfill the biblical requirement.

The Mishna (Berakhot 20a) states unequivocally that women are required to recite *Birkat HaMazon*. The Gemara (20b) raises the issue of whether women are required to do so by force of Torah law or rabbinic enactment. Rashi explains that since *Birkat HaMazon* includes a section about the Land of Israel, perhaps women, who did not receive a share in the land, are exempt from the biblical requirement. The *Tosafot*, however, reject this interpretation in light of the fact that the daughters of Tzelofḥad received their father's share in the land. Clearly, then, women also have at least the potential to receive a portion of the land. Moreover, *kohanim* also did not receive a share and yet they certainly must recite *Birkat HaMazon* at the level of Torah law. The *Tosafot* therefore explain that since women are exempt from the mitzvot of *brit mila* and Torah, two integral themes of the second *berakha* of *Birkat HaMazon,* the Torah obligation perhaps does not apply to them.

The Gemara then asks, once it's been established that women are required to recite *Birkat HaMazon,* what difference does it make whether they are obligated on the level of Torah law? The Gemara explains that this issue will determine whether a woman can recite the *berakha* and fulfill the obligation on behalf of men. Since men must recite *Birkat HaMazon* according to Torah law, women can exempt them only if they share the same level of obligation.

Rabbi Yeḥezkel Landau (*Tzelaḥ,* Berakhot, ibid.) questions why the Gemara had to resort to this issue as the practical difference between a Torah obligation and a rabbinically ordained requirement. After all, a general rule in halakha dictates that in a situation of doubt, one must act stringently with regard to biblical law but may be lenient when it comes to a rabbinic law. Why didn't the Gemara point to this classic principle as the practical ramification of the issue concerning the nature of a woman's obligation of *Birkat HaMazon*? Rabbi Landau suggests that since, as the Gemara mentions, Moshe composed the first *berakha* of *Birkat HaMazon* in the desert when the Jewish people ate manna, this *berakha* is certainly obligatory upon women. They, too, were obliged to thank the Almighty for sustaining them in the wilderness. The Gemara questioned only the origin of women's obligation to recite the second *berakha,* the blessing over the land, *brit mila,* and Torah. Therefore, in a case of doubt, a woman must certainly recite *Birkat HaMazon* in order to fulfill her biblical requirement, and for this reason the Gemara had to search for another practical ramification of this issue. Although Rabbi Landau ultimately dismisses this theory, we nevertheless see from his discussion an interesting conceptual difference between the various sections of *Birkat HaMazon.*

Parashat Re'eh

Tzedaka

We are obligated to be more meticulous about the mitzva of tzedaka than any other *mitzvat aseh*, since tzedaka is the identifying characteristic of the descendants of our father Avraham" (Rambam, *Hilkhot Mattenot Aniyim* 10:1).

The Torah told us that there will always be needy people, and we are required to supply them with their needs. In fact, the Torah forbade us to "harden our hearts" or "close our hands"; rather, we must give tzedaka (Devarim 15:7–11). Rambam (*Sefer HaMitzvot*), therefore, enumerated two separate mitzvot. There is a *mitzvat aseh* (no. 195) to give tzedaka and there is a *mitzvat lo taaseh* (no. 232) not to withhold tzedaka. Although Rambam combines the prohibitions against "hardening our hearts" and "closing our hands" as one commandment, the *Behag* and others count them as two separate *mitzvot lo taaseh*.

The Gemara (Bava Batra 8b) tells us that Rava coerced R. Natan to give tzedaka. The *Tosafot* (ad loc.) ask: How could he force someone to fulfill this mitzva? There is a general principle that *beit din* does not force someone to fulfill a mitzva whose reward is directly mentioned in the Torah. Since the Torah (Devarim 15:10) said that there is a special blessing bestowed upon a person who gives tzedaka, it follows that there should not be any coercion to fulfill this mitzva.

Rabbenu Tam answers that Rava did not actually coerce R. Natan: he merely persuaded him to fulfill this obligation. He also suggests that there may have been a communal commitment to give tzedaka, and the members of the community had accepted upon themselves that they may be coerced to give tzedaka. A third answer, proposed by the Ri, is that one may not coerce someone to fulfill a *mitzvat aseh* whose reward is specified. However, in the case of tzedaka, there is also a *lo taaseh* (or perhaps even two separate prohibitions) to refrain from giving tzedaka, and one may use coercion to avoid transgression of a *lo taaseh*. The Ritva answers the question by saying that *beit din* may coerce someone to fulfill any *mitzvat aseh*. The rule means only that *beit din* is not *required* to force people to fulfill mitzvot whose rewards are specifically noted. However, they may certainly do so if they feel such a course of action is warranted.

Many other answers have been suggested by Rishonim and Aḥaronim. The Ritva (Ketubbot 49b) says that we may coerce people to give tzedaka since the poor are in dire need. Rabbi Moshe Goldstein, the editor of the Mossad HaRav Kook edition of the Ritva, said that this may be in keeping with the Ritva's opinion that the *beit din* always may coerce people to fulfill any mitzva, but are not required to use force in a mitzva that has a reward attached to it. However, whenever there is a special need, as in the case of the poor, the *beit din* should coerce people to fulfill their obligations. It would follow that in the case of honoring one's parents (which also is a mitzva that has a reward mentioned specifically), the Ritva would think that the *beit din* should coerce a recalcitrant child if the parents are in dire need.

The Ritva adds that we have a specific commandment to force people to give tzedaka. The Gemara (Rosh HaShana 6a), referring to the phrase "You shall keep your statements and do [them]" (Devarim 23:24), says specifically that the *beit din* is required to employ force in connection with tzedaka. Although the Torah was relating to a case where the person had taken a vow to give tzedaka, the Ritva said that this teaches us that coercion may be used in general for tzedaka since the indigent are in dire straits.

The Radvaz (*Hilkhot Mattenot Aniyim* 7:10) and the *Ketzot HaḤoshen* (39:1) raise the possibility that there is an actual monetary obligation to support poor people, and not only a mitzva. Therefore, we may force people to give tzedaka, just as we may force people to pay their debts.

There are many obvious practical distinctions between the various explanations of the Gemara. For instance, if it was a local *minhag* that a particular community had accepted, it would apply only in communities that accept a similar custom. Conversely, according to Rabbenu Tam, only persuasion would be allowed: it would be prohibited to use actual coercion or to take money by force.

Rambam (*Hilkhot Mattenot Aniyim* 7:10) rules that if someone does not want to give tzedaka, or does not give an amount commensurate with his wealth, the *beit din* should coerce him even by use of physical force. They also may take his property from him in his presence and give it to the needy. The *Baḥ* (*Tur, Ḥoshen Mishpat* 248) interprets this statement to mean that the court may force someone *even* in his presence: they need not wait for him to do it himself. If he were not present, they could certainly take his property and give tzedaka. This explanation is based on the question of whether a person fulfills the mitzva of charity if his money is taken by force (see *Shulḥan Arukh, Yoreh De'ah* 249:2; *Taz* and Gra ad loc.) Because of this question, we might have thought that we should not forcibly take his property if he is present and could give it himself. However, if he is not present, the *Baḥ* feels that the court may certainly seize his possessions in order to fulfill his obligation of tzedaka.

The *Beit Meir* (*Even HaEzer* 71) disagrees with the *Baḥ*, and interprets Rambam in the opposite manner: the court may take someone's property for tzedaka *only* if he is present. (The *Arukh HaShulḥan, Yoreh De'ah* 248:5, cites various opinions regarding this issue.)

This dispute probably revolves around the question of why *beit din* coerces one to give tzedaka. If this is an example of the general rule that they are to use coercion for certain mitzvot, it would seem likely that this could be done only in the presence of the obliged donor. However, according to the understanding of the *Ketzot*, namely, that there is an actual monetary obligation, this obviously could be collected even if the owner were not present.

Rambam explains that there is a great mitzva to accompany travelers. He writes (*Hilkhot Evel* 14:3) that *beit din* may coerce people to accompany guests just as we coerce people to give tzedaka. The comparison seems to indicate that the concept of coercion is due to the nature of the mitzva, and not due to a financial obligation. This seems to support the opinion of the *Beit Meir*, as opposed to the *Baḥ*.

The Gemara (Bava Batra 9a) says that someone who is instrumental in getting another to give tzedaka is actually greater than the person who gives it. Rambam (*Hilkhot Mattenot Aniyim* 10:6) seems to cite the Gemara, but changes the language and style somewhat. He writes, "He who coerces others to give tzedaka and causes them to do so has a greater reward than the actual donor."

Parashat Shofetim

Appointing a King

When the Jewish people entered the Land of Israel, they were commanded to fulfill three mitzvot: to appoint a king, destroy Amalek, and build the *Beit HaMikdash* (Sanhedrin 20b, as codified by Rambam, *Hilkhot Melakhim* 1:1). Rambam goes on to say that the mitzva of appointing a king precedes and is a prerequisite for the other two mitzvot.

It has been asked why God was angered at the people's request to appoint a king in the time of Shmuel. Since there is a mitzva to appoint a king, it seems they were performing God's will (see I Shmuel 8:4–8; *Sifrei* Devarim 17:28; Rambam, ibid. 1:2; Me'iri Horayot 11b). Rambam answers that their request was not motivated by a desire to fulfill the mitzva. Rather, it was indicative of a rebellion against God, as it says, "They despised Me" (I Shmuel 8:7). Therefore, their request was considered improper.

The Me'iri (ibid.) suggests that kingship is reserved for the tribe of Yehuda. Apparently, at that particular time, there was no appropriate candidate from this tribe to serve as king. Therefore, the request to appoint a king at that time was improper. God's response was that they may appoint a temporary king who could rule until a suitable person from *shevet Yehuda* would emerge.

In the Gemara (Sanhedrin 20b), there are three opinions regarding Jewish kingship in general. R. Neḥemya said that the entire issue of appointing a king was written in order to alert the community to the dangers inherent in monarchy. The mitzva is phrased as a conditional statement that is not obligatory: "When you enter the land that Hashem, your God, is giving to you, and possess it and settle in it, and then say, 'I wish to appoint a king'" (Devarim 17:14). According to this reading, there is no mitzva to appoint a king, but you have permission to do so if the people wish to. The *navi* then warns of the absolute power of a king, who may conscript soldiers, confiscate property, etc. (I Shmuel 8:11–18).

R. Nehorai agrees with R. Neḥemya that there is no obligation to appoint a king. He says that it is always better not to have a king. However, if the people choose to have a king "like all the other nations in our area" (Devarim 17:14), the Torah allows it. Since the Torah added this phrase, it implied that any request to appoint a king is motivated by a desire to emulate other nations. It is more appropriate for Am Yisrael to retain its unique identity and proclaim that God alone is our king. Human beings should be political and military leaders, but kingship should be reserved for God.

R. Yehuda says that there is a positive mitzva to appoint a king.

It seems that Rambam codifies the opinion of R. Yehuda, even though the majority opinion is that monarchy is not the desirable form of government. On the other hand, Rabbi Yitzḥak Abrabanel was strongly opposed to monarchy. He claims that there is, in fact, no opinion in the Gemara that there is a mitzva to appoint a king. He points out that the Torah actually said that *if* the people ask for a king, then we are allowed to appoint a Jewish king, and emphasized that we may not appoint a non-Jewish king.

In fact, Abrabanel (Devarim 17) claims that even Rambam did not think that appointing a king was a mitzva. Rambam did not state simply that there is a mitzva to appoint a king. He said that there is a mitzva to appoint a Jewish king. Abrabanel understands this to mean merely that if the people ask for a king, the appointee must be Jewish. Many people have disputed this opinion of Abrabanel, and especially reject his understanding of Rambam (see Rabbi Saadia Gaon's *Sefer*

HaMitzvot, III:230). There are variant texts in the Frankel edition that read that there is a mitzva to appoint a king for the Jewish people. This text would certainly contradict Abrabanel's understanding.

There definitely does seem to be a prohibition against appointing a non-Jewish king: "you may not appoint a foreigner who is not your brother" (Devarim 17:15). Rambam explains that this excludes converts as well as non-Jews. In fact, Rambam codifies that a convert may not be appointed to any position of authority (*Hilkhot Melakhim* 1:4).

The Jewish monarchy is reserved for the Davidic family. The Gemara (Yoma 72b) and Eikha Rabba (7:1) say that David attained the crown of kingship, and Rambam (*Hilkhot Melakhim* 1:7) rules, "Once David was anointed, he attained the crown of kingship, and kingship belongs to him and to his male lineage [if they are fitting] forever." In fact, Rambam polemicized that "anyone who believes in the Torah of Moshe, the master of all prophets, has no king other than from the lineage of David and Shlomo" (*Sefer HaMitzvot, Lo Taaseh* 362). It seems from his wording that if we would appoint a non-Davidic king, we would transgress this prohibition.

Of course, Rambam recognized the fact that kings from other tribes were appointed by prophets, such as Yerovam, who was appointed by Aḥiyya HaShiloni. Rambam (ibid. 1:8–12) rules that such appointments are valid and all laws of monarchy do apply to them. He apparently understood that David's kingship is eternal, while other families could rule as kings for limited time periods. We are enjoined from giving the permanent crown of David to someone from another family. However, there may be temporary kings from any family.

Another example of a non-Davidic monarchy is found at the time of the Second Temple. "The Hasmonean high priests overcame [their enemies], rescued the people of Israel, appointed a king from among the kohanim, and the monarchy of Israel was restored for more than two hundred years, until the second destruction" (Rambam, *Hilkhot Ḥanukka* 3:1).

Ramban (Bereshit 49:10) completely disagrees with the opinion of Rambam. According to Rambam, kings are to be appointed by a prophet in the name of God. Ramban asks, if that is so, why was it necessary to forbid appointing a non-Jewish (or non-Davidic) king? A *navi* certainly would not appoint such a person. Perhaps Rambam felt that it was only preferable for the *navi* to appoint the king. However, if there were no *navi*, the king could be appointed by the people. They were therefore instructed not to appoint a "foreigner."

This approach could lead to a discussion regarding a situation where there is no *navi* and the general populace elects a leader. In such a situation, what is the status of the leader? Could he be considered a king (temporarily at least, since he is not of the Davidic line) at all? Would the laws (or at least some of them) apply to him? While this issue is beyond the scope of this article, the interested reader may see Radvaz (*Hilkhot Melakhim* 3:8), Rabbi Kook's *Mishpat Kohen* (144:15), and Rabbi Federbush's *Mishpat HaMelukha BeYisrael.*

Another answer to the question of Ramban could be suggested if we follow the reasoning of R. Neḥemya, R. Nehorai, or Abrabanel's interpretation of Rambam. There really is no mitzva at all to appoint a king. However, if there is a popular request for a king, the Torah tells us that we may (or should) appoint one. However, the Torah forbade us from appointing a non-Jewish king. This may mean that if the community asks for a foreign monarch, we need (should) not acquiesce to their wish. While it is unthinkable that a *navi* would appoint a foreigner, it certainly is possible that the community could request such a personage, and the *navi* would not then have to appoint anyone.

It is interesting to note that a king is appointed. The Vilna Gaon points out that a *melekh* (king) is appointed, but a *moshel* (dictator) is self-appointed. When Yosef related his dreams to his brothers, they asked him, "Do you plan to be a *melekh*; do you think you will be a *moshel*?" (Bereshit 37:8). Ibn Ezra comments that the question is not redundant. They first rejected any suggestion that they would appoint him. They then added that he should not think that he would rule by force.

God is a *melekh* to the Jews, who accept His kingship. However, He is only a *moshel* to non-Jews. We anticipate and pray for the day that God's kingship will be accepted by all mankind. Then God will truly be one and His name will be one. This is the meaning of the short prayer recited daily following *Az Yashir*.

Parashat Ki Tetzeh

Kiddushin

The mitzva of *peru urevu* (procreation) has been stated a number of times in the Torah. However, the laws of *gittin* (divorces) and *kiddushin* (betrothal) were mentioned only in our *parasha*. "If a man marries a woman and lives with her… and he writes her a bill of divorce" (Devarim 24:1). The Torah did not phrase this in absolute terms of requirement or obligation, but simply explained the fact that if a man marries and later wishes to divorce his wife, this is the proper way to proceed.

The Rosh therefore explains that there is no mitzva at all to marry. The only mitzva that is incumbent upon us is *peru urevu*. Since people could indeed have children out of wedlock, marriage is not even a necessary prerequisite for this mitzva. It should be noted that the Rosh is obviously alluding to single people whose sexual union would not involve any specific biblical prohibition. The Rosh points out that the text of the *berakha* recited at *kiddushin* is "who sanctified us through His mitzvot and commanded us regarding forbidden relationships." A normal *berakha* prior to performing a mitzva would state clearly that we are commanded to fulfill a specific mitzva. Since this *berakha* does not mention any mitzva of *kiddushin*, but refers only to the prohibition of forbidden relationships, this certainly cannot be considered as a *berakha* prior to a mitzva. Rather, it would seem to be categorized as a *birkat shevaḥ* (a *berakha* that is recited as praise to God when we encounter special phenomena).

The Rosh discusses various opinions regarding the need for a *minyan* to recite the blessing over *eirusin* (*kiddushin*). The *kiddushin* itself obviously can be performed in the presence of two witnesses, and there is no requirement to have a *minyan* present. However, there are opinions that the *berakha* can be said only when there is a *minyan*. This, too, would indicate that the *berakha* is not a *berakha* on the *kiddushin* itself (which may not even be a mitzva), but is rather a *birkat shevaḥ* that may be recited only if the ceremony takes place within a community, and therefore a *minyan* is required for the *berakha* (Rosh, Ketubbot 1:12).

Rambam (*Sefer HaMitzvot, Aseh* 213), on the other hand, holds that there is a positive mitzva to perform *kiddushin*, and he counts it as one of the 613 mitzvot. In fact, he counts it as one of the sixty mitzvot that absolutely must be fulfilled by ordinary people under normal circumstances. At the end of the *mitzvot aseh* section of *Sefer HaMitzvot*, Rambam explains that only sixty of the 248 mitzvot actually must be done by people at all times and in all situations. The mitzva of *kiddushin* is included in that list.

Rambam (*Hilkhot Ishut* 3:23) rules that whoever performs the actual *kiddushin* – the groom or his *shaliaḥ* (agent) – must recite the *berakha* prior to the *kiddushin*, "just as we make the *berakha* before performing all mitzvot." If a person did *kiddushin* without reciting the *berakha*, he may not say it after the *kiddushin*, as that would constitute a *berakha levattala* (a *berakha* made in vain), since what was done was done.

Rambam obviously disagrees with the Rosh, and maintains that there is an actual mitzva of *kiddushin*. Moreover, he thinks that the *berakha* is an ordinary *birkat mitzva*, even though it is phrased in negative terms ("commanded us regarding forbidden relationships"), and does not refer directly to the mitzva of *kiddushin*.

The customary practice that a rabbi (*mesadder kiddushin*) presides at the *kiddushin* ceremony and recites the *berakha* seems to follow the opinion of the Rosh. If the *berakha* is made due to the uniqueness of the wedding ceremony, it could presumably be said by any person. In fact, the obligation of saying this *berakha* would fall upon the entire congregation. However, according to Rambam, it seems that the *ḥatan* (groom) should actually recite the *berakha* himself. After all, he is the person who is fulfilling the mitzva now, and therefore should recite the *birkat mitzva* himself. The *Noda BiYehuda* (*Even HaEzer Tinyana* 1) cites a responsum of Rambam that says that if anyone other than the *ḥatan* recites the *berakha*, it is actually a *berakha levattala*. The custom in Yemen, Krotochin, and other communities was that the *ḥatan* himself makes the *berakha*. I was present at a wedding where Rabbi Yosef Kapaḥ, the eminent Maimonidean scholar and adherent, served as *mesadder kiddushin*. I asked him how he could make the *berakha*, which according to Rambam is a *berakha levattala*. He responded that in Yemen he would not have done so, but in Israel, the Yemenite community did not retain all their customs. He added that there is no responsum of Rambam that actually states that this would constitute a *berakha levattala*, despite the testimony of the *Noda BiYehuda*.

In the title description of *Hilkhot Ishut*, Rambam defines the mitzva "to marry a woman through *ketubba* and *kiddushin*." This phrase implies that men are obligated to fulfill the mitzva of *kiddushin*, but women are not. It is obviously impossible for a man to fulfill the mitzva without the consent of a woman, but he must find a wife, whereas a woman may remain single if she so desires. This is similar to the mitzva of *peru urevu*, which is incumbent only on men and not on women. Rambam (*Hilkhot Issurei Bia* 15:2) codifies, "A man is commanded to fulfill the mitzva of procreation, and a woman is not [commanded]." Rambam (21:21) writes similarly that a man is not permitted to live without a wife. However, a woman has the right to stay single all her life. Although the general context of the laws in that chapter refers to proper moral behavior rather than biblical law, nevertheless, it seems clear that Rambam holds there is no obligation at all for women to marry.

It is therefore noteworthy that Rambam specifically mentioned that women are exempt from fourteen of the sixty mitzvot that are incumbent upon all people under normal circumstances. He did not mention that women are exempt from *kiddushin*. Inasmuch as he was quite meticulous in enumerating fourteen mitzvot from which women are exempt, and he did list those fourteen, it would seem that he thinks that women are obligated in *kiddushin*, and this would reflect that Rambam later changed his mind about this issue. It should be noted that Yaakov Levinger, in his seminal article on the sixty mitzvot that are always obligatory (in *HaRambam KePhilosoph UKhePosek*, Jerusalem, 1989), questioned the accuracy of the list as we have it.

In any event, in *Mishneh Torah* and *Sefer HaMitzvot*, Rambam clearly thinks that there is a real obligation for a man to marry. In general, a young man who reaches the age of bar mitzva is obligated to perform all the mitzvot. However, the well-known mishna (Avot 5:21) says that the age of eighteen is the proper time to marry. Rambam (*Hilkhot Ishut* 15:2) codifies that a man is obligated from the age of seventeen. He adds that if someone reaches twenty years of age and has not married, he transgressed and negated a *mitzvat aseh*.

Our Sages apparently felt that lack of maturity and financial independence are sufficient grounds to exempt young men from the mitzva. In fact, the Ḥida (*Birkei Yosef, Even HaEzer* 1:7) says that we should not marry today at the age of thirteen. It is obvious that the obligation of learning Torah is also a major factor to consider in determining the proper age of marriage (see Rambam, *Hilkhot Ishut* 15:2–3; *Shulḥan Arukh, Even HaEzer* 1).

Parashat Ki Tavo

Mutual Responsibility

Moshe and the Elders commanded the nation to write the Torah on stones at Mount Eival, where they were also obligated to bring a sacrifice and rejoice before God (Devarim 27:1–8). Our *parasha* further cites Moshe's instructions regarding the blessings and curses declared on Mount Gerizim and Mount Eival. Rambam (*Sefer HaMitzvot*, principle 3) establishes that only eternally binding mitzvot are enumerated among the 613 mitzvot. Therefore, these commandments in our *parasha*, which applied only at a specific time, are not to be counted, just as the mitzvot with which the people were charged as part of the preparations for the giving of the Torah at Mount Sinai are also not counted.

However, the *Behag*, who omits the mitzvot of *mattan Torah* from his list, does count the mitzvot concerning Mount Eival. Ramban (ad loc.) attempts to explain this position. He suggests that although we were explicitly commanded to draw a boundary around Mount Sinai and to make various preparations to receive the Torah, those measures had no lasting effect and are therefore considered temporary obligations, and thus do not qualify for inclusion in the list of 613 mitzvot. Writing the Torah on the stones, by contrast, has a lasting, permanent effect. These stones were to have remained with us forever, and the blessings and curses entail an eternally binding acceptance of the Torah. Although there is no specific action that we are required to perform today, mitzvot intended to have a lasting effect are, according to Ramban's understanding of the *Behag*, counted among the 613 mitzvot.

Rabbi Saadia Gaon also includes the mitzva "to establish a covenant of the blessings and curses" in his list. As we have discussed several times, he divides all mitzvot into three categories: *mitzvot aseh* (positive mitzvot), *mitzvot lo taaseh* (prohibitions), and mitzvot that apply to the community as a whole, but entail no personal responsibility on individuals. He includes this mitzva in the third category.

Rabbi Perlow explains (based on the Gemara in Sota 37b) that the specific eternal mitzva involved here is the concept of *arevut*. When the Jewish people received the Torah at Sinai, they obligated themselves merely as individuals; only once they entered the Land of Israel did they truly become united into a single nation with mutual responsibility for one another. Rabbi Perlow finds this idea to be so self-evident that he expresses wonder over Rambam's omission of this mitzva. As he notes, however, according to this line of reasoning, this mitzva should be included in the general list of *mitzvot aseh*, rather than in the list of communal obligations. After all, it is each person's obligation to accept responsibility for every other Jew.

To resolve this difficulty, we must address one basic question concerning the inherent nature of *arevut*: does the concept of *arevut* constitute a separate, individual mitzva, or should it be viewed as a broad, overarching principle? Perhaps the acceptance of any mitzva automatically includes an obligation of *arevut* with respect to that mitzva. If so, then *arevut* should be seen not as an independent mitzva, but rather as a feature common to all the mitzvot. Indeed, the Gemara (Sota 37b) states quite clearly that each mitzva included 600,000 covenants, as each member of the nation bears responsibility not only for himself, but for the entire Jewish nation, as well.

One ramification of this question involves the status of women with regard to *arevut*. The Gemara (Berakhot 20b) discusses the issue of whether women are included in the Torah obligation of *Birkat HaMazon*, or are obligated by force of rabbinic enactment. It explains that this question determines whether they can recite *Birkat HaMazon* on behalf of men. If the Torah exempts women from *Birkat HaMazon*, then they may not recite it on behalf of a man, given their lower level of obligation. The Rosh took this to mean that the concept of *arevut* does not apply to women. Generally, he writes, a person included in a given mitzva by force of rabbinic enactment may, in fact, perform it on behalf of someone included on the level of Torah law. Thus, for example, a man who ate only a minimal amount of food, who is obligated on the level of rabbinic law to recite *Birkat HaMazon*, may nevertheless recite it on behalf of someone who ate a quantity requiring *Birkat HaMazon* according to Torah law. The concept of *arevut* means that he bears responsibility towards others, and he may therefore fulfill the obligation on others' behalf, even if his obligation applies at a lower level. Women, however, do not bear an obligation of *arevut*, and they may therefore not fulfill a mitzva on behalf of those with a higher level of obligation in that mitzva.

The *Noda BiYehuda* (*Dagul MeRevava, Oraḥ Ḥayim* 271) interpreted this to mean that *arevut* does not apply to women at all. He even raised the possibility that men might not bear the responsibility of *arevut* with respect to women. Rabbi Akiva Eiger (Responsum 7), however, rejected this interpretation of the Rosh. He understood the Rosh to mean that *arevut* does not apply regarding a mitzva that one is not obligated to perform. Only when a person is individually obligated in a given mitzva does he become obligated through *arevut* to help others perform that particular mitzva. Therefore, if women are not biblically required to recite *Birkat HaMazon*, they have no obligation of *arevut* for that mitzva and therefore cannot fulfill the obligation on behalf of those included in the obligation. Regarding, however, those mitzvot that obligate both men and women (such as Kiddush, the specific point of debate between the *Noda BiYehuda* and Rabbi Akiva Eiger), *arevut* applies to women as much as to men.

This debate between the *Noda BiYehuda* and Rabbi Akiva Eiger clearly hinges on the aforementioned question of whether *arevut* constitutes an independent mitzva or is simply part of the specific mitzva involved. According to Rabbi Akiva Eiger, the concept of *arevut* exists within each mitzva, and thus everyone included in a given mitzva bears as well the obligation of *arevut* concerning that mitzva.

This perspective resolves the difficulty noted above regarding Rabbi Perlow's approach. Generally, there is no specific mitzva of *arevut*; it is, rather, part and parcel of each individual mitzva. If Rabbi Saadia did list an independent mitzva of *arevut* incumbent upon the community at large, he must refer to a special type of *arevut*, separate and apart from the standard obligation that applies to every individual concerning every mitzva. Rabbi Saadia here speaks of a unique obligation cast upon the community leaders to work towards ensuring the nation's compliance with the mitzvot.

Indeed, the Me'iri (Sanhedrin 43b) writes, "The judges, scholars, and leaders must constantly check and inquire about the actions of their townspeople... since all of Israel have *arevut* toward one another." Evidently, in addition to the general obligation of *arevut*, there exists a specific obligation of *arevut* incumbent upon the leaders, and this obligation may perhaps be counted as an independent mitzva.

Parashat Nitzavim

Teshuva

This mitzva that I command you today is not beyond your understanding, nor is it distant from you…it is very close to you, in your mouth and in your heart [so that you can] do it" (Devarim 30:11–14).

To which mitzva does this verse refer? Rambam (*Hilkhot Talmud Torah* 3:8) seems to have understood (based on Eiruvin 55a) that it refers to the mitzva of *talmud Torah*. He interprets the sentence "it is not in heaven" (v. 12) to mean that Torah knowledge is not found in haughty people, and the phrase "it is not across the sea" (v. 13) to indicate that Torah scholarship is not found among people who frequently travel. We may therefore assume that according to this approach, the clause, "it is very close to you" likewise refers to Torah knowledge, and informs us that it is attainable and within our reach. Indeed, the Talmud (Nidda 30b) teaches that every child studies Torah while in his mother's womb, meaning that the Torah is innately part of the human personality.

The verse continues, "in your mouth and in your heart." Perhaps the phrase "in your mouth" alludes to the idea that Torah should be studied verbally, out loud, as the Gemara (54a) comments that Torah serves as a "source of life" for those who study out loud. Finally, the verse's final word, "to do it" could refer to the fact that one should study Torah not merely as an intellectual exercise, but with the intention to put what he learns into practice and observe all the laws he studies. There are different versions of the text of the mishna (Avot 4:5) regarding a person who studies Torah for purely intellectual purposes ("*lilmod ulelammed*" – "to learn and to teach"). However, it is clear that the Mishna places "*lilmod laasot*" – learning for the purpose of fulfilling Torah – on a higher level.

Ramban suggested – but then dismissed – an alternate understanding of this *parasha*. He said that this "mitzva" might be a generic term for all of Torah. In that case, Moshe here does not introduce any new concept or idea, but simply admonishes the Jewish people to observe the entire Torah. For grammatical reasons, however, Ramban rejects this interpretation, and finally concludes that the mitzva spoken of is really the mitzva of teshuva, the topic addressed in the preceding verses. Ramban adds that the Torah describes the Jewish people's teshuva in narrative, rather than imperative form, thus alluding to a divine promise that ultimately, the nation will perform teshuva. Rambam similarly writes in his *Mishneh Torah* (*Hilkhot Teshuva* 7:5) that the final redemption will arrive only in the merit of Benei Yisrael's teshuva, and the Torah promised us that we will, eventually, do teshuva. Rabbi Soloveitchik (*Al HaTeshuva*, Jerusalem, 1975, pp. 95–96) notes that this comment of Rambam becomes ever more significant in light of his inclusion of the belief in redemption among the Thirteen Principles of Faith. If we are obligated to believe in redemption, and redemption can occur only through teshuva, then it turns out that we are obligated to believe this divine promise that the Jewish people will collectively do teshuva.

In any event, Ramban, after establishing that this section refers to teshuva, proceeds to explain each phrase as it relates to teshuva. According to his understanding, Moshe informs us that teshuva is not a distant, foreign concept: one can perform teshuva at any time and in any place. "In your mouth and in your heart" means that we must orally confess our sins, return to God with all our heart, and accept the Torah forever.

Rabbi Ovadya Sforno agrees with this general idea but explains the actual verses somewhat differently. He writes that the expression "teshuva is not found in heaven" implies that one does not need scholars (who are in "the heavens," or in ivory towers) to facilitate his teshuva.

And "it is not found across the sea" teaches that one can do teshuva anywhere, and need not consult scholars living in distant lands.

In any event, both Ramban and Sforno understand the word "mitzva" in this context as a reference to teshuva, and thus maintain that there is a mitzva of teshuva. By contrast, Rambam (*Sefer HaMitzvot, Aseh* 73) famously counts *viduy* (confession) as one of the mitzvot, but omits the mitzva of teshuva. Many Aḥaronim (e.g., *Avodat HaMelekh* of Rabbi Menaḥem Krakowsky; *Minḥat Ḥinnukh* 364; *Mishpat Kohen* of Rabbi Kook) also hold that there is no need for a specific mitzva of teshuva. After all, if a person sinned once, he certainly would not be allowed to continue sinning. It is inconceivable that a person could exist in a state of sin: he obviously would have to rectify the situation as best he can.

The Ḥida (cited by Rabbi Kook) adds a brilliant proof to the idea that there is no mitzva of teshuva. We know that there is no punishment of *makkot* (lashes) for any transgression that can be rectified by performing a *mitzvat aseh* (this is known by the term *lav hanittak laaseh*). For example, if a man divorces his wife in a case where the Torah forbids doing so (see Devarim 22:29; Makkot 15a), he would not receive *makkot*, since he must rectify the situation by remarrying her. Thus, the Ḥida writes, if there were a mitzva of teshuva, there would never be a case of *makkot*, since every prohibition must be rectified by teshuva. Of course, one can easily debate this point and explain that *makkot* are not administered when there is a specific *mitzvat aseh* that requires correcting the violation. Teshuva, however, even if it were an independent mitzva, would constitute a generic form of atonement and would not fall under that category.

A completely different analysis of Rambam's position is found in Rabbi Soloveitchik's *Al HaTeshuva* (pp. 38–45). Although some writers, as we have seen, think that Rambam did not view teshuva as a mitzva, the situation seems to change on Yom Kippur. Rambam (*Hilkhot Teshuva* 2:7) writes, "Yom Kippur is the time for individual and communal teshuva.... Therefore, everyone is required to do teshuva and recite *viduy* on Yom Kippur." Thus, although Rambam does not generally consider teshuva a mitzva, apparently an obligation of teshuva does apply on Yom Kippur.

Rabbenu Yona (*Shaarei Teshuva* 2:14) states quite clearly that there is a mitzva to perform teshuva on Yom Kippur. He later (4:17) remarks that although the mitzva of teshuva applies all year round, there is an additional obligation on Yom Kippur to attain *tahara* (purification). Wherein precisely lies the distinction between teshuva, which applies all year, and the special mitzva of *tahara*, which applies only on Yom Kippur? Rabbenu Yona may have meant that all year round, a person who commits a sin bears an obligation to perform teshuva for that particular sin. On Yom Kippur, however, we are required to attain a state of purification from all our sins (see Vayikra 16:30). If a person performs teshuva for only part of his sins, he does not meet this requirement and does not fulfill the mitzva. Rabbenu Yona (1:9) indeed writes that forgiveness is granted for any type of teshuva, whereas purity requires much more. To illustrate this point, Rabbenu Yona draws an analogy to a soiled garment. Standard laundering may remove some stains, but the garment will remain dirty until it is thoroughly laundered and all stains are removed.

Four possible perspectives regarding the mitzva of teshuva emerge from this discussion. Rabbenu Yona (and perhaps Rambam) thinks that there are two separate mitzvot of teshuva, one that applies all year and another that is unique to Yom Kippur. Ramban and Sforno maintain that there is a single mitzva of teshuva all year round. Rambam (as explained by some Aḥaronim) holds that there is no such mitzva at all. Yet a fourth possibility, as we suggested in Rambam, is that the mitzva of teshuva applies only on Yom Kippur, but not throughout the year.

Parashat Vayelekh

Hak'hel: The Torah Reading of the King

Moshe commanded them, saying, "At the end of seven years, at the time of the *Shemitta* (sabbatical) year, during the festival of Sukkot, when all of Israel comes to appear before Hashem, your God, in the place that He will choose, you shall read this Torah before all of Israel, and they shall hear it." (Devarim 31:10–11)

While Moshe clearly demands a public reading of the Torah, he does not identify who should read it. The *Bekhor Shor* and *Ḥizkuni* claim that Moshe was directing his charge to Yehoshua, who essentially became the king of Israel. Therefore, the obligation was forever incumbent on future kings. From this perspective, the role of the king is fundamental to the mitzva of *hak'hel*. In contrast, Rambam (*Sefer HaMitzvot, Aseh* 16) enumerates the commandment "to gather the entire nation…to read some portions of [Torah]," but does not mention who is to read them. Similarly, in *Hilkhot Ḥagiga* (3:1), he writes that "there is a positive commandment to gather all men, women, and children…to read portions [of the Torah] that encourage them to perform mitzvot and strengthen their commitment to the true religion." The fact that the king reads the Torah does not appear for another two halakhot, implying that it is a mere detail of the law, rather than central to it.

The *Sefer HaḤinnukh* (612) generally follows Rambam in his formulation of mitzvot, and quotes Rambam in this mitzva almost verbatim. Yet, he adds that "any man or woman who does not come at this time to hear the words of Torah transgresses [this law]. So, too, a king who does not want to read has neglected his commandment." Thus, while like Rambam he formulates this mitzva as focusing on the assembling of the nation, he highlights that the king's role is critical, something that does not emerge from Rambam. It is almost as if the role of the king and the role of the people are two separate mitzvot!

Indeed, the *Yere'im* counts two separate mitzvot – the gathering of the people (Mitzva 433) and the reading of the king (Mitzva 266), the latter being an obligation that applies to the king alone. As proof, he points to several *pesukim* (II Melakhim 23:1–2) in which King Yoshiyahu gathered many of the people and read "the book of the covenant that had been found in the house of Hashem." This mitzva even precedes the mitzva of the people to gather together.

Another interesting question that is discussed is whether the king is to stand or sit during *hak'hel*. The *Semag* (*Aseh* 230), based on the Mishna (Sota 7:8), writes that when the king was given the Torah scroll he had to stand. However, he did not have to stand when he read the Torah, but if he does so, this is meritorious. This is based on the Mishna's record of the Sages' praise for King Agrippas for standing when he read the Torah during *hak'hel*. The *Tiferet Yisrael* (*Yakhin*, Sota 7:54) asks why this would be considered meritorious. In general, anyone who does an action from which he is exempt is considered a *hedyot*, a fool (Y. Berakhot 2:9). He answers that Agrippas was not legally fit to be king. Thus, he was obligated to stand in the Temple; only proper kings of the Davidic line are allowed to sit. Therefore, Agrippas was following the letter of the law rather than going beyond it. From this analysis it follows that a proper king should specifically sit rather than stand during *hak'hel*. This, however, seems to contradict Rambam, the *Semag*, and the *Ḥinnukh*.

The *To'afot Re'em* (266:1), a commentary on the *Yere'im*, notes this difficulty in the explanation of the *Tiferet Yisrael* and suggests an alternative interpretation. He cites the Vilna Gaon (*Shenot Eliyahu*, Berakhot 1:3), who explains that someone is only criticized for doing something he is not obligated to do if the action is not inherently valuable. However, there are some actions that are fundamentally valuable, but the halakha does not obligate us to do them. However, if someone does do them, as he would be doing something that is a mitzva, he is praised rather than censured. Noting that the Gemara (Megilla 21a) claims that ideally one should always stand when studying Torah, the *To'afot Re'em* argues that standing for *hak'hel* is a mitzva and praiseworthy, even if not required.

Why is there no rabbinic mitzva in commemoration of *hak'hel*, as there is regarding many other mitzvot? Rabbi Eliyahu David Rabinowitz-Teomim (known as the Adderet), father-in-law of Rabbi Kook, published an anonymous pamphlet entitled *Zekher LaMikdash* in which he suggests two reasons: *hak'hel* fundamentally requires the presence of the entire Jewish people in Israel, and it also requires the laws of *Shemitta* to be in place. Today, neither is true, as most Jews do not live in Israel and most *posekim* rule that *Shemitta* is in effect only rabbinically. (In his time this was the case. Now, it is unclear whether the majority of Jews live in Israel or in the Diaspora. We are definitely reaching the halfway point, if we have not already passed it.)

Rabbi Shlomo David Kahane (in the above pamphlet) adds two more reasons: First of all, we are not able to go to the section of the Temple Mount where the Torah must be read (it is beyond the scope of this article to discuss the question of where on the Temple Mount it is permitted to walk). Additionally, we do not have a king, and, as we have seen, it is possible that the obligation fundamentally applies to him. The Adderet rejects this, arguing that even if this were to be the case, the nation might be able to fulfill their obligation by hearing the Torah from a different leader, especially if they have a separate mitzva from that of the king, as suggested by the *Yere'im* (above).

Parashat Haazinu

Birkhot HaTorah

Ramban adds seventeen *mitzvot aseh* that, in his view, Rambam mistakenly omitted from his list of mitzvot. Among them is the obligation to recite a *berakha* when learning Torah, a mitzva that the Gemara (Berakhot 21a) deduces from a verse in *Parashat Haazinu*: "When I proclaim the name of Hashem, give praise to our God" (Devarim 32:3). Ramban emphasizes that *Birkhot HaTorah* should, indeed, be counted as an independent mitzva, rather than simply as part of the mitzva of *talmud Torah*. Just as eating the *korban Pesaḥ* and relating the story of the Exodus constitute two separate mitzvot, Ramban argues, so must Torah study and *Birkhot HaTorah* be counted as two separate, independent mitzvot.

It is interesting to note that Ramban (based on the Gemara) interprets the phrase "When I proclaim the name of God" as referring to Torah study. This interpretation is consistent with the kabbalistic concept expressed by Ramban himself (in the introduction to his commentary to the Torah) that the entire Torah is composed of names of God. There seems to be an alternate, hidden method of reading the Torah in which the name of God is the basis of every verse.

The position of Rambam, who does not count *Birkhot HaTorah* as one of the 613 mitzvot, may be understood in one of two ways. It could be that he agrees with Ramban that *Birkhot HaTorah* constitute a Torah obligation, but felt that inasmuch as *Birkhot HaTorah* are a necessary prerequisite for Torah study, this obligation is naturally subsumed under the mitzva of *talmud Torah*. Ramban, as mentioned, explicitly dismisses such a notion, but this may very well have been Rambam's rationale. Indeed, the *Sefer HaḤinnukh* (430), who generally follows the opinion of Rambam, states explicitly that *Birkhot HaTorah* are of biblical origin. Following Rambam's view, he does not count this as a separate mitzva; this comment concerning *Birkhot HaTorah* appears amidst the *Ḥinnukh*'s discussion of *Birkat HaMazon*. Alternatively, one might claim that Rambam denies the biblical origin of *Birkhot HaTorah* entirely, and holds that the Gemara only quoted the *pasuk* as an *asmakhta*.

The practical ramification of this issue arises in a situation where a person is unsure of whether he is obligated to recite *Birkhot HaTorah*. Generally, in situations of uncertainty, halakha permits one to follow the lenient possibility regarding rabbinically mandated obligations, but requires that one act stringently with regard to Torah obligations. According to Ramban, a person in doubt concerning *Birkhot HaTorah* certainly must recite them, since a Torah obligation is at stake. However, the *Shulḥan Arukh* (*Oraḥ Ḥayim* 209) seems to have ruled that *Birkhot HaTorah* are not a biblical obligation. He writes, "In regard to all blessings, if someone is in doubt as to whether he has recited them, he should not recite them … except for *Birkat HaMazon*, which is required by the Torah." By not singling out *Birkhot HaTorah*, the *Shulḥan Arukh* strongly implies that they are included under the category of "all blessings." On this basis, Rabbi Ovadia Yosef (*Yabia Omer* III:27) ruled that *Birkhot HaTorah* are rabbinic in nature and need not be recited in situations of doubt. On the other hand, the *Mishna Berura* (47:1) ruled that *Birkhot HaTorah* are biblically mandated.

A second fundamental issue regarding *Birkhot HaTorah* involves the nature of these *berakhot*. We generally classify *berakhot* into three categories: *berakhot* recited before the performance of mitzvot, *berakhot* recited before deriving some pleasure (such as eating and drinking), and *berakhot* expressing praise and gratitude, which one recites upon encountering some extraordinary phenomenon. Into which category would we place *Birkhot HaTorah*? Of course, this question becomes more acute if we assume that these *berakhot* are rabbinic in origin. The only *berakha* that we know to originate from the Torah – *Birkat HaMazon* – may be of a distinct, unique nature and thus need not fall into any group (though it is certainly a *berakha* of praise and gratitude). Likewise, if we were to assume that *Birkhot HaTorah* constitute a Torah obligation, we would not necessarily be compelled to classify them into one of these three groups. Assuming their obligation originates from *Ḥazal*, however, we must determine their essential character and nature.

The *Tosafot* (Berakhot 11b) ask why we do not recite *Birkhot HaTorah* every time we learn, just as we recite a *berakha* every time we enter and eat in a sukka. By drawing this comparison between *Birkhot HaTorah* and the *berakha* recited over the mitzva of sukka, the *Tosafot* appear to take the position that *Birkhot HaTorah* should be seen as a *birkat mitzva* that we recite over the mitzva of Torah study.

The *Shulḥan Arukh* (*Oraḥ Ḥayim* 47:14) rules that women also recite *Birkhot HaTorah,* despite the fact that women are exempt from the formal obligation of *talmud Torah* (Kiddushin 29b). The Vilna Gaon (ad loc.) explains the *Shulḥan Arukh*'s ruling as based on the tradition that women who perform mitzvot from which they are exempt nevertheless recite the *berakhot* over those mitzvot. Clearly, the Gaon also considered *Birkhot HaTorah* akin to other *birkhot mitzva.*

Earlier, the *Shulḥan Arukh* (47:2) codified that one does not recite *Birkhot HaTorah* if he merely thinks or meditates about Torah: only when a person studies verbally or writes Torah does he recite the *berakha.* The Gaon (ad loc.) questions this ruling and argues that inasmuch as one fulfills the mitzva of *talmud Torah* even without verbal articulation, why does one not recite the *berakha* over thinking about Torah? Once again, the Gaon here takes a clear stand regarding the nature of *Birkhot HaTorah,* viewing these *berakhot* as *birkhot mitzva* that should be recited whenever the mitzva of *talmud Torah* is fulfilled.

We should note, however, that the Gaon's argument concerning women's obligation to recite *Birkhot HaTorah* seems very difficult to understand. In this context, he addresses the ruling of Rabbi Yosef Karo, the author of the *Shulḥan Arukh,* and argues that women may recite this *berakha* just as they may recite the *berakha* over any mitzva they perform, even those from which they are exempt. However, the *Shulḥan Arukh* (*Oraḥ Ḥayim* 17:2) explicitly rules that women may *not* recite a *berakha* over the performance of a mitzva from which they are exempt. If the Gaon merely intended to say that halakha follows the Ashkenazic custom permitting women to recite a *berakha* in such a case (Rema ad loc.), we would still need an explanation for the *Shulḥan Arukh*. If the *Shulḥan Arukh* generally forbids women from reciting a *berakha* over mitzvot from which they are exempt, why does he require that they recite *Birkhot HaTorah*?

Rabbi Velvel Soloveitchik (*Novellae of the Griz, Hilkhot Berakhot* 11:16) cites an explanation from his father, Rav Ḥayim. Rav Ḥayim claimed that this *berakha* is not a standard *birkat mitzva*. Rather, it stems from a unique halakha, that Torah requires a *berakha*. Although Rav Ḥayim did not use this exact terminology, he appears to consider *Birkhot HaTorah* to be *berakhot* of praise and gratitude. It therefore follows that women, although they are not obligated to learn Torah, must nevertheless recite these *berakhot* when they study, since the very encounter with Torah requires the recitation of *Birkhot HaTorah*. On this basis, we might explain the *Shulḥan Arukh*'s ruling that meditation about Torah does not require a *berakha*. True, as the Gaon argued, one indeed fulfills the mitzva of Torah study by simply thinking about Torah. However, the interaction with the Torah (the *ḥeftza shel Torah*, in Brisker terminology) must be done verbally or by writing in order to create the phenomenon of Torah in the world, and thus generate an obligation of *Birkhot HaTorah*.

The text of the *berakha* according to Rambam (*Hilkhot Berakhot* 7:10), which is codified by the *Shulḥan Arukh* (ibid.), seems to corroborate this explanation. Whereas the Ashkenazic custom is to say, "who commanded us to occupy ourselves with Torah," Rambam's version reads, "who commanded us with regard to the words of Torah." This phraseology strongly implies that *Birkhot HaTorah* do not fall under the category of *birkhot mitzva*, but rather constitute special *berakhot* recited on the very concept of Torah.

We have thus seen two fundamental disputes concerning *Birkhot HaTorah*: whether they are biblically required or were instituted by the Rabbis, and whether they should be viewed as *birkhot mitzva* or as *berakhot* recited over the phenomenon of Torah. One might suggest distinguishing between the three (or four) different *berakhot* over Torah recited daily. Our discussion revolved mainly about the first *berakha* ("*laasok bedivrei Torah*" or "*al divrei Torah*"). Many Aḥaronim maintained that there are a number of important differences between the various *berakhot,* and thus the points raised in this chapter would not necessarily apply to the other *berakhot* (see, e.g., *Baḥ,* OḤ 47:4; *Minḥat Ḥinnukh* 430; *Lekaḥ Tov* 11).

Parashat Vezot HaBerakha

Temple Service by a Disqualified Kohen

Ramban (Vayikra 21:1) notes that in the context of the prohibition for *kohanim* to become impure, the Torah calls them "the children of Aharon." It does not do so when discussing their role in offering the *korbanot*. Based on this distinction, he concludes that only the prohibition to become impure relates to the intrinsic holiness of the *kohanim* that is lacking in a disqualified *kohen* (one whose mother was forbidden to marry a *kohen*, such as a divorcee), known in halakhic terminology as a *ḥalal*.

The *Keli Ḥemda* (ibid.) explains that according to Ramban, *kohanim* have two distinct types of holiness. The first is the ancestral holiness that comes from being descendants of Aharon. The second is the intrinsic holiness that each one of them personally has by virtue of being a *kohen*. A *ḥalal* has the former but lacks the latter. Since he does not have the intrinsic holiness of a *kohen*, he is not proscribed from becoming impure, and is also forbidden to serve in the *Beit HaMikdash*. Nevertheless, if he does serve, as a descendant of Aharon his service is valid post facto.

This is because the role of *kohanim* in the *Beit HaMikdash* stems from their status as descendants of Aharon.

Rabbi Soloveitchik posited that there are two different aspects to the holiness of *kohanim*. First, all Jews are obligated to honor those related to the tribe of *kohanim*. A *ḥalal*, due to his problematic lineage, is not a *kohen* for these purposes. The second aspect is that every *kohen* who works in the *Beit HaMikdash* becomes a *keli sharet*, a service vessel. He suggested that the honor due to *kohanim* because of the former can be waived, but the latter cannot, as it is the honor of God. With this logic he explains why Rabbenu Tam allowed a *kohen* (when there was no *avoda*) to waive his honor and wash Rabbenu Tam's hands (Mordekhai, Gittin 461).

By combining these two formulations, we can conclude that a *ḥalal* is not a *kohen*, though he is a descendant of Aharon. Thus, his service in the *Beit HaMikdash* would be valid and, if he served, he would be defined as a *keli sharet*.

The Gemara (Kiddushin 66b) offers different sources to explain why the service of someone who thought he was a legitimate *kohen*, and discovered afterwards that he was not, is valid. Each of the three opinions sheds light on a different aspect of *kehunna*.

R. Yehuda citing Shmuel derives this halakha from the verse "It shall be to him and his children after him" (Bemidbar 25:13).

Shmuel's father derives it from "Bless, O God, *ḥeilo* (his resources), and desire the work of his hands" (Devarim 33:11), which is understood to mean that even the *ḥullin* (invalid ones) from among the *kohanim* shall be desired.

R. Yannai derives it from "You shall come to the *kohen* who will be in those days" (Devarim 26:3). He asks, would one have thought that someone would go to a *kohen* not in his days? Rather, R. Yannai says, this refers to "one who was valid and became invalid."

The Yerushalmi (Terumot 8:1) cites only the latter two opinions, the second in the name of Rav and the third from R. Yoḥanan. Some Aḥaronim (*Even HaAzel, Hilkhot Biat Mikdash* 6:10; *Devar Avraham* 26:9) suggest that these latter two sources reflect fundamentally different conceptions of this law. The last source refers to the *ḥalal* as a *kohen* until it is discovered otherwise, implying that until he reveals the problem he is considered a full *kohen*. In contrast, "even the invalid ones shall be desired" implies that his service is valid even though he is not a *kohen*.

The Yerushalmi (ibid.) draws this distinction almost explicitly, with ramifications. According to the final source offered by R. Yoḥanan, the *ḥalal* would be considered a *kohen* even in situations outside the Temple. The rule would apply to *kodshei gevul*, holy things that *kohanim* are entitled to outside the Temple, and would also apply nowadays, after the destruction of the Temple. For Rav, the dispensation is limited to the context of *avoda*. (We may speculate that the first source is similarly limited.)

Rav's opinion can be understood in light of Ramban's distinction mentioned above: the *ḥalal* lacks the intrinsic holiness of *kohanim*, but is a descendant of Aharon. Based on Rabbi Soloveitchik's approach, we could add that though not personally a *kohen*, if he does serve, he will attain the status of *keli sharet*.

This logic can then be employed to explain several other issues.

The Gemara only mentions the case where a *ḥalal* thought he was valid when he served. What would happen if he knew he was a *ḥalal* beforehand and served anyway? Rambam (*Hilkhot Biat Mikdash* 6:10) claims that even though it is forbidden to do so, his service would be valid. The *Kesef Mishneh* notes that this follows from the source "even the invalid shall be desired," which has no limitation.

This works for this source, which specifically validates *ḥalalim*. However, the source of "the *kohen* in those days" clearly depends on the *ḥalal*'s lack of knowledge that he was invalid when he served. The *Minḥat Ḥinnukh* (267) cites an opinion that indeed disqualifies *avoda* when a *ḥalal* knowingly serves in the *Mikdash*. It is worth noting that Ramban goes farther, claiming that anyone who finds out he is a *ḥalal* disqualifies his *avoda*. The dispensation in the Gemara only validates the service of someone who found out he *might* be a *ḥalal*. This position makes it impossible for Ramban himself to subscribe to the thesis we constructed based on his comments (as he clearly does not grant the *ḥalal* any positive status as a *kohen*), though the theory could be adopted independently.

This question also affects whether a *ḥalal* who served without *bigdei kehunna*, the special garments worn by the *kohanim* when they served in the Temple, would disqualify his service and be liable to the death penalty, both of which would happen if a regular *kohen* were to serve without these garments. The *Minḥat Ḥinnukh* (99) rules that his service would be invalid, just like that of a regular *kohen*. This makes sense if we believe that the *ḥalal* is considered a *kohen* (at least until he found out he was a *ḥalal*); in this respect he is no different from any other *kohen*. However, he does not think that he would be liable to the death penalty, as a *ḥalal* is not obligated to perform the service and cannot be commanded to wear the garments. However, if our analysis above is correct, we could argue that until he finds out he is a *ḥalal*, he is a full *kohen* for the purposes of *avoda* and would be obligated to wear the *begadim*. (The *Tzafenat Pane'aḥ* [second edition, *Hilkhot Yesodei HaTorah* 5:6] argues that the *ḥalal* does not have to wear the garments at all, as the lack of garments normally disqualifies service because they render the *kohen* a *zar*, a non-*kohen*. The *ḥalal* is not a *kohen* but his service is valid anyway, so he does not need to wear the *begadim*. This conclusion seems impossible to accept.)

Another implication would seem to be whether the service of a *kohen gadol* who served on Yom Kippur and found out he was a *ḥalal* would be valid. If the dispensation is derived from "the *kohen* in those days," which implies that he is a full *kohen* until he finds out otherwise, it might be valid. This is the position of the *Minḥat Ḥinnukh* (*Kometz HaMinḥa* 185). If, on the other hand, there is a special exception that validates the service of a *ḥalal*, this would presumably be limited to ordinary *kohanim*, but it could not make the *ḥalal* a *kohen gadol*. Thus, his service would be invalid, a position taken by the *Hafla'a* (cited in *Kometz HaMinḥa*). There is also a parallel discussion about whether a *kohen gadol* who discovered he is a *ḥalal* can release accidental killers from cities of refuge.

In general, regarding laws that require a *kohen*, and not just a son of Aharon, a *ḥalal* should be invalid. For example, the Griz (Rav Velvel Soloveitchik, beginning of *Parashat Metzora*) argues that only someone with the status of *kohen* can purify someone who has *tzaraat*. Thus, a *ḥalal* cannot. One could wonder whether *pidyon haben*, the redeeming of the first born, requires a *kohen* or a descendant of Aharon.

There are two semi-*avodot* that must be mentioned. The Gemara (Pesaḥim 72b) discusses whether someone who did not know he was a *ḥalal* and eats *teruma* is liable to pay the fine a non-*kohen* pays for eating *teruma*. R. Eliezer obligates him to do so, while R. Yehoshua exempts him, arguing that *teruma* is an *avoda,* so the rule of "even the invalid among them" applies. Here Rambam (*Hilkhot Terumot* 10:12) limits the exemption to cases where he did not know he was a *ḥalal.* He seems to have thought eating *teruma* is not really an *avoda,* a position found in the Yerushalmi (Terumot 8:1), making it stricter than actual Temple service. *Nesiat Kappayim,* the *kohanim*'s blessing of the Jewish people, is also compared to *avoda* in certain respects, and we must wonder whether these laws apply to it.

About the Author

Rav Binyamin Tabory, a *talmid* of Rav Joseph B. Soloveitchik and *talmid-chaver* of Rav Aharon Lichtenstein, received *semikha* from Yeshivat Rabbeinu Yitzchak Elchanan and a Master's degree in Jewish Philosophy from Yeshiva University. For more than thirty years, he gave an advanced Gemara *shiur* in Yeshivat Har Etzion.

He previously served as *rosh yeshiva* in Toronto, Canada, at Yeshivat Or Chaim and Ulpanat Orot, and was the founding *rosh kollel* of the Torah Mitzion Kollel in Cleveland, Ohio. For one year he served as the Rav of Kehillat Alei Tzion in Henden, London.

For over twenty years, Rav Tabory taught at Midreshet Moriah, a women's learning center in Jerusalem, and more recently at Sha'alvim for Women as well. His *shiurim* have appeared in various publications and websites devoted to Torah study.

Rav Tabory's encyclopedic knowledge, clarity of thought, clever and concise style of teaching, and warm personality have made him a popular scholar-in-residence in the USA, UK, Switzerland and South Africa.

Rav Tabory and his wife Naomi live in Alon Shevut. They have two children and nine grandchildren.

The fonts used in this book are from the Arno family